I0569283

# THE FOUR RS OF PARENTING

## CONVERSATIONS
## WITH PARENTS, YOUNG ADULTS,
## AND ELDERS

CARMEN E. BYNOE BOVELL, PHD

PRIMIX
PUBLISHING
THE WRITE CHOICE

Primix Publishing
East Brunswick Office Evolution
1 Tower Center Boulevard, Ste 1510
East Brunswick, NJ 08816
www.primixpublishing.com
Phone: 1-800-538-5788

Published by Primix Publishing: 06/05/2025

ISBN: 979-8-89194-479-4(sc)
ISBN: 979-8-89194-480-0(hc)
ISBN: 979-8-89194-481-7(e)

Library of Congress Control Number: 2025909853

To my mother, Ismay Elizabeth Bynoe, and my grandmother, Anne Mahala Ouseley—the two women who raised me—and to all parents who have the extraordinary responsibility of raising the world's children to be productive citizens.

Train up a child in the way he should go, And when he is old he will not depart from it.

—Proverbs 22:6, Holy Bible

# Contents

# FOREWORD

Dr. Carmen Bovell is an expert in her field. She has spent more than fifty years in the field of early childhood engaging with, advocating for, and fostering relationships with young children and their families. Most of her years engaging in this work were with Head Start, a locally operated but federally funded program for young children and their families. Therefore, Dr. Bovell is an expert who is steeped in parenting information, parenting advice, and parenting advocacy and is by far the best person to write such a compelling account of what "real parents"—current, past (grandparents), and future parents—have to say about the subject.

Dr. Bovell has held positions both inside and outside of the classroom; therefore, this book and the research she conducted to birth this book required her to return to the basics…back to where it all started—with parents. As we all know, being a parent is the most challenging job that there is. It has been said repeatedly, "Parenting is the hardest job I have ever had!" Parenting is a mystery! Dr. Bovell's book has taken the mystery out of parenting! In fact, she offers us an assist to help future parents and early childhood professionals serving young children and their parents. In this book, Dr. Bovell coins the term "intentional parenting."

As an early childhood professional, I am familiar with the term "intentional teaching" coined by Dr. Ann Epstein (2014). According to Epstein, intentional teaching is planful, thoughtful, and purposeful (p. 1). Fundamentally, it means that teachers act with specific outcomes or goals in mind for all children for all developmental domains. In comparison, intentional parenting suggests that parents act with intention. Parents should be thoughtful, purposeful, and strategic as they parent their children with respect, responsibility, reciprocity, and restraint in their interactions with their children. In her book, Dr. Bovell declares that we need to "go back to basics and give priority to how we raise our children." She further states that "paying attention to parenting practices in our society is not the only solution, but it is a critically important aspect of the problems we face in our society today.

When I read through the chapters of this book, I knew that it was timely and very special. I predict that this book will help a lot of parents. I am happy to be a part of it. When I read the interviews from current parents, grandparents, and future parents, I hear authentic values and beliefs from them. I am excited about getting this book in the hands of a new generation of parents. As a parent and a grandparent, I find the book helpful as I coparent my grandchildren with their parents. This book is about parenting with a purpose! Parenting with the values of respect, responsibility, reciprocity, and restraint is a winning strategy.

Dr. Bovell does a wonderful job of laying out the Four Rs of Parenting and their impact on parenting. Parenting is more challenging today than ever before, but Dr. Bovell addresses how the Four Rs of Parenting can help by going back to basics, as she says so eloquently.

I think this book is critically important, bringing much-needed attention to the mystery of parenting. I hope that parents will read the words of the different parents in these pages and have a powerful standard for parenting for the rest of their lives. This book will help parents as they deal with how to raise their children. In the end, what's most important in life isn't going to be how much money you make, how many material things you own, or how many sexual conquests you have. It's going to be the way you raise your children. They are a reflection on you.

Dr. Marsha Carter McLean
Early Childhood Consultant, Trainer, Mentor, Coach
Building Blocks Learning
http://www.building-blocks-learning.com

# FOREWORD

Dr. Carmen Bovell's book, *The Four Rs of Parenting: Conversations with Parents, Young Adults, and Elders*, is a timely addition to the literature of child-rearing which, as we know, comes with no instructions. Oftentimes, parents bring up their offspring the way they were raised. However, in some cases, parents are determined to depart from tradition, especially if their experiences were traumatic. Regardless of this, experiences deep in their subconscious sometimes surface when they least expect it, causing them in some cases to essentially "become their parents."

The author's questions, based on what she terms the four *Rs*—respect, responsibility, reciprocity, and restraint—elicit cogent responses from forty-two parents, adults, and young adults that many can relate to. These interesting, practical responses reflect the views of the respondents who vary in age, and although many of the adults are old-school, some acknowledge changes that they have made while parenting in the twenty-first century. It is also heartwarming that the young adults interviewed demonstrate a depth of thought that spells progress for the next generation.

Overall, the responses emerge from places of deep consciousness and highlight the challenges we all face when bringing up the next generation. This book is not meant to be a blueprint, but it can function as a guide for those on their parenthood journey.

Carmen Barclay Subryan, PhD
Retired Faculty, Howard University
Published Author

# ACKNOWLEDGMENTS

My sincerest thanks to the parents, young adults, and elders whose willingness to be interviewed and wholeheartedly share their thoughts and experiences made this book possible. Thanks also to my son, Marlon Bovell, for his patience and tireless efforts in assisting me with the technical aspects of securely saving the oral and written transcripts of all interviews and formatting the first draft of the book. Finally, a million thanks to Cyndi Mercado, professional transcriber, who made it possible for me to utilize all interview recordings by transcribing those that were difficult for me to convert to print.

# INTRODUCTION

I have heard it said over and over again that parenting is hard work. When you stop to think about it, raising children can be a challenging responsibility. It is hard work, for sure, and can be intense for at least the first twenty-two years of your child's life, that is, from birth through the first four years of college. Most young men and women I have talked to about having and raising children in the future have expressed a desire to have children; however, many have also stated they may not have what it takes to be successful at fulfilling such an important responsibility.

Raising children can be challenging; however, it doesn't have to be. If parents utilize certain strategies from the very beginning, their parenting experience should be less bumpy and more satisfying. There are many parents and grandparents who will agree with this statement, and I selected a sample from among them to be contributors to this book based on my experiences with them over many years and my knowledge and observations of how their children and grandchildren live their lives as responsible, respectable, productive citizens. I selected the young adult contributors for this same reason, that is, how they live their lives as the embodiment of the values I espouse in this book.

Parenting is as important today as it has been in the past and will continue to be in the future. In fact, "intentional parenting" is of critical importance today as our society is riddled with issues of violence—both domestic and in our schools and neighborhoods, school dropouts, bullying, and substance abuse, to name a few. Not that these issues are new to this era, but they appear to have escalated and have become more difficult to contain and remedy.

"Intentional parenting," a term and concept I have coined, is values-based. It refers to parents being guided by certain principles or values by which they raise their children. That is what this book is about. *The Four Rs of Parenting* documents conversations about parenting or child-rearing beliefs and practices I have had with parents, young adults who are not yet parents, but who plan to have children in the future, and grandparents who I refer to as elders. My conversations with all three groups centered on the importance of the four values of respect, responsibility, reciprocity, and restraint in the process of raising children; however, there was a different emphasis with each group. With the parents, I emphasized how and why they applied these values in raising their children; with the young adults, I focused on what they would and would not carry over from how they were parented to their own parenting of their children and their thoughts about whether the four values were relevant in today's world among children, youth, and young adults. With the elders, I centered more on what twenty-first-century parents could do to raise children who internalized and practiced these four values, as well as the kind of external support that would be beneficial to parents in raising their children.

I firmly believe that although some may consider the four values "old school," they are still relevant in today's world because they are basic human values that have assured a decent, caring society; however, there has been an erosion of these values, and here are a few examples. As I walk through my neighborhood every morning, I pass a community college, and every day there is so much litter on the grounds as well as in my neighborhood. As I ride on trains and buses in my city, visit community stores and shopping centers, watch the news on television, or even walk on the sidewalk, I hear adults verbally abusing young children and cursing in their presence, I see adults physically abusing children, and numerous other abusive, unhealthy behaviors. What's going on in our world? How can we turn it around? I believe paying attention to parenting practices in our society is not the only solution, but it is a critically important aspect of the problems we face in our society today. So let's go back to basics and give priority to how we raise our children.

The values presented in this book are in the social emotional domain and although there is little reference to academics, the areas discussed are essential in supporting and reinforcing children's successful academic development. So read and discuss the opinions and recommendations in this book with family and friends and come up with your own opinions and recommendations concerning the positive and successful rearing of children in your family.

Be open-minded when reading this book. You will find thoughts and opinions from a range of individuals representing diverse ages, ethnic groups, and of course, both genders. You will find similarities and differences in some responses to the same questions, and I encourage you to consider the similarities as reinforcing and the differences as unique and refreshing, providing more food for thought, deliberation, and decision-making. I hope this book will speak to today's twenty-first-century parents, because I feel our society is in trouble and we need to make absolutely sure that the present and next generations will restore values, beliefs, and practices that are important in raising children to be productive citizens.

—Carmen E. Bynoe Bovell

# Section 1

## CONVERSATIONS WITH PARENTS

In this section, parents respond to the following questions:

- What are your thoughts about parenting?
- As a parent, how do you define the concept or value of respect, including self-respect?
- How do you show respect for yourself, your child or children, and others?
- As a parent, how do you define the concept or value of responsibility?
- How important is responsibility?
- How important is it for you to be a responsible parent and for your child/children to develop and demonstrate responsible behavior?
- How do you or how have you demonstrated responsibility in your own parenting? Give examples of your own responsible behavior?
- As a parent, how do you define the concept of reciprocity, or "the Golden Rule"?
- How do you model reciprocity as a parent?
- As a parent, how do you define the concept or value of restraint?
- How important is restraint?
- Give examples of how you practice restraint when relating to your child/children and other family members.

- How important is it for your child to practice restraint—not only within the home as they relate to each other, but outside of the home, when they go to school, and are older and interacting with their peers and others in the community?
- How would you like your child to express negative emotions?
- What practical parenting advice do you have for twenty-first-century parents? These must be things parents can actually do.

# CHAPTER 1

## How Parents View the Role of Parenting

What are your thoughts about parenting?

*Marguerite Anderson*

I think, generally speaking, we basically approach parenting as we approach anything in our lives. We are the sort of people who like to travel; we believe in a very broad worldview and caring for people and showing our caring through basically how we treat each other and how we interact with others in the world. And we want our son, George, to understand that, and we want him to mimic our behavior and absorb how we treat others in the world. So parenting is about caring. I guess my main thought is, I like it, it's rewarding, it's worth the hard work. My husband, Sean, and I agree it's the most rewarding hard job we've ever had. We give up a lot to do it, but we get such great rewards for doing it. I love seeing the person he's becoming. George is kind; he's a thoughtful child; he likes to share. I can see that he likes to make his playmates feel happy, and he's a jovial child, and it's wonderful seeing him grow into the person that he is going to be. I think I like parenting, and I feel lucky that I'm able to raise a child, and we got lucky with the kid that we have. He's a very easy baby, a very easy toddler so far. He's fourteen months old.

*Christopher Blanchard*

I would say, I think parenting is probably the best thing that ever happened to me. It's a life-changing experience, being a parent, being that person that your child looks up to, and you know, I'm happy to be there to provide and care for that person that I cocreated, and I definitely enjoy the experience. I say it's a life-changing experience for me because of having created another human life and being one of the main persons that need to care for, nurture, and be there for the person that I cocreated. So it's something that's very, very important and special to me, in that I definitely got something I always wanted. It's more than everything I thought it would be, and I see parenting as a very, very important responsibility.

*Holly Blum*

From my personal experience as a parent, one of the things I think parenting has made me much more aware of, and intentional about, is figuring out what were my values and what I really want to intentionally and thoughtfully impart to my daughter. Somewhere in my mind and in my heart, I knew what my values were, but then what does that look like? And more intentionally, when I'm trying to communicate those values, how does that affect my behavior? I'm looking for consistency between my behavior and my values, and this is what I think is important. Her father and I had quite a few conversations about that because I didn't know whether we shared the same values. It was a talk we had never had, but I didn't think he was as thoughtful about parenting, and maybe that was partly influenced by the fact that I was an early childhood teacher. I think I parented in a way that tried to provide opportunities where her experiences would be consistent with those values. For example, when I first moved into Virginia, I was naive and assumed that the world was pretty well integrated because that had been my experiences in most of the places I lived, so it never occurred to me to really take a look at the demographic of the neighborhood. I was just focused on what I could afford, but when we moved, I looked around me, and I was surprised by how homogeneous the community was. To this day, her dad reminds me I was ready to pack our bags when I realized the lack of diversity and worried about what if the neighborhood doesn't change.

Respect for diversity is one of the values that guided my parenting socioeconomic and cultural diversity; I don't think I gave a lot of thought to language diversity. That awareness came when I started to experience the impact of culture and language and how they interacted. That came a little bit later in the game when I had the fortunate experience to find work with the Fairfax County Head Start Program.

Another value was being respectful of other people's thinking and ways of doing things; therefore, I wasn't uncomfortable, for example, sending my daughter to a Lutheran Preschool, although our cultural heritage is Jewish. The Lutheran preschool was the best and most developmentally appropriate preschool in my community that I knew of, and I wasn't intimidated by having the conversations about her having to go to chapel twice a week. Other people live other ways; not everybody in the world is Jewish. When she came home from preschool, she asked questions and made comments, and I saw it as an opportunity to have conversations with her about other people may think differently, or let's look at what we have in common, everybody is special, etc. I felt that those were fine messages that afforded us a chance to talk about different religious backgrounds, experiences, and traditions.

Respect for your elders was another of my values. You don't have to like everybody, but you have to be respectful of everybody.

*Marlon Bovell*

As a parent, you are fully responsible for your child, to teach them to be successful or responsible contributors to society. I think parenting is a 24-7 job. It's tougher than you would ever think it would be, both before becoming a parent, and as a parent, I now see where my parents were coming from with all the things they used to say. I still hear those things in my head today, and I repeat some of those same phrases to my kids. I understand now what I did not understand as a child, and I try to keep that in perspective when I discipline or talk to my kids even though it's tough. I keep in perspective that kids don't really understand what you're telling them because they can't project into the future. I try to use terms they understand and explain to them the possible outcomes to their actions. I have a lot of information, and I can project into the future what will or can happen based on their current actions—for instance, not wanting to clean their room or not wanting to put their device down and do homework without us having to tell them to do it. Also, one of the main things I always tell them is, do now what you can do today. For instance, my daughter may have an assignment that's not due until Wednesday and it's Monday; she would do very little or none on Monday. I tell her do as much as you can today; if you can finish your homework on Monday, finish it, because you never know what's going to come up on Tuesday, so do as much as you can today to be prepared for the next day.

*Robert Bovell*

I believe parenting takes the collective effort of both mother and father. In that way, a child understands the roles of man/father and woman/mother who together raise the child using a balanced approach. When parenting is one-sided, sometimes we leave out certain components, whether it's from a male role-model standpoint or a female role-model standpoint, and the child has to rely on outside sources for those things that make them function with a balance in and out of the household or with other family members. So I believe it's key that both parents play a very active role in the upbringing of the child, whether they're married or they're not living together.

The role of parents is very vital, because if parents don't take an important stance, we then rely on the streets, the church communities, the schools, and peers to play a role in raising our children, and that's when we complicate things. When there's one parent, if that parent merges the components and balances the roles of mother and father and interjects that education equally into the child, you can get productivity from the child, but I find it to work better when a father, whether the mother and father are married or divorced plays an active role in the upbringing of a child.

There are things that a child can ask a mother and a mother can give a more subtle or passionate response to the child that helps the child better understand a particular behavior or situation. A good way to look at that is the following. A lot of times when we talk to our children, whether it's a mother or father, a father may say, "I think you may need to ask your mom when she gets home or when you can find time to talk to her," and the mother may say, "I think you need to talk to your father," or "I'm going to let your father know." Once we understand the importance of each parent's role, we get a better reaction from the child, and that adds an important dimension to the upbringing of the child...

*Shanice Bovell*

Well, for me as a single parent, parenting has been hard, but I've learned through the years that parenting is as hard as you make it. We all have struggles, but as with anything in life, it's how you handle it. It's the most precious thing. For me, it's the most precious thing that I have because I am the one responsible for molding two individuals who will go out into this world and make an impression.

Parenting has been joyous for me because I have two great sons who have made it so. Even though there have been some scary and tough times, for the most part it has been pure joy raising two boys to become respectful men and teaching them about manhood. I needed to be a good example when teaching them to treat people the way they want to be treated and to respect girls/women the way they would want a man to respect me. I had excellent examples in my father and brother, who of course learned from their fathers, and I've been thankful to have them around to teach my boys about manhood.

Both of my children's fathers for the most part were absent. They were around enough so that their children knew to call them daddy. They have different fathers, and both weren't the best at being providers. My oldest would spend quality time with his father but those days didn't last long and visits were far in between. As he got older his dad pulled away and left everything on me. I struggled a great deal, even as a wife. I struggled to raise them and take care of the household. Being diagnosed with chronic illnesses when my children were five and two put a huge burden on me because I needed tremendous help. My ex-husband was never around for assistance. Thankfully, I had an excellent support system in my family. Trying to get financial help for the most part was difficult, so I took both of them to court for child support, and back then the courts weren't as helpful and strict as they are now. I didn't start to get financial support for my children until they were in middle and high school. By then, their dads came back around to develop a relationship. I did appreciate what they could provide, a few dollars here and there, but it was never enough.

*Dorel Campbell-Adams*

I think when you first become parents, your parenting style comes from what your parents passed on to you. You become the parent that your parents were to you, and as your children grow and mature, you begin to develop your own parenting ideas and views, and they may not mimic or mirror the ideas and views that you grew up with. I had many discussions with my mom about this and her views about how we should treat certain situations, and we agree on some and disagree on others. So I think it all depends on the time that we are in and whatever is going on in the world and in our environment, because it's ever evolving, and parenting is ever evolving. So it's just what our kids are exposed to at that time and how we choose to tackle it. There are, of course, the base values that we carry on from generation to generation that this book addresses, such as, respect, reciprocity, and responsibility. These are the foundation, but of course, there are many different variations in how we pass along these values.

So there is a difference between the way I was raised in the Caribbean by older parents compared to parents today and with these kids who are all high tech and the experiences that they have. I never had these experiences as a child, and my parents had different experiences as well. So the values they passed on to me were based on different scenarios, but hopefully it's the same values that I'm passing on to my children. I'm talking about different variations of different scenarios that we have to tackle with these kids, but we are trying to pass on the same values.

*Desiree DeFlorimonte*

Parenting is an ongoing process in which a child is nurtured, protected, and guided in preparation to become a well-rounded adult. Although there are some instinctive responses to being a parent, I believe that I learned many of the necessary skills about parenting from my mother and through trial and error. I am grateful that she was there to guide and support me for my daughter's birth and through the first nine months of her life. Through that experience, as well as recalling my upbringing as a child, I learned much about parenting.

Just as many teachers teach the way they were taught, I believe many mothers parent the way they were parented. As a new and young mother, I learned the importance of taking care of and raising Angel through each developmental stage of her life. In college, I studied Maslow's Hierarchy of Needs, which included being responsible for my child's basic needs of food, clothing, and shelter. In addition, I learned to provide her with a firm foundation, grounded in the Christian faith. The Good Book tells us to "train up a child in the way she should go and when she's old, she won't depart from it." Throughout the years, this verse was central in my mind as I strived to raise my daughter to become a caring, capable, responsible, and independent young woman. Teaching Angel values, showing her affection, but not being afraid to discipline her when necessary were all part of the course. I instilled in her the importance of education and always supported her in school. I can recall the time I spent a morning observing in one of her middle school classrooms, at a boarding school she attended. At the end of the visit, she asked, "Mommy, when will I be old enough for you to stop sitting in my classrooms?" My response was, "When you are in college." Of course, I did sit in one of her college classes since I was also teaching in the adjacent building.

As a parent it was also important to protect my child and keep her safe from the myriad of obstacles, challenges, and dangers she would encounter. However, I had to find a happy balance and not be overly protective but encourage Angel to make good choices and learn from mistakes. There were times when nonnegotiable rules that were established were not adhered to and the resulting consequences had to be painfully accepted. I had lots of fun times, providing mommy time while reading to my child, traveling, visiting museums and family members, and giving unconditional love. All these matters are integral to the process of parenting.

I believe I will always be a parent. Even now, my daughter is forty-three years old, and I'm still parenting her…giving advice, especially when asked. It's truly an ongoing process as I'll never stop parenting.

*Ryan Dickson*

For me, parenting is an amazing opportunity of discovering not only how I show up for my kids but what vision I have for their future as well. As a single parent, I call myself a decentralized parent, in that I have two girls with my ex-wife and a son from a previous situation. So with my daughters in the Virgin Islands, we are geographically separated, and I look at myself more as a facilitator between the relationships with my kids.

In my life, my father had children outside of his relationship with my mom—and I've seen this in other situations as well—so that the nature of the relationship amongst the siblings is in direct correlation with whichever parent they live with that similarly facilitates that relationship. So obviously if you're in a household with your mom and your siblings may have different fathers, your mom may facilitate the relationship among you and your siblings. If you happen to be somewhere else, there has to be an active effort from the parents to facilitate relationships with and among the children. So I look at my role as a facilitator, and I continue to reinforce the love and connectedness between my son and his sisters. As a single dad and also as an attorney, when I had my son out of wedlock, and was not in a serious committed relationship with his amazing, fantastic mom at the time she was pregnant, I instantaneously thought that warranted a fifty-fifty custody, and looking at how much value society placed on fathers at that time, it was impactful to me. I think it actually impacted my desire to want to be married and have more children and to not only have the full fatherhood experience, which to me meant waking up with your kids, and so forth, but also being a stand for other fathers who may be frustrated with the system and how much time and connectedness they're allowed to have with their children.

All that being said, as a human being, I definitely identify right now as being a father who facilitates relationships with my children with multiple moms, and that pretty much runs a large part of my identity in terms of my commitment to expanding my business empire, so on and so forth, so I can fly back and forth between my kids with ease and show up one day and get on a plane and be here in the morning and just move in those types of ways and travel with them to where I want to go. Parenting requires teamwork. To fully integrate it is definitely a team experience and I definitely have my kids' moms and their families on my team, and I'm committed to maintaining those relationships.

But co-parenting is a whole other topic, and that's a huge part of the deal. I've seen many persons whose relationships with their children suffered because of their relationships with their co-parents. So the advice I'd give to fathers around co-parenting is based on my own experience as a co-parent. I have an ex-wife who is the mother of my two wonderful, beautiful daughters, and then there is the previous situation with my son's mom. We didn't really know each other when we first met—she's great, she's amazing, but there was a lot of drama in the beginning. I mean, you don't know each other to a core in the beginning, and then when you add in the stress of the pregnancy and you're still trying to discover how you're going to work out not only the aftereffects of parenting but this kind of situation, this pregnancy, that's another aspect, you know.

*Richlyn Emanuel*

Parenting on a whole is not easy. You do need a village. It doesn't matter if you're a single parent, or if you're co-parenting, or if the father is in the home. You need more than that; you need a village;

you need outside support. You need to expose your kids to other family, other individuals, because as a parent, you don't know it all. But we're not born, or we don't grow up knowing, okay, this is how you parent. It's trial and error. It's asking for help, asking the right questions or the wrong questions. It's making mistakes, because I've done that. The one thing that I've tried to do as a parent is to do all the things that my parents did not do, good, bad, or indifferent. I tried to do things that parents have not done, because how I was raised and how I wanted to raise my child were totally different. His dad said that from birth, I've raised a well-rounded child and he was jealous. He's actually jealous of his son because of all the things that I've allowed him to experience—every sport, regardless of whether or not Giovanni wanted to do it—because that's the only way you grow, when you come outside of your comfort zone. And you do that from the inception; you expose kids to everything so they don't have a narrow view of the world. From the time he could understand words I didn't do the baby talk thing with Giovanni. I didn't do goo-goo, ga-ga—none of that. I remember his pediatrician walking into the examining room one day when Giovanni was maybe two, and she said, "I thought you were having a conversation with an adult." That was because of how I was speaking to him.

Growing up around people and actually having conversations, I think, is very important. Exposure to the world is important; letting them know that they're not privileged is very important. It's also important to have a routine: Saturdays we clean house, Sundays we go to church, then we rest early to bed. Those things are important, and you can't stray from them, because I've learned the hard way that once you break a routine, or you add things to a child's routine, or there is a lot of confusion within the household, it drives your child crazy. We had a period of time in our lives when Giovanni was in the fifth or sixth grade and he went through the confusion of "this is what Mom said," "these are Mom's rules," "this is what Dad says," "this is what Nana says," "this is what Grandma says," and it was overwhelming because he had four adults plus school telling him what he could and could not do, what he should and should not do. So as a parent, you have to set the standard. I appreciate the fact that you think I should do things this way or that way, but you don't bring it to the child. As a parent you need guidelines—yes, this is how other people think it should be done. That doesn't mean that it's right; that doesn't mean that I'm right. I could be wrong, but be open enough to accept ideas and try different things.

Parenting is not easy, regardless of who is in the house, and it's especially not easy in this day and time when kids are exposed to so much, and it's hard to limit that. But you can't truly limit what they want; you can't limit the influences that they get outside of the home. All you can do is set the guidelines and lead by example and have faith that when they leave your home or when they leave the house that they're putting on their best face and showing the world how it should be.

Yes, for me, parenting has been difficult, but I've had a village, and I appreciate my village. It seems small, but the amount of experience in that small village is remarkable. Giovanni has been xeposed to his great-grandparents all the way down, up and down the line on both sides, everyone.

*Raymond Fisher*

Parenting is a journey that takes commitment, sacrifice, and a strong belief in shaping and molding lives to be productive. I take it as the ultimate responsibility, and being a spiritual person, I also take it as a gift. The greatest gift you can have in life is to cocreate another person and then nurture him and raise it in a positive way. For me it's the driving force of who I am at this point in my life as an individual and as a person. The interesting thing about it is I'm coming to the point where my children don't need that much effort on my part because of the foundation I laid early in their lives. I think it's important that the responsibility of parenthood is not something you can share that you don't share it at eighteen or twenty-one. You never shared it. It is ever evolving; that's why I call it a journey. But the cornerstone of that, I think, is based on the foundation you lay with your children. The boundaries of respect, love and discipline come in many forms, and it's an all-encompassing journey that constantly evolves.

*Martine Gordon*

My initial thought is just that it's the hardest thing I've ever done—the most rewarding and the hardest, simultaneously, thing I've ever done. For me it's the knowledge that someone's life and development is so heavily dependent on what you're directly giving them at this young age. You know, my daughter is very young; it's just the ultimate responsibility, and I really feel a lot of pressure to not mess it up. So it's the hardest thing and simultaneously the most rewarding thing that I think I've ever done and I probably ever will do.

By saying "not messing it up," I'm thinking that I didn't have a great childhood experience myself, and when I reflect on how I was raised, I don't feel that I was supported and encouraged in a way that could help me get to my full potential, so I feel a lot of pressure to not repeat what I view as mistakes with my child. So for me it's a constant, everyday sort of gut check for me… Am I acting in a way that's demonstrating for her that she should be confident and healthy and she's supported and safe? And you know, with everyday stressors outside of family life, some days it's harder to do than others.

I take my role as a parent very seriously. It's the most important thing in my life.

*Justin Hampton*

Parenting for me is a learning process, and I try to always be open to learning new and effective ways of doing it. I've had the advantage of having a lot of my friends get married very young and have children very young in their early twenties, so I've gotten opportunities to observe them. Their children are now teenagers, and I've had the opportunity to see how they raise their kids, some of their successes and failures, and to see the kind of children that are the fruit of their lives and their parenting efforts. I get to see and glean from them some positive things that work and some things that didn't work. This allowed me to kind of have an advantage. So what I try to do is just create a hodgepodge of successful techniques that I've seen firsthand, and I do listen to the advice of others. But like I said, I have the advantage of seeing firsthand the outcomes of their parenting; therefore, for me parenting is a learning process. It's about trying to do your best in the moment and not be led by your emotions and to really think about what the long-term consequences or outcomes are of what you are instilling in your child.

The way I look at it, every interaction is a learning experience for the children; every interaction is a training. Even if it's not intentional, every conversation, every time we go to the park, I'm training them, I'm teaching them something, I'm instilling something, and it is not necessarily on purpose. For instance, they've gotten used to going to the park every week, and that's something they will take to their parenting when they grow up. They're going to remember that, and it's going to be impactful, as those things leave a lasting impression. So I try to be cognizant of the fact that everything I'm doing has the potential to be impactful in their thinking and I just have to be really careful and intentional as much as I can about what that means and what the outcomes of could possibly be for the children.

*Leticia Herrera*

Being a parent is very important, because parents are the children's first teacher and play an important role in their early development. How you spend time with your child and what you say, how you express yourself is what will make a big difference in everyday life for your child. One example is, when a child asks a question, make sure that you give the right answer, or if you don't know the answer, just say, "I will check and get back to you." For me what was always important was spending quality time with my son. I remember the way I was raised. I was raised with a lot of siblings by a widow in a big house. The widow did not have time to spend with me individually. My son was very lucky. He was the only child, and I was able to give him lots of attention.

As a young single mother, I had a very hectic life working seven days a week but always looking into what was the best for my son. One of the things that I noticed about the Jewish family I worked for was how they raised their children. After observing how they parented their children, I decided to incorporate some of those strategies into my parenting style. I admired this family I worked for. They were open in conversations with their children. That is something that I really liked. At one time my son wanted to become Jewish because he had a lot of good times with this family, but I always made sure he knew he was Hispanic and that his mother born in El Salvador, not in America. I'm very happy to have been able to put all the pieces together because this has helped him understand and appreciate the Hispanic culture as well as others. Right now it is fantastic. We live in an ethnically and culturally diverse world, and he is able to work and function very effectively because of his exposure to various cultures and racial groups at an early age.

One of the things that I did with my son at a very young age, I think when he was eight months old, was actually to read to him every night, because that's what I saw the Jewish parents do. Each parent took a turn to read to the children every night, and I loved that, and I was asked to read to one of the children at nap time every day. I noticed when this five-year-old spoke, she had the vocabulary of a middle school child, and I liked that. So I did that with my son starting when he was eight months old. By the time he went to kindergarten, I had read a collection of Bernstein Bears books to him, but I didn't know that he really knew how to read, until after he went to kindergarten and he started to read back to me. I wondered if he memorized the books or he really knew how to read. Now I think he knew how to read, and I feel so proud of that. I'm not a reader, but he is a fantastic reader. He reads a lot, and he writes a lot. I do believe it is because I followed the example of Jewish family and read to him every day.

I was raised in a huge family. There was no time to say "I love you," because there were just too many of us. But I saw the love the Jewish family had for each other and the kinds of things that they did together. I liked what I saw and did all these things as a single parent. I did them because I put my son first. It was not his fault that I was a single parent. I always felt that he was not to be blamed. He was first always. I wanted him to be successful. He didn't ask to be here, so it was my job to make sure that he got everything and was exposed to everything that was important so that he could be successful in the future, and that's what I did. He met a lot of wealthy people and a lot of very poor people, a lot of families and friends, so he could see the differences and learn that there was a price you have to pay to be able to earn what you wanted in life, and by having some of these examples, I was able to show him that he could be anyone he wanted to be, but he would have to work hard for it. That was my plan, and he was first in every way. Finally, I could not have done a successful job raising my son without support from family, friends, and the Head Start Program. The preschool education my son received in Head Start made a significant contribution to his social and cognitive development. My involvement in the program sharpened my parenting skills and helped me be a good role model for my son.

*Joseph Kijewski*

I don't want to point fingers at anyone, but I think a lot of people go into parenting not realizing the true commitment it takes to successfully raise children. Being a good parent requires three things. You have to be a friend, but you also have to be a disciplinarian. You have to be gentle, but you have to be stern. And you have to be able to set rules, but you have to be able to look at those rules and bend them at the right times. There are so many contradictory things that go into it. And it really requires dedication to the calling. I think some people are more suited to be parents than other people just because it's something that they're truly willing to embrace.

I keep remembering the dialogue in the movie *Guess Who's Coming to Dinner*, where Sidney Poitier was talking to his father and his father reprimanded him about the way he was speaking to them and what Sidney Poitier owed him for everything he and his wife had done for him. Then Sidney Poitier came back and said, "I owe you nothing. If you carry that mailbag to the moon and back from the day you brought me into this world, you owe me and if I have a son, I will owe him." I think that's the way I look at parenting as well. I think once you take on that responsibility of being a parent, you owe your everything to that child or to your children. Not meaning that you get in and give them everything they want, but you owe them your full attention. You owe them your time. You owe them your love, you owe them your consideration, you owe them all these things, and you really have to pour yourself into your children's lives.

I don't know that a lot of people think about that when they think about becoming parents. It's a full-time job, the full twenty-four hours, seven days a week, 365 days a year. It doesn't end when they turn eighteen or twenty-one years old. You still get the calls at 1:00 a.m. You still get the crying over this or that happened, and you still have to be there, and you want to be there. I think if you're a good parent, you want to be there. But it really is, once you want to take it, a full-time call.

*Errol Marks*

It's the most important job that anyone could ever have, and it's an extreme responsibility. I would say it's the most important job that anyone could ever have. Most of us go into it lightly. We don't take it as seriously as we should. It's the most rewarding job, filled with pride, especially if your child does something great that makes you proud. That feeling is immeasurable. Like when my child finished at the top of her class in fifth grade, she had a nice GPA, and that made me very proud. So yes, it's the most important job and the most rewarding job and the lowest-paying job, but ultimately, it's a labor of love.

*Maxine Maloney*

My thoughts on parenting are from two perspectives—a spiritual perspective and what we would say would be a theoretical perspective. From a spiritual perspective, parenting, I would say, is a gift. It is a gift and an honor that's bestowed upon us by the Father. And many of us get to parent because, you know, but there is something significant about the role of the parent, and I think when we are in tune and whether we're spiritually grounded or on a spiritual journey, our Father grants us that gift, that opportunity to parent. Then there's the theoretical, that parenting is caring for our children, whether it's a biological or adopted child. I'll also say that parenting is a powerful relationship that has to be approached with care and great caution because as a parent, you have the ability to give life or destroy life.

We give life from a physical sense, and we give life through the care and the nurturing and building of our children; then as parents we can destroy the life of a child—whether it be from the way you look at a child, the things you say to your child, the relationship or lack thereof. And so, you know, combining all that, I think parenting is a gift that should not be taken lightly.

*Virgil McDonald*

First of all, I must admit that parenting is a joint effort by my wife, Kelley and me. Fortunately, we agree on most things about parenting. In our courtship years, we had long conversations about having a family and the number of children we wanted. She wanted six children because she is an only child. I wanted three children, we had three, and she thanks me until this day. We were not ambitious for our children. Instead we wanted them to develop good character. Respect, responsibility, reciprocity, and restraint were among the characteristics we hoped that they would embrace. I have to give Kelley credit because she was a stay-at-home mom who spent a lot of time substitute teaching at the elementary school where our children were enrolled. She was engaged in virtually all our children's activities as they were growing up. The feedback that our children gave to me is that they could rely on me going to work every morning and coming home for dinner every evening. They remember fondly our family vacations, visits to the museums, and picnics along the Potomac River that I usually planned.

Have fun with your children. Don't be afraid to let them see your silly side. Challenge them intellectually. Set high standards for them. Expose them to new and different things. Prick their interest and curiosity. Teach them about money. Let them know that death is a part of life. Teach them that "life ain't no crystal stair." Don't shield your children from the unpleasant side of life. You're lucky if you are a parent at thirteen and a friend at thirty. Expose your children to religion, but impress upon them that the choice is theirs and theirs alone. Allow your children to grow up—it will broaden your horizons. Tell your grandchildren preposterous stories—real and imagined. Remember your grandchildren love to hear about the devilish things their parents did as children. Let your children and grandchildren teach you new things; it keeps you young. Be more an example than a disciplinarian. Show your children how to love and not to be afraid to express it.

*Lawrence Rawlings*

I think parenting changes with each generation. We look to the past as a guideline, looking at what our parents did and seeing where they made mistakes and where we could improve upon what they did. Each generation should build upon all the positive aspects and influences of the previous generation, such as dedication, hard work, and perseverance. These are the things that my mother instilled in me even though they were the archaic way of doing things, but I built a foundation for myself, and I'd like to continue that foundation for the next generation. It's a good thing when your parents have a brick wall for you to run your head into, like when they say this is the limit and you know that is a line you don't cross. And if you cross that line there should be some kind of punishment that instills in you, "Okay, well, I want to do this, but maybe I don't."

It makes you think about the consequences of your actions and how you instill that into the next generation without putting out those heavy consequences. I talk with a friend of mine about parenting all the time. We talk about positive reinforcement and giving our kids other tasks outside of school for self-betterment and also having good conversations and open dialogue with our children. We are working at building that open dialogue. For me the open dialogue came late in the game because I've had this issue with my wife, but the open dialogue with my daughter has been created. Sometimes just walking and doing simple things cause me to reflect on things like, "Do I love her enough?" "Am I getting enough positive energy?"

Build the energy in your home for the child to feel comfortable and welcome and figure out, "Are we actually in a bubble or are they in a bubble?" Break that bubble and get to the child; speak their language so they can feel more welcome. Most importantly, build experiences with your child; that's your job. This is more important than the material items you get. Material items should only be tools to create experiences.

*Jacqueline Rose*

Parenting is a lifelong endeavor. One's parenting role shifts and changes over a lifetime. One needs to understand and have wisdom at each age and stage of their child, youth, and adult development over their parenting experience. Seeking to understand yourself and your child builds effective communication and strengthens trust in your relationship. The most important thing is to listen to your child and your own inner voice. That's the place to start.

*Halima Thorne*

Parenting is extremely difficult. You do need your village to help you out. It's very important to have that. You cannot do it alone, especially in 2018, 2019. Things have become more and more difficult to do on your own, financially and emotionally. I don't know what I will do if I didn't have my mom, my dad, and my sister throughout this whole process of having Carter, birthing Carter, and currently dealing with Carter. Not that he's a bad child, but you know, there are sleepless nights, he gets sick, and he needs day care. You have to think about all those things, and you can never be hundred-percent prepared to be a parent, no matter what people tell you.

Having a child is definitely rewarding. Every time I see Carter, I see myself, his dad, my sister, my mom, and a little bit of my dad. And you know the smile that he gives you when he wakes up, just the hugs and the slobbering kisses are very rewarding at his age, because he's only six months old. But you know, just like everything in life, there are pluses and minuses. As he gets older and as I become older too, my thoughts will definitely change. But this is how I currently feel and have experienced right now with Carter being six months old.

As Carter gets older, as he starts progressing and having his own opinions, and as I become older, my thoughts will change, and parenting will definitely become easier. But there are still going to be challenges. The only thing, I think, that will become a little bit easier is maybe sleep. Everything right now is difficult because he's only six months old; he's so young.

*Joseph Shields*

My thoughts about parenting are different since I've become a parent as opposed to how I thought about it before being married and having children. I feel a lot about the way environmental factors and social factors can influence and change a child or an individual. One of a kind, hard, but I would say, among the valuable lessons that I've learned as a dad has been that kids are kids based on who they are coming out of the womb, given the kind of DNA and RNA of how they're shaped and their personalities. There are a lot of ways, from being God's creation when they're born, that we can influence their personalities, that we can shape it and guide it, but I've become much more respectful of the fact that, you know, my son and my daughter have their own personalities, regardless of what I thought they should be or where they should go from the get go. I think that's a learning process in terms of parenting. And so it shifts how you want to approach nurturing and caring for a child as a result of that. And it really makes you more of a guide and an influencer and obviously a good example, as opposed to somebody that's trying to change everything your kids are going to be by the spot. So that's my perspective.

*Barbara VanDyke*

It's a blessing to be a parent, and it's a gift that you get for a lifetime. It's a gift because parenting provides the parent with opportunities to grow and develop in areas in which they wouldn't have ordinarily grown without being a parent. And the reason I say so is because some of the beliefs and maybe even some values I didn't hold fast to before becoming a parent because the reality of being a parent in and of itself was a lesson—a lesson to live my life by or to guide me in my own life and to move from one stage of development as a parent or as an adult to another. I don't think I had, for example, the patience or the degree of patience I have now before I became a parent. I am not so sure that I saw things through the lens of a child like I did after I became a parent. When I interacted or worked with children before, I might not have been as empathetic as I should have been to their needs, but once I became a parent, I learned very quickly to feel and see things through the lens of a child's eyes and understand what they may be going through and understand that like me, like an adult, they have emotions, they sense fear, they have difficulty with changes and transitions, they see and recognize when you don't care about them, they see when you're unfair, and you know those things help you do your own self-reflection if that does occur in your parenting relationship and help you to grow.

# TEN THINGS ABOUT PARENTING

- Parenting is joyous, rewarding, and challenging and the most important responsibility anyone can ever have. Parenting is about caring. As a parent, you make many sacrifices but receive many rewards. Parenting is a life-changing experience. Parenting is a 24-7 responsibility, and it is tougher than you may think.

- There is a spiritual perspective to parenting, in that the cocreation and nurturance of another human being from infancy to adulthood, and at the same time parents themselves grow and develop in various ways, is the greatest gift given to us by the Father.

- Parenting is an all-encompassing journey…it is ever evolving. One's parenting role shifts and changes over time. Although we tend to parent the way we were parented, parenting in today's world may require different parental behaviors to pass on the same important values we acquired from our parents. Parenting changes with each generation, as the younger generation tries to improve upon what they view as mistakes their parents made.

- Parenting must be taken seriously, and parents must think about the long-term consequences of what they are instilling in their children. Children will observe their parents' behavior and mimic how they treat each other and how they interact with others in the world. As a parent, you are fully responsible for your child, to teach them to be fully responsible, successful contributors to society. You are your child's first teacher, and you play an important role in their early and ongoing development.

- Parenting includes setting high standards for your children; it is therefore important to think about what you want to intentionally and thoughtfully impart to your children, as well as how you are going to demonstrate consistency between your values and your behavior. Some persons may be more suited to be parents than others because they are willing to embrace the commitment that parenting requires.
- Parents need outside support. They need "a village" to support them in carrying out their parenting responsibilities and should not be timid or afraid to ask for assistance.
- Single parenting can be one-sided, and certain components may be left out; therefore, it's important for both parents to be actively engaged in raising their child.
- Divorced parents co-parent in separate households; therefore, it's important for both parents to facilitate the relationships between and among the adults and children.
- It's important to note that young children may not fully understand what parents are trying to impart to them, because they do not have the background experiences to facilitate their projections into the future.
- Parents should also be aware that children have their own unique personalities from birth and their main focus should not be on changing the things they don't like about their children; rather, they should be more of a guide, an influencer, and the best example in the lives of their children.

# CHAPTER 2

# Parents Share Their Views on the Value Respect

## Respect

> Respect is a positive feeling or action shown towards someone or something considered important, or held in high esteem or regard...it is also the process of honoring someone by exhibiting care, concern, or consideration for their needs or feelings. (Wikipedia 2018)
>
> Respect your efforts. Respect yourself. Self-respect leads to self-discipline. When you have both firmly under your belt, that's real power.
> —Clint Eastwood

It's important to begin with the value respect, as it is the foundation for positive human relationships and the building block for warm, nurturing, effective parent-child relationships. Parents need to understand and accept the value of first respecting themselves so they can fully understand and accept the value of respecting their children. Respect is a positive force in the child-rearing process. When parents have high regard for themselves and understand the critical role they play in the lives of their children, they will, most likely (naturally), demonstrate respect for their children in the way they relate to them,

44

that is, holding them in high regard and taking adequate care of their needs and concerns to the fullest extent that they can.

Parental self-respect leads to their demonstration of respect for their children, which in turn leads to children's development of self-respect and in turn their respect for others. It is a winning continuum.

As a parent, how do you define the concept or value of respect, including self-respect?

How do you show respect for yourself, your child or children, and others?

*Marguerite Anderson*

Respect for me is understanding other people's boundaries. It's a general way of interacting with other people. For me it always comes back to kindness and understanding that different people have different things that work for them. So just bearing in mind that what works for you may not work for someone else and just having the overall view that you should be mindful of that. You should be caring when dealing with other people. So in terms of how we teach George respect, we basically set boundaries for him; we tell him, "Now, George, you can't do these things because you would hurt Mommy," or "If you're trying to hit Mommy that hurt," or "You can't throw your utensils on the ground because that's disrespectful, other people have to clean it up. It's not what we do when we're at the table. We use our manners." That one is a little more challenging. He's not throwing food as much as he did even a week ago. He's learning the word *done*, so he's following instructions now; he's now saying "Done" before he starts throwing and hitting me with things. But he has paused, which is good. With respect you have to repeat often; you have to teach them rules.

*Christopher Blanchard*

Having respect is being there for another person and not doing the wrong thing but doing what's right for that person, not just doing your own thing. It's about being loyal to that person and following the rules and orders you set for yourselves. Self-respect is also very important. It's being important to yourself and doing what you feel is right. It's very important because you need to set a good example for your children so you're the person that they look up to, and they need you because they need to learn how to behave and how to act so they look at you as the person to show them what having self-respect means and setting the example of what is right and what is wrong.

*Holly Blum*

Respect is in your heart. Holding people in high esteem. And I think there's an expectation, as far as I'm concerned, that you treat everybody respectfully. You don't have to respect everybody, and you don't have to agree with everybody, but you should treat them with respect. Everybody deserves to be treated that way; whether you agree with somebody's values or whether you agree or disagree with somebody's way of doing things, you still treat them respectfully. My expectation was that my child would treat other people respect-fully too, even if she didn't agree with them. It's important because it's closely connected to kindness and a willingness to understand, empathize, and be compassionate.

*Robert Bovell*

Respect is important for both parents and children. As a child develops, we look for how he/she is learning to be respectful. Children learn to respect parents from infancy, you know, "Don't touch that, if you touch that, there's an end result," whether it's punishment or maybe a corporal spanking on the bottom, or taking away a prize possession. So from these experiences children learn that "Oh, if I listened and obeyed my parents, these things won't get taken away from me or I won't be disciplined in this manner," and that is a form of respect. Also, the manner in which we respond to our children and the person with whom we live, whether fiancée, or husband or wife, teaches a child how he should behave if he expects a certain response from others. This is what makes respect an important value and why parents should establish respect within a child by monitoring their behavior and their response to behavior around children. We need to underline the word *respect* when it comes to raising children. Once children hear cursing, or once they see abuse, they later find out that that's a disrespectful behavior. So the more you teach of something, the less of the negative side you're going to get to it.

*Marlon Bovell*

To me respect is a big one because I tend to use that word sometimes with the kids. I don't think I say it to them; I probably say it around them and more so when I say, "You're not going to disrespect me." I think that's what I may say to them.

Respect to me is appreciating what others do for you and with you and allowing them to make their own decisions, or allowing them to be their own person without damaging their well-being. When it comes to the children, I talk to them about respecting other people, and I also stress that they should not disrespect their parents. If we tell them something they should not talk back, or if they show attitude or certain tone of voice, I tell them that that's not respectful. I explain to them that we're telling them these things because we know better and for their well-being.

As a husband and father, in thinking of how I demonstrate respect I always think about what a good friend of mine told me, my friend Sean. We talked before I got married. I was already a father, because I was stepping into the role as a stepdad. He said one thing that still resonates with me. He said, "You have to instantaneously be the person that you want your kids to become." Those words resonate with me because I can't be around my children and curse, smoke and hit their mother, or show lewd and bad behavior and then tell them not to do it. You know, there's a time and place for everything. I leave certain language and certain behaviors behind when I'm around my kids, so my way of showing respect is to carry myself in a way that will not disrespect others I'm around or hurt their feelings. And I always try to be helpful when I can and show a positive attitude toward family, friends, and my kids. I try to carry myself in a way that I would want my kids to carry themselves.

One way that my children show me respect is that they listen when I speak to them. At this point in their lives, they don't have a lot of responsibility outside of doing their homework and being respectful of people. So their main responsibility is cleaning their room and doing their homework. And if we tell them clean your room or do your homework and we have to say it over and over again, it seems to be disrespectful. But what I'm learning is that it's not necessarily disrespect. It's more so that their young mind is on something else and to them that particular thing is more important than what you as a parent ask them to do. I don't think it's intentional.

*Shanice Bovell*

Respect is something that I have taught my boys. I have taught them that to get respect, you have to give respect. As young black men, they have to always be respectful, especially to their elders. I think that's a very important trait to have, as they're already stereotyped as being the opposite. Respect is a way of life. It's about how you treat other people and carry yourself.

*Dorel Campbell-Adams*

Respect includes self-respect. Whatever your kids see in you on a daily basis, they mimic, and they become you as individuals. They do what they see in their father and/or their mother. They use their father as an example of a male in society, and that's what they carry on. That's why I think it's important that we exhibit self-respect. Of course, self-respect starts from within. First, respecting your body in the way that you take care of it, respecting your mind and the way you feed it with knowledge on a daily basis, and if that's a routine in the home, it becomes routine for the kids. We carry children along up until they leave the home, and then they develop their own views on life, and we hope they will take with them good habits developed from these family routines, such as self-respect, and that these will become routine in their own lives. It's going to carry them longer into life than if you are inconsistent with your views on certain things during their foundation years.

An example of consistency when it comes to self-respect or respect generally is parents being respectful to each other and not letting the kids see them being disrespectful to each other, such as being physically or verbally abusive to each other. If I accept that, then I am not valuing who I am, he's not respecting me, and I don't have enough self-respect to stop that behavior. I think sometimes it's good that they see that we have disagreements, and they follow through and can see how the disagreements start and how they end. It shows that we still have a solid relationship and everything is fine. It's okay to have disagreements, but mutual respect must be shown during disagreements.

*Desiree DeFlorimonte*

Respect can be defined as having the assurance and demonstrating high regard or confidence in yourself and others. I believe that showing care and consideration by thought, words, and deeds show that you value yourself and others. If you value yourself, you will think, say, and behave in ways that reflect this quality. I show respect when relating to myself, my child, and others. For example, I never use curse words or vulgarity, and when I overhear persons who do, to me they are exhibiting a lack of self-respect and respect for others. My personal mantra of "Divine Order" that comes from my love and respect for God emanates to my child, my family, and others. Respect begins with me. I am therefore more capable of respecting others if I first respect myself.

When I think about respect between my child and me, it was imperative that I lead by example and demonstrate how to be respectful. One aspect of being a good parent was to train my child to be respectful to me, her elders, and those in authority. Again, I think about my mother teaching me the basic manners of saying, "Excuse me," "Please," and "Thank you" when requesting something and when the request is granted. Disrespect was never tolerated in our home, and I had the same expectations for Angel. At an early age, she was required to be respectful to family members and other adults, including her teachers. Once, when she refused to eat her dinner and her grandmother scolded her stating, "Do you know how many children are starving in Guyana and you are wasting good, good food?" Angel rudely responded, "Well, send it to them." I immediately intervened and let her know that it was inappropriate to speak to her grandmother in that manner and she needed to apologize. I believe if a child is permitted to be disrespectful to her parents/grandparents, then she will not be respectful to any adult. It was important for me to nip disrespectful behavior in the bud and talk about more acceptable ways to speak with adults, void of screaming and losing my cool…not always an easy thing to do.

As Angel grew older, I realized that to show her respect, I had to be considerate of her feelings and show respect for her individuality, opinions, and accomplishments. There were occasions when my respectful relationship with my daughter meant being positive, giving praise, being supportive, showing empathy, and even apologizing when I made mistakes. Through the years, I learned and taught my child that respect should not be demanded but earned. I had to be the role model for my child to emulate being a respectful person.

*Ryan Dickson*

Respect is a sociological, cultural creation that is warranted and needed. I have an open view of respect—be flexible, listen, follow rules, do what works for human beings in the society as a whole, definitely respecting elders. Everybody is going to be one. Everybody was young at one time; it just makes sense. Elders have more knowledge, they've seen more things, and even that has value, so does respecting other people and respecting people's space and giving them enough space to feel comfortable. You may not know their background or where they're from and what their norms and traditions are, but there's universal value in giving people space physically and getting consent for hugs and things of that nature. Then there's creating space for people to speak up. You have a voice and a choice, and no matter what, choose to use it. And if you're teetering on the brink of speaking up, or staying silent, consider strongly speaking up. Then there is respect for your life, to live your dreams, to live your lives to the fullest. When we don't know how to do something, it's okay to seek out the solution. That's how I live out respect in my own life.

I'm always seeking out development—mentally, spiritually, emotionally, physically, socially—and I have an attitude of curiosity. That's how I live in my own life. Of course, holding the doors for people, saying please and thank you, being respectful to my mom, and doing so as a parent as well. I practice respect with my children and other family members, and I think this is pretty much a way to command respect.

*Richlyn Emanuel*

I don't talk bad about people. I respect his face; he respects mine. I'm respectful to everyone around me, even if we don't like each other. You don't tear each other down, you say hello, you don't walk away. I'm meeting self-respect. I don't allow people to disrespect me. Once they do it one time, I leave them alone, because as a single mom, you can't allow others to disrespect you and you can't have your son see that because then he'll think, "Well, that's the way I treat women."

I don't allow him to disrespect me because the majority of his teachers in school are women. All the male role models in his life have shown him this is how you treat people, and this is how not to treat people. I try to maintain that; it's hard sometimes, but I try.

*Raymond Fisher*

Respect is probably the cornerstone of all these four values. You have to have self-respect. You have to love yourself and know yourself and always be seeking self-improvement to show and teach others, especially your children. Respect is a two-way street. You have to give it to get it. It sounds like a cliché, but it's very simple in its complexity. You set boundaries, and you have to adhere to them. What you most often see in a lot of homes of people who have challenges with their children is, as the boundaries are set, there is not a clear line on who the adult is and who the child is and people have to learn something that I don't think is in any book. It's something that you learn early on, that the children in your life will push those boundaries. They're going to challenge those boundaries, and you have to be steadfast in things, such as setting curfews and building expectations of what you want from your children, such as educational excellence, spiritual growth, being able to take care of yourself, cleanliness, and so on. There's a unique science to it. The respect aspect, like I said before, is the cornerstone because it helps you to build on everything else. In the end, it's the most important dynamic of the parent-child relationship.

I demonstrate respect for my children by being transparent and honest with them. That's the first part. I let them know that we're all human and we're not perfect. I don't know that their generation does it, but I know in my generation, we put our parents on a pedestal. Mom and Dad could do no wrong, and when they did wrong, it was a great disappointment. I experienced that in my life with my father. The biggest letdown with my dad was when he fell prey to alcoholism, had a nervous breakdown, and suffered through that emotional challenge. It was very disappointing because I had set him up on such a high pedestal. So I am very transparent and honest with my kids. And I do that to teach them the ways of the real world. You have to be honest and transparent to a degree with everybody that you deal with in relationships. It comes with trust and honesty on both sides. I tell my kids that they're going to make mistakes; the key is not to keep making the same mistakes. I tell them to take counsel when it's given to them and in the vein that it's given to them, in love, not because I'm trying to be strict or hard on them, but I know what it takes to survive and sustain productively in life.

*Martine Gordon*

For me, first and foremost, when you say respect in the context of parenting, I think immediately of the respect that I can demonstrate and show to my child. That includes demonstrating self-respect for myself so that she can also understand that you should respect yourself in addition to feeing others should respect you. You shouldn't assume people won't respect you. Culturally, I come from a family in which the children are not necessarily their priorities or their needs aren't considered first, and that's a cultural thing in my background, and I as a parent try to disagree with that. I try to consider how my daughter might be feeling in new situations, consider that she might not remember Auntie So-and-So from last year, and so I'm not just going to throw her in her arms when auntie comes to visit; you know, she might be intimidated by that. So for me, it's both demonstrating that as a role model, I should respect myself, but also thinking from her perspective that I respect her as a person even though she's very young.

I've always struggled with being self-deprecating in my language, not necessarily in my professional life, but when I'm home or with my family, and as I've become a parent, one example of how I've tried to demonstrate self-respect is by not being self-deprecating, not apologizing for things that don't require an apology, and just demonstrating that I am worthwhile as a person in small ways, obviously not being over the top and having all sorts of hubris, but demonstrating that I'm a person, I'm an individual, and I think for a woman raising a daughter, that's really important for me to demonstrate to my daughter that she can be a strong, respected individual.

*Justin Hampton*

Respect is treasuring, as valuable, the uniqueness and position that someone has. I try to make sure that I'm doing so in front of my children and I'm getting better at it. In reference to me and my wife in terms of how we respect one another and one another's opinion in front of the children, we have to get better at that because we disagree a lot. We're not one to yell or scream or argue outright, but our disagreements can probably come to each other at times, and I can see that in the way the kids interact with each other. I can tell they're mirroring and gleaning certain things. I try to pull them to the side and try to get to the bottom of it. I may say, "Is this something you learned at your school?" "Was somebody in school saying that?" "Why do you say that to your brother?" "Where do you hear that?" If I can identify something they learned at home, I try to correct them, but I make sure that I don't belittle them in the way that I correct them, in the way that I address them, to make sure that I'm building them up in whatever sort of correcting I'm doing so that they never feel like, "Well, when Daddy has something to say, or when I mess up, he doesn't care about me," or "He doesn't love me." In correcting, it's always comes back to "You know I love you, right? But we have to fix this." So I try to make sure they understand they are also respected.

*Leticia Herrera*

Well, self-respect, I believe that is the key for every individual. If I do not respect myself, I will not expect to be respected. So I set a standard for myself and passed it on to my son to ensure that he knows the difference between respecting himself and his expectation to be respected. It doesn't matter what age. I emphasized throughout David's childhood how important it is to respect other people. That's the way I raised him, to respect himself and make sure that he will respect everyone else regardless the age, race, or the place or region the individual comes from. He can show respect to people by taking time to look at the person or listen to the person and respect what they have to say. Then he can talk back and share his views and how he feels. Just make sure the other person, regardless of their education or background, will be able to feel respected and valued.

I do believe that by him seeing the way I treat myself and how I treat all people has given him an example of how to treat himself and other people, and that's what he's doing because he respects others and he respects himself. When he and I have a conversation, if he doesn't agree with what I am saying, he will respect that, but then he will come back to me and say, "This is my point, but I respect your opinion because that's the way you were raised. I know that you grew up in a different time, but this is a different time, and I do respect what it is right now, and I know that you don't agree." That's how we communicate. He will show respect, and he will take whatever is useful for his life. He will also respect what his stepfather says, also anyone who will give him advice, like my family and friends and his friends, because he has seen me do that.

*Joseph Kijewski*

I think you always have to teach by example, and that's the best way to teach in any situation, but especially with children. Be the person you want them to grow up to be. Model that person.

Going back to my own childhood, I came from a family with an alcoholic father and a lot of issues with physical abuse and things like that, and I always knew what kind of parent I didn't want to be. I wanted to be a parent, and I thought I could do it much better.

The behaviors that my father modeled, I would never want to take up myself or pass on anyone else and increase the sentence. He grew up in the same kind of household, and that's what he saw, that's what he learned, and that's what he lived with us growing up. Luckily, my mother was very much the opposite. She was an excellent parent. I didn't have a good model as a father, but I think you have to model for your child conduct that you want to see from them. If you're not respectful toward your spouse, you're raising someone who, when they're married, is not going to be respectful toward their spouse. If you're having temper tantrums in front of your children, they're going to have temper tantrums. If you're disrespectful, or dismissive of others, that's what they're going to adopt. I've seen it across the spectrum of my family. I've seen it with my siblings and my cousins, I've seen their traits showing up in their children, and I believe it's the modeling that you do in front of your children that's going to influence them more than anything else.

So with something like respect, I've always tried to be respectful to my wife. We disagree on things at times, but we're never disrespectful toward each other. We disagree on things like adults, you know, we're on the same page when it comes to the children, and the children are always free to disagree with me. They're free. They've always been free to disagree with me, but in a respectful fashion. And it's my hope that in their relationships as adults, they'll be carrying on that same behavior as parents.

There are certain parental behaviors that I consider to be disrespectful toward the children, the worst being anything involving physical abuse or physical violence. Children should never be seeing that. It doesn't have to be you doing it yourself; it's what you allow them to watch on TV. It could be choosing to expose them to that what you watch on TV in front of them, what movies you take them to, what music you listen to. I think it all goes into that. So if you're taking enjoyment in something that is of questionable value, something that is demeaning of somebody else, whether or not you're the person doing it, I think that the example for your child will be that "This is fun, this is something to be enjoyed, this is something that can be done," you know, speaking disparagingly in the crudest ways about this person or that person. It's fine. But it's really not fine. You're setting up a pattern that is going to be harmful to them. It's not making them a better person in the world.

*Errol Marks*

Well, respect starts with self-respect, and if you don't have any self-respect, you can't expect anyone to respect you. And I think you should work on the core value of self-respect. Once you understand yourself and understand how to respect yourself, you'll find that respecting others is automatic, and it's applied to the children as well. I've learned that the strategy to earning their respect is actually letting them know what you will accept and what you won't accept without being domineering, without having to force of coerce that from them. And that would play into reciprocity as well.

I treat my children differently from how I was treated as a child. I treat them somewhere in between contemporary and conventional parenting. I appeal to their intellect, as in saying to them, "You know how you enjoy spending time with me at my house," "You know why you're coming here," "You know what motivates you to want to be here," and "You know what you love about being here." So if something were to happen that would cause you to not act according to what will allow a good time, ask yourself, are you willing to risk that? Are you willing to spoil everyone's mood or spoil everyone's fun? I tell them simply, "Don't make me do my job." It's something I learned from being a corrections officer; I would tell the inmates, "Don't make me do my job. Everybody will be fine if you do what you're supposed to do, what's expected of you. Then you can do whatever you want afterward." It's a simple rule, but I'm not like a warden when it comes to my girls. I ask them, "Well, hey, you didn't clean up your room, tell me how that makes you feel. Why wouldn't you care about that?"

I start a conversation because I'm not so strict on the rules and I don't want them to live in fear of me and fear of my wrath. Of course, they know when they cross a certain line that I go into that mode and they are well aware of that, and they have an understanding that if they don't do this or that, Dad's going to be upset, and when he's upset, nobody has fun, and he doesn't want to be upset either. So I never let them cross my boundaries. I always stand by my boundaries, and that's it. There are hard and fast, and I help them to understand that. My boundaries are hard and fast, but there's a lot of room in between to enjoy the space they're allowed to live in. It's not respect derived from fear. It's not oppressive, it's not respect derived from fear, because I give them the respect as well, so it is reciprocal. And you should not think of them as your property as some people do. I call that third world parenting, especially being Chinese. I know some parents can be in total control of their kids. I don't want to control my kids. I don't want them to be controllable. I want them to be independent thinkers; however, they are free to do what they want to do within certain boundaries.

I'm not raising my kids in any way that I was raised, more or less. I'm kind of questioning everything and doing what I think is right because I remember what it was like being a child growing up with certain personal attributes, like fears. I had fears and certain behavioral patterns that developed as a child that I attribute to how I was raised. But that's blaming. I could blame my parents as a child, but I can't blame my parents as an adult. So taking responsibility, I have managed to curtail certain learned behaviors so as to not have them waterfall down onto my children. I've learned to stop myself and to do the opposite. For example, instead of yelling at them, I would appeal to their intellect. I don't want my kids to feel inferior or incompetent; I don't want them to rebel as I did growing up.

*Maxine Maloney*

I define respect as how we approach and treat others and how we feel and then even treat ourselves. I want to share a caveat that I started with my daughter from very young from when she could speak, and she spoke very early—she started talking at ten months. There's something that we have, and those are values and characteristics tied to our family values; there's respect. And it was important that she learned very young about having respect for others—and *others* means humans, animals, the environment, the earth, and all the things that you have. So it's treating others as you would like to be treated, and she's been having that notion of empathy be part of that notion of respect. When it came to self-respect, it's having pride in who you are and what you do, and so who you are is carrying yourself in a way that people will treat you well and recognize your gifts and not give them opportunities to disrespect you. I model that by how I speak to my daughter, Zaria, how I speak to others, and then when I see those behaviors that are disrespectful or lack self-respect, I will immediately point those out. I started that really early and even used open-ended questions, like, "How did you feel when you saw that?" or "How did you feel when you said that?" or "How do you think the persons felt when this happened?" Because that notion of respect has to be an anchor in who we are so that we learn to treat others well and first and foremost treat ourselves well.

From very early on for Zaria, I would use that word *respect*— even before she could fully even understand the notion of respect is just part of our vernacular—"I respect you," "I respect that you did that, but here's how I feel." And then when she did things, I would say, "Do you think that was respectful?" Respect is really part of our core family values and part of our character. Building character very early on is what I always did with Zaria before she could even really say full sentences. And thinking of that notion of respect for parents comes even when your babies are infants—respecting that when they cry, the cry is their way of speaking, and we respond to it and respect is listening and understanding the different tones, because there's crying that I'm just expressing myself; there's crying when I'm in pain; there's crying when I'm hungry; there's crying when I'm tired; and from early on being able to really hone in and be in tune to those cries and your baby's rhythm, I think, is an anchor and the beginnings of respect. Now that Zaria is a teenager, you know, respecting that she needs her own space and her own time; respecting that she needs to express herself, but she has to express herself in a respectful manner; and then when she does feel angry, or anxious or overwhelmed, recognizing that she's human and it's okay to feel that way. But expressing it in a respectful manner shows it doesn't hurt others' feelings, and when she does, in recognizing that she's human, that when she does do it, I will say, "You know, Zaria, did you think it was respectful that you did that and did you think about how I felt?" Then when I realize that I had done something that wasn't what I would consider respectful, being able to apologize to her and say, "I'm really sorry that I lashed out. I was angry" or "I was agitated" or "My mind was not able to take in what you were saying."

*Virgil McDonald*

I had the opportunity to talk with our sons (unfortunately, our daughter passed away at a relatively young age) about these four concepts because I wanted to get their feedback. I was very pleased with what I heard from them. In general, they said that we did not teach them respect; they learned to be respectful from us. They were clear about what we would do and not do out of respect for each other. These patterns of behavior guided them, and they apply the same principles with their children.

Respect is being, first of all, respectful to you. If you respect yourself, you can easily respect others. One of my favorite quotes and a principle I have tried to live by is from Hamlet by William Shakespeare, "This above all to thine own self be true and it must follow, as the night the day that thou canst not thence be false to any man." There are standards that you establish for yourself and your children. For example, we did not want our children to use profane language. Therefore, we did not utter vile words in their presence. I think my children were adults before they ever heard me curse. I learned that from my father. So I define respect as honoring the dignity of all persons.

I grew up in a family with both brothers and sisters, and my parents insisted that we respect each other—our privacy, dreams, and aspirations. In our family, modesty forbade us from being undressed or partially dressed in presence of each other. It was required that we get fully dressed before leaving our bedrooms in the morning. My children understood that this was the kind of respect we would show each other. If they had a goal, a dream, or an aspiration, we respected that. If we had to point out pitfalls, we always tried to do so without disparaging, belittling, or trivializing them or their dreams. We were supportive, but at the same time, we did not neglect our responsibility to lead and guide them.

*Jacqueline Rose*

I truly believe in Namaste.

The God, love, light, truth in me honors the God source in you as my child or my grandchild.

This intention is the cornerstone of RESPECT.

*Joseph Shields*

Respect, I think, is a lot about how you carry yourself and how, whether you want them to or not, how people are going to perceive you. We talk a lot about respect with our son, Christopher, as he gets older. Christopher is obviously biracial, and the perception of a black child matters differently in this world than it does, I would say, for white children and people of different races and ethnicities. So I think we are really trying to make sure we focus on both how Christopher presents himself and on him being aware of his social surroundings. That's because he can easily be judged by other people as being highly articulate or as someone who gets himself in trouble. Because I've worked in the criminal justice system, I know people that get themselves into trouble are often enough affected by people, places, and things. So as a parent I'm mindful of being intentional about what I think is really, really important. Fortunately for us, both our children have been really, really good about that, particularly our son, as he gets older and thinks of being intentional about how he engages his folks and his friends, and in building peer support for himself and interacting with all the elders and family members. For myself, I would say, respect goes into some of the other values, and hopefully, I show myself to be and carry myself in a way that sets a good example within the family.

I'm probably the quietest one in our family dynamic, and sometimes my kids are surprised by the kind of a personality I may show to the public. Sometimes it's a different dynamic; it's business. I run my own company, and I'm very much a kind of alpha male and assertive, so it's a different dynamic. And I try to share that with my kids as well, particularly my son; he's seen me in a bunch of different environments, from professional settings coming to work, owning and running a $100 million agency, working in the private sector or at home, then out socially.

We don't have an around-the-kitchen-table lesson learned time where we'll work through issues; it's really facing issues calmly, hopefully facilitating a process where my son and daughter know what things mean and how they want to execute solutions.

*Halima Thorne*

I've always been taught to have respect for others. That is something that was shown in my household. Not that it was taught in a book; it was basically demonstrated and shown to have respect for others. If we didn't show respect for others, there were consequences. My parents definitely taught me to have respect for others.

Now for self-respect—I definitely have respect for myself, but I think that I had to learn that going through life. Of course, there were some challenges that I had to find out by loving myself. Since I didn't love myself at one time, I didn't respect myself. I'm going through that phase in my life where I figured it out by seeking therapy, just talking and being more open about what is going on with me and how to improve myself. So working on myself, I've learned to love myself and have more respect for myself. It's not to say I was doing incriminating things out there, but you know, what helped me was knowing my self-worth, being aware of it, acknowledging it, and getting help when I needed it.

I show respect to Carter by loving him, giving him all the hugs and kisses that I can, making sure that he has everything he needs at the current moment, from diapers to having a roof over his head and clothes on his back. I show my respect to my child. I will go above and beyond for him if I have to, just to make things right for him.

*Barbara VanDyke*

For me, self-respect is demonstrating or modeling the type of behavior that you are teaching or training your child and demonstrating the same values you're instilling in your child. And I know respect goes across a wide spectrum, but I'm keeping it narrow to the parent/child relationship. I believe it's disrespectful to demonstrate all the things that are unlike what you're teaching and the expectations that you have for your child. For example, if what you're teaching is, "You are special," "You are God's child," "You are beautiful," then you need to exemplify or demonstrate to your child that you are the same way and you feel the same way about yourself and not demonstrate behaviors that teach the child or show examples to the child that you don't have those same beliefs of yourself.

As parents, there are behaviors that we don't encourage, and we try to ensure that our children don't inculcate these behaviors. So we kind of manage their social relationships and peer groups because we feel that we can see that that may not be right for them. Then we set those expectations and violate them ourselves in our own lives. I think it brings disrespect to the parent. It is disrespecting yourself, but disrespect, like I said, is vast. I probably should give vignettes to explain more about respect, but I'll put that on hold and get to the next question.

# Ten Things about Respect

- Respect is about showing care and consideration in thought, word, and deed. It's about showing that you have high regard for yourself and others. Respect is about honoring the dignity of all persons.
- Showing respect is doing what is right for others. It's about kindness, understanding, empathy, and compassion. It's about having concern for the well-being of others and being mindful of how you behave in their presence.
- Teaching respect requires that parents teach children rules and frequently repeat these rules. It takes more than one lesson for children to learn the rules. The more parents teach what is expected, the less negativity they'll get from the children.
- Respect is an important dynamic of the parent-child relationship in which parents teach by example. When parents fully understand the value of self-respect, their respect for the children and others will become automatic.
- Parents can show respect for their children by allowing the children to share their views, opinions, and feelings and by attentively listening to them. Parents can also allow their children to disagree with them as long as they do so in a respectful manner. Parents should respect their children's goals, dreams, and aspirations.
- Parental respect for their children begins during pregnancy and is openly expressed in infancy through their responses to the infant's crying and other behaviors that place demands on the parents.

- If you respect your life, you will live it to the fullest. You will live out your dreams, and you will also focus on your personal development as an example for your children. Parents ought to be mindful that they model the expectations they express to their children and that they do not violate these expectations in their own lives.
- It's all right to have disagreements in families as long as there is no physical or verbal abuse. When children witness the resolution of conflicts between their parents, they get a sense of how mutual respect is demonstrated in relationships.
- Consider the cultural aspects of respect when interacting in culturally diverse settings. These include, but are not limited to, physical space, acceptable ways of greeting someone, and cultural differences in parental beliefs and practices.
- Respect for racial and cultural differences is played out in our society's criminal justice system, and it is important for parents to teach their children how they are perceived and judged within and outside their communities, as well as the ramifications of their behavior outside their homes.

# CHAPTER 3

# Parents Share Their Views on the Value Responsibility

## Responsibility

> A responsibility is something you are
> expected to do...or a way you are expected to act.
> (Talking with Trees, LoveWell Press 2013)

Responsible people do what they need to do, or have to do, without being told. They have a sense of duty to do what is expected or required of them. They also understand there are consequences, both positive and negative, attached to fulfilling or not fulfilling their responsibilities.

Parents have a multitude of responsibilities related to raising their children. The word *parent* provides a concise, concrete list of specific parental responsibilities and is an excellent way for parents to remember major responsibilities they are expected to fulfill.

*Some Important Responsibilities of Parents*

PROVIDER—parents are expected to meet the basic needs of their children, such as food, clothing, housing, health care, education, guidance, and nurturance.

ADVOCATE—parents are expected to speak on behalf of their children to responsible individuals and agencies within and outside the home to ensure their children are receiving the necessary services of high quality.

ROLE MODEL—parents are the first adults with whom children interact and are considered their children's most influential socializing agents. Children are always listening and watching; therefore, parents must always be setting the example by what they say and do.

ENCOURAGER—parents are expected to "be there" for their children, to listen to their challenges as well as their successes. Parents are expected to be cheerleaders for their children, championing their causes and pointing them in the right direction as often as needed.

NURTURER—parents are expected to give their children warmth, support, and understanding. Children thrive on love; it is a powerful variable in their lives. Love includes setting boundaries that are in each child's best interest. Parents must get to know each child's unique temperament so as to respond appropriately by giving each child what is necessary for them to thrive.

TEACHER—parents are considered their children's first teachers. When children enter school for the first time, they bring with them the knowledge, skills, attitudes, and behaviors they learned at home from these important first teachers.

As a parent, how do you define the concept or value of responsibility?

How important is responsibility?

How important is it for you to be a responsible parent and for your child/children to develop and demonstrate responsible behavior?

How do you or how have you demonstrated responsibility in your own parenting? Give examples of your own responsible behavior.

*Marguerite Anderson*

We basically divide up chores in our household. I am responsible for certain things, and Sean is responsible for certain things—so for instance, I cook dinner, I do the majority of the laundry, Sean cleans up after dinner, and basically, we've been showing George how to clean up. He's very good at it—he actually has a set of toys that we purchased him, like brooms and mops and a dustpan. And he uses them and he goes one further—whenever there's a spill, he gets the cloth and he just starts wiping it up. And I think that's great—that's something that I want him to continue to understand that we're all living in this household together. We all have a responsibility to keep the household in a neat and tidy way that makes for a calm environment. I really think that those aspects of responsibility are important. Also, you know, I am responsible for myself in my relationship, and Sean is responsible for himself and also for each other. So we approach it like we approach everything. We look at the world as if there are the two of us and we are a partnership working together, so what do we have to do to help each other to be responsible for each other. And I think, I hope, that George sees that because we are a partnership better taking different aspects, taking different roles in our relationship, that he'll understand that he too is part of our unit and that he will have responsibilities, and as he grows up—he's still quite small—he doesn't have a lot of responsibilities, but you know, I do appreciate that when I say, "George, it's time to clean up," he starts putting toys away. So he does understand that for him to live in our environment he has to clean up, and that's a pretty good thing.

*Christopher Blanchard*

Raising a child is a lot of responsibility. You have to be there for your children, and it's not always easy. It's a team effort, and there are lots of things to do to be there for your children and to teach them to be responsible. Being a father for the second time is a lot of responsibility, always doing right and leading by example are very important to me. As a father, I see our responsibility in raising the girls is to show them what is right or wrong, showing respect to others, and leading by example.

It's our responsibility to teach them, and when they do something wrong, there has to be consequences. But I also understand that because my older daughter is two years old, she's going to have tantrums at times, and we have to have patience. The most important thing is being there, and that's a big responsibility to always be there and be a part of their lives growing up and leading by example.

I would definitely like my girls to be responsible adults. I would want them to follow the rules and laws and have good values so they know what's right from wrong, to lead by example and to treat others how they want to be treated. I definitely believe it's my responsibility now, as well as my wife's, to lead by example, to do what's right so that when the girls are older, they will stay on the right path.

*Robert Bovell*

As far as responsibility is concerned, we as parents must illustrate to or teach a child what is responsibility, and it can be something as small as your favorite toy—if you leave your favorite toy in the middle of the floor after you play with it, without putting it up and putting it in its right place, you risk or take the chance in that toy being destroyed, or misplaced, or misused by others, but if you pick this toy up and you place it back in your room in your toy chest, or in a safe corner in your room, then that toy stays in the same condition as when you pulled it from the corner to play with it and not risk other things happening to it. That's the first step of responsibility. The next thing in responsibility is teaching them the timetable of life. If you wake up every morning to watch cartoons as a child and prepare yourself for the day, you must set a time regiment that you should be able to watch your show, get dressed, brush your teeth, clean your room, do your grooming, and be ready on time when Mommy or Daddy is ready to go out the door. If you don't follow that rule or you break that cycle, and you hear Mommy or Daddy holler, "Come on, I told you!" then your responsibility timetable becomes disrupted.

At age four and five years old, children already have a sense of what they want, what they want to play with, and what they want to eat. While they're developing in these areas, parents can provide a model of how these things can be done. What I'm saying is, if your child's favorite show comes on in the morning, then the child needs to rise up earlier and make sure he takes care of his responsibilities so he can enjoy the show—if not, he can't watch the show. Parents much teach children the timetable of life, and these responsible behaviors will carry over to their school and adulthood lives.

I reward responsible behavior with things children either like to do or places they like to go, for example, trips to Sesame Place or Great Adventures. But for these bigger rewards they have to fulfill their responsibilities on a daily and timely basis. Usually, young children get excited about and want things they see on the television, such as Great Adventures, or a favorite toy, or Mickey Mouse or Disney World. I use these opportunities to remind them to keep their rooms clean, get good grades, or attend to their hygiene. I use a reward system.

As for my own behavior, I model responsible behavior by never disrespecting their mother and by taking care of my other responsibilities, such as paying the bills, keeping the house clean, and keeping the grass cut. I let the children see these behaviors on a consistent basis, and then they too will act in that same manner. It's best to never introduce children to a comfort zone where you're constantly disrespecting one another, because it's going to result in one of two things for the child—either they develop the mind-set that it's acceptable to disrespect people and continue what they think is normal behavior (the mind-set), or when they start to see or hear disruption, they remove themselves from that situation because they see it as not being normal behavior and they prefer to be associated with behaviors that they view as good and acceptable to them, or what is normal for them. That's why I always talk to their mother with respect; at least I always practice that. If there's anything they need, we come together to discuss it, and if I can't do it and you can do it, or you find complications in doing it, let's collectively see if we can get it done or explain why we can't do it at this time. For example, their mother may say, "I thought I told you that the car needed to be fixed so I can take the kids to Sesame Place which is seventy-five miles away. I need tires." I would say, "I apologize, honey, for not getting it done in a timely manner," but explain that other things came up that prevented me from doing it at the time, and maybe we should consider pushing the schedule back for a bigger trip after we do thorough maintenance to the car and I don't have to worry about you getting a flat tire or getting in an accident. It's important for a child to understand that parents may not be able to get everything done at the time they need to be done, but they will get it done when they have the time and the money to do it. It's important for them to understand that if Daddy makes a promise to Mommy, if my parents make a promise, they may not be able to keep it right away, but they will keep it. They give you their word, and they're going to follow through on their word.

Another thing a child learns from this example is that their parents had the discipline to attend to something more important like having lights in the home, food on the table, and a roof over their heads. Kids start to understand that early on, and they carry that over as they grow up.

*Marlon Bovell*

As a parent, I define responsibility as providing for my family, waking up in the morning and going to work, making sure they have everything they need to sustain them, food, electricity supplies for school, clothes, help with homework, taking them to activities, and so on. You know, those basic needs.

I don't feel responsible for going over and above the basic need, but sometimes I find that we do go above the basic needs, and I'm really not sure why. I think I tend to believe that we want them to have things that we didn't have, but the funny part about that is, a lot of those things don't exist now. So generationally, when parents say that some of those things never even existed, for instance, video games, they started to come out when we were younger, we did have video games, so I can't really use that as an example. The cell phone, my wife and I discussed it, and we got cell phones for the kids because she was more concerned that she couldn't get in touch with them. One day our son missed the school bus and he had to borrow someone else's phone to call her, and I was out of town. So now she's convinced he needs one. I never had a cell phone when I was a kid, so giving him a cell phone is going beyond basic needs.

Then the question becomes, do you want your child to be the only one that doesn't have a cell phone when all their friends are on their cell phones and they're sitting there not getting paid attention to? That's just the way that modern kids are nowadays. There's peer pressure and as a parent, you kind of want them to not feel like they don't fit in. But at the same time, I'm telling them not to give in to peer pressure, but I'm feeding into it. It's like a catch-22. So I guess I'm going above and beyond with something like a cell phone, but not necessarily with clothes. We don't buy expensive clothes. We explained to them that name brand clothes aren't necessary. I remember my mother used to tell me those same things when I wanted Jordache jeans. Now, with the information that I have, I can tell them that these jeans are made in the same places as the other more expensive jeans; they just put a name on it, and it becomes more expensive. When it comes to clothing and things like that, we don't go above and beyond, maybe except for some sneakers. If they want a nice pair of sneakers and have good grades, we may get them. At Christmas, their mother goes above and beyond and gets them so many toys. She said that's because when she was a child, her mother did the same thing. So I pulled back from the toys. They weren't expensive; it was just the quantity, just so many of them, and it sets a bad expectation for the kids. That's where we disagree, and we do go above and beyond.

In terms of giving the kids responsibility, now is the time where we're starting to put more responsibility on them. I'm not really sure at what age you start trying to give kids responsibility, but I think no matter what age, if you start with small tasks, they will catch on, and they will respond because kids are resilient. I wouldn't like my kids to feel entitled. I tend to use the word *entitled* and say to them, "You are not going to be entitled kids, we're not raising entitled kids." I tend to say that a lot, but at the same time some of our actions give them all the entitlements. We are going to start giving them more responsibility outside of their homework, such as small things to do around the house. Currently, we're having them put their own clothes away. We haven't shown them how to use the washer and dryer to wash clothes as yet, but we told our son since he just turned thirteen, we're going to start showing him how to wash clothes. We showed his older sister at a young age. Right now, when we wash the clothes, we put their clothes on their beds and have them put them away.

We've shown them how to sort clothes before washing. We have two baskets, and they put the darks in one basket and the lights in the other basket. They do a good job; that is a very small task, but they do it well. When it's time to wash the darks, lights and whites are already separated. Soon we'll be teaching them how to wash the clothes and then how to load and use the dishwasher. I remember my sisters and I had a day each week when we alternated washing the dishes and doing other small tasks. We want to start doing that with our kids.

They have to make their beds every day. They know they need to brush their teeth and take a shower every day. So little things like that, but we haven't given them chores, per se. That's something that we're going to start doing.

They go with us to the grocery store, but we haven't shown them how to assist with grocery shopping as yet, like selecting items off the shelf. We get what we want, they push the cart. They remain with us, but we haven't shown them how to help with getting things off the shelf.

Being responsible for small tasks at home teaches them how to be able to take care of themselves, including when they live on their own later on. It also takes a little bit of slack off of the parents and gives us time to do other things.

*Shanice Bovell*

I define responsibility as taking care of yourself and your loved ones. It shows you care enough and want the best for yourself and others. It also means taking action for your mistakes and doing what's best when it matters most.

My responsibilities as a parent, especially when my children were small were, of course, making sure they were fed, clothed, clean, and educated and making sure that they treated others with respect and carried themselves as responsible young men.

*Holly Blum*

I think responsibility is related to having respect for yourself and others. You become more responsible, more thoughtful about your own behavior and responsible for showing respect and kindness to others. As a parent, you model what respect and responsibility looks and sounds like.

If you take parenting seriously, then you know it goes hand in hand with taking on the responsibility for parenting a child. My own responsible behavior as a parent probably manifested itself in trying to communicate the importance of responsibility and in paying attention to things like who was my child's teacher, paying attention to the things she liked and was interested in and attentive to how I could nurture that and be responsible for finding the right match in terms of, for example, a babysitter, a club and/or school program that encouraged and enriched her interests.

I think some parents are more sensitive or overly sensitive to these things, and others take them for granted. I've come over the years to realize that people that I think are well educated and smart because they do such and such and such and such are clueless, not because they're not respectful and responsible and want the best for their child, but because they come from a very different perspective. These are people who may be an economist, maybe a construction worker, etc. They don't have the background knowledge of these things that seem very obvious to me. And I used to think, "Well, how come they're not paying attention to these things?" I think maybe some of us are hypervigilant because of our background and training or our own personal interests that manifests itself in intentionality and a consciousness about it. Being a thinking, compassionate, passionate, responsible adult is eventually what parents are hoping will happen for their children.

We ate dinner together every night as a family, and I remember reading every night to Jordan, my daughter, but those were things that I think came so naturally from the way we were parented. So when Jordan started to do gymnastics—and it meant that she was going to be eating dinner five o'clock or five thirty and then not be home until nine o'clock, which meant Bill and I would be eating dinner in between together without her—I remember being a little concerned and having a conversation about her really wanting to do this gymnastics. It was a big commitment, and I really understood the commitment, but part of what I had a bit of a problem with was it meant that three or four nights a week, she was not going to be having dinner with us. We were not going to be eating together as a family.

*Dorel Campbell-Adams*

I consistently tell the children, "This home is our little community, and we have to take care of each other, and we have to take care of everything that's involved in the community. That means if you see that the sink is full of dishes, put them in the dishwasher. I shouldn't be telling you to do this on a consistent basis. If the trash can is overflowing, you know you need to empty the trash. This is our community. This is our environment, we need to get accustomed to seeing a clean environment. We know what is normal and what's not normal." I think the responsibility starts with kids knowing what their chores are and being able to navigate that on a daily basis without thinking there's nothing to do when they open their eyes in the morning. I encourage them, now that they're old enough to be responsible for their own chores. Nevin has been washing his clothes since he was tall enough to press the buttons on the washer. It's having certain goals every day and them knowing that they have to do—a, b, c before they do e, f, and g. I think it's important because that's how I was raised, and that's the one thing, compared to all the rights and wrongs when I was growing up, that kept me always busy and focused.

And it also encouraged me to finish something that I started and kept me on task. When you know that you need to do something, you do it; you complete it. If there's something else to be done, you do it. It shouldn't feel like laborious work because you should always, in a consistent way, be doing something; you should always be in a mode of business because that's what keeps your mind active, even if it's chores. It could be anything, but I think for kids, it starts with chores in the house.

As a parent, my responsibility is to ensure that my kids have a comfortable home, have food to eat every day, have clothes on their backs, not necessarily designer clothes. I tell them I give you everything that you need not necessarily what you want. In this day and age, the kids want what they see, you know, everyone's wearing designer items, Gucci belts, and Gucci this and that. I tell them they don't need it and we've at least talked about succumbing to peer pressure. There are many forms of peer pressure. When you say that you want to dress like this and wear these clothes, you're succumbing to peer pressure, and it's okay to be different. It's okay not to do these things.

My responsibility is also to make sure they get the right education that they deserve. If I see that one child has the potential to go farther, then I will encourage that, and I try not to put too much pressure on each of the kids. I'm now realizing their individual potential, and I expect them to put the effort into their work. I'm teaching them not be afraid of hard work. I'm not going to indulge them. Drew likes to move around with me every so often, and on the weekends we would go to the store and be out for a couple hours. She said to me, "Mom, you know, I like shopping with you a lot. We don't have to shop for lots of things, and we don't have to go buying lots of things." She just enjoys the act of being there with me, and we don't have to spend money to enjoy the time.

*Desiree DeFlorimonte*

Some basic responsibilities of parents include providing a safe and loving home, food, clothing, as well as making sure the child has a good education. As a child growing up in a two-bedroom house with five siblings was difficult, but there was a lot of love shared in my home. I learned from my parents that a house is a home if love is infused there. It was my duty to shower Angel with unconditional love as we shared our home. In addition, giving my child healthy meals (although she would have much preferred to eat pizzas, macaroni and cheese, and Mac-nuggets daily) was my responsibility. Teaching her that nutritious meals would contribute to her growing into a strong and healthy person was my duty. Another basic responsibility was to have my daughter wear appropriate and comfortable clothing, but on occasions I would get "pushback" from her. Recently, we viewed an old picture album, and she lamented that I had dressed her in a navy blue and white polka dots dress with knee-high polka dots socks. I admit, sometimes I got it wrong. ☺ My obligation to provide Angel with a good education was one of my most important responsibilities. In addition to being educated at home, she was also educated at a private school, a boarding school, and several public schools. It was my responsibility to immerse myself in her education by supporting her financially, making sure she was on task with her homework, communicating with her teachers, encouraging her when she talked about giving up, and praising her when she was successful.

As Angel's first teacher, there were a number of fundamental skills and concepts she learned from me… I modeled how to be responsible. Beginning at a young age, I incorporated responsibility into her life and provided routines and structure. She observed me, participated in chores around the house, and could be seen putting away her toys after playing and hanging up her clothes, instead of leaving them on the bed or floor. Later, she was responsible for such chores as washing dishes, sweeping the floors, helping to prepare meals, and saving monetary gifts to purchase things she wanted. I did not want my daughter to grow up feeling entitled or that she could just get by because Mommy was there to do everything.

It was also important to teach Angel how to be the best she could be as she grew into a responsible young woman and citizen of the world. We talked a lot about "choices and consequences," and she learned, very quickly, that whatever decision she made, the consequence was always her responsibility.

*Ryan Dickson*

The way the way I look at responsibility, especially as a parent, is more as a causative model, meaning there are always consequences to any action and consequences to nonaction. It's really just creating a world of cause and effect. For example, my child knows that we can live this type of life or this type of life. Let's track the things that we need to do to live this type of life and see if it's worth it.

Responsible behavior, I think, is honoring your word. I still sometimes struggle with honoring my word. For instance, if I'm going to be late, do I always communicate as soon as I know I'm going to be late that I'm running late? Or if a deadline is past, do I always acknowledge deadlines and fulfill promises to get documents in on time? I do not. Some people are committed to their word on a higher level than I've ever played. If they say, "I want to be a nuclear physicist and discover a new power source," they do it. And if they say, "I want to be an entrepreneur and I want to start this," they do it. If they say, "I will run a marathon next year," they take the actions required to live their fantasies. That's what responsibility does—being responsible for your word in the matter and your word in the world. That's what I want to cultivate in my children—people who thrive in any circumstance. I'm really responsible for how they show up in every situation.

Being responsible for your life comes back to being one hundred percent responsible for your life without anybody else needing to do anything for you for you to feel whole. Your children learn that from you, the parents, and through practice and experience. We are the lid on our children, on what they know. They know their father cannot teach them how to run a multimillion-dollar business if he's never had a multimillion-dollar business. He might be cultivating a worker, because that's all he's cultivated. That's not a judgment; you have empathy for the circumstances that come up.

We're talking about responsibility, and as a segue we have a responsibility to discover in ourselves the conversations that we inherited that don't serve us anymore. For instance, I was telling my mom that one of the things she says is, "When you go out, don't show off." When I discovered that conversation was playing in the background, I had empathy for my mom, because her mom told her that, and her grandma told her mom that, and her mom's mom told her that because it was necessary to save her child's life during the days of slavery when young black boys couldn't show off. Today, with the stars, and definitely with individuality, specialization and talent, all these lead the way to Instagram and being a star; the marketplace welcomes a star. So if you're still being run by conversations in the past that don't serve you, recognize and distinguish that, and get it out the way. We have a responsibility to know the conversations we're still perpetuating that don't necessarily serve us, our vision for our children, or our vision for ourselves.

## Richlyn Emanuel

How do you define responsibility other than making sure that you follow your set of values, the ones that you were raised on or the ones that you have developed over time? I'm responsible for making sure we don't live beyond our means, responsible for doing me personally—I'm studying, I'm being responsible as a student, I'm going to work, the way I conduct myself when I'm at work, and to make sure that I keep my job.

As it relates to my parenting role, I don't know whether or not that's difficult making sure that my child has food in his stomach, clothes on his back, and making sure he has a place to live. I'm making sure he has all his supplies for school, making sure that he goes to church even though some days he doesn't want to, making him finish things that he starts (that's very important), having a study schedule, then ensuring that he has the things that he needs, and giving him the guidance that he needs to be a responsible adult—going into young adulthood—whether it be these are your chores or this is what you have to do to maintain life, teaching him the ropes of finances, saying don't do these things because I did them and look what happened. I've said these things to him a number of times, and I've even told him about my high school days. I said to him, "My high school days, I didn't have my parents there making sure I went to school or I got my work done, they weren't at parent teacher meetings, they weren't involved in my school life, but I'm going to be involved in yours. My responsibility is to make sure you finish high school and you move on to something you want to do, whether it be college, a career, another career that's not a choice to go to school for four years, or whatever the case is, just making sure that you get to that point."

## Raymond Fisher

Like I said earlier, I've been given the gift of being a parent, and I firmly believe, as a Christian, that when I stand to give an accounting for my life and the things that I was blessed with, especially my children, God is going to ask me, "What did you do with the gifts that I gave you?" So I take the responsibility of being a parent very seriously, because of the healthy fear and reverence I have for my Creator, but also because it's a life I'm shaping and I can't take short-cuts. It's hard work. It's never easy. And there's no romantic way of dealing with it. Whether you have a child that has illnesses or adolescents with substance abuse issues or all the things that they encounter in this world, you have to be on guard and be vigilant to be able to give them a clear and objective perspective as a parent for everything that they have to go through. So responsibility as a parent is all-encompassing when it comes to developing your children. It comes with sacrifice and commitment. You have to be responsible enough to know you can't party all the time. You can't burn the candles at both ends and be there for your kids. You have to sacrifice hanging out with the fellows and all those things.

I remember early on in my marriage and being a parent when some of my friends weren't married. Before my marriage, we had established lifestyles where we could do the things we wanted to do. But with the kids came responsibilities, and they told me, "Ray, you never go out anymore." But I'm not in that that space anymore. My responsibilities have shifted, and my focus has changed. Now those hundred dollars a nighttimes four nights a week have to go toward the college fund and time being at home to help with a math problem... That became my focus as a parent. It's my responsibility to be there because that might be the challenge that makes a difference of him being an engineer or jag. So I take, and took, my responsibilities in developing and shaping and molding my kids seriously. I'm a deep thinker. So I gave it a lot of thought when I realized that I had to shape and mold, and based on my experiences of not having my parents through certain years of my life, I knew what I wanted to give to my children for the time that I would have them in my life and they had me in their life.

Parenting requires sacrifice, as I was alluding to earlier. You have to have a sincere, consistent commitment to sacrifice so that you can shape and mold your kids, because there're so many things that they need from a social, physical, emotional, spiritual, and financial standpoint, especially in this area where it's ultra expensive to do anything. I'm not saying give them everything, but you have to give them fundamental things, and it comes with a cost. So you have to be willing to sacrifice to sustain that cost. For me, spirituality, good health, a safe haven, and stress-free zone to come home to are worth sacrificing for. I consider wherever I live a stress-free zone, and I've always told my kids drama doesn't come through the front door. Leave the drama outside when you're home. Home is your refuge from the chaos and confusion. So my commitment is to doing those things, be it living in a room in somebody's house or having a 5,500-square-foot house. You have to sacrifice to make that space you exist in as a family unit a place of comfort and peace where everyone feels welcome and comfortable.

It wasn't as challenging as I'm articulating. You know, when I look back in hindsight, because like I say, it comes with the commitment, I don't remember what life was like before my kids, because I've been so focused and in tune with trying to develop them as best I could. Through all the circumstances that I've gone through being a parent and a single parent, the responsibilities of parenting are no harder than anything else, I think, once I committed to it. Commitment is the key.

*Martine Gordon*

I think similarly to respect, I view responsibility both from a parental perspective and then also from a child's perspective. From the parental perspective, I feel fully responsible for helping to guide my daughter. I think part of the responsibility I have is also to help her to learn how she can be a responsible person, appropriate to her age, you know, but she is part of a family, she is part of a community, she goes to school, she is part of the school, so what my responsibilities are to her, what my responsibilities are to the family, and similarly, what her responsibilities are to the family, to her school, to her community. So I view responsibility as both me being responsible as a parent to her but also helping her to understand what responsibility means and why that is an important factor in her life as well. Responsibility is meeting the expectations you set for yourself and that your family or community sets for you—that is, doing what's expected of you both because you internally set that expectation and you feel like it's what needs to happen and also because you know there are definitely things like laws we need to abide by and things like that. There are both external and internal expectations we need to meet.

*Justin Hampton*

Again, I try to model for the kids. For me, responsibility is when I don't feel like doing it, I still have to do it, because it's best for everybody, and so I try to make sure they understand at times when things just have to get done and you don't want to do it. Whether that's the kids cleaning their rooms or me cutting the grass, there are times when we have to do things we may not feel like doing; like when I have to go to work and the kids want me to just play with them all day. But I have to do this because this is what we are trying to do together. And this is why I have to do this. This is a responsibility for me, and we all have responsibilities—it's homework for Victoria, for Justice it's cleaning his room, and obviously the baby…we'll have to figure that out. But as it is, when you don't feel like doing something, but it has to get done, they need to understand they're not the only ones that have to do that. And I feel like for me, as a kid, I didn't understand that concept. I thought, well, I'm only doing this because you're telling me to; you're making me do this. And that's true, and there's a certain level of respect to that. But at the same time, I try to impress upon my children that there're one hundred things that they fall into that category for them, and that's necessary in order to become the person you want to become and do what you want to do. You do what you have to do so you can do what you want to do. Denzel Washington said that.

*Leticia Herrera*

That is very easy. One of the ways to teach responsibility is to be a good example, always being responsible with everything that I've done in life. I do have a few regrets, but that's okay. I used those mistakes to improve myself. But at a very young age I taught him to be responsible. One example is that he was given the opportunity in our Head Start office to come and fix computers when he was in middle school. He was given a lot of hours to work, but because he knew what he was doing he was able to do it in a few hours, he said, "Mom, I'm finished." I said, "David, but you only worked a couple of hours." He said, "That's okay, I will charge only for a couple of hours that I worked." That's how he was at a very young age. He got that very clear. It doesn't matter if you don't have a supervisor in front of you. If you are given ten hours of work and you finish the work in two hours and your job is done and there is nothing else to be done, you must report that your job was finished. That's how it was in his mind then, and as an adult right now, that's who he is. He's very responsible for what he says and for what he does all the time. Every day he's just so conscientious because he knows he has to be responsible. It is the key to success for any individual. That's the way I raised him. And I'm so proud to say that he's very responsible all the time.

*Joseph Kijewski*

Again, you model for your children what you want them to be. As parents you have responsibilities. You have to make sure that they're dressed; you have to make sure that they're fed; you have to make sure that they have all the physical things and, perhaps even more important, all the emotional pieces; and that they're loved. And you have to give them the opportunity to take on some of those responsibilities, to be contributing members to the household, you know. They see you working and doing all these things for the betterment and for the security or the happiness of the family. Well, they have a responsibility to do what they can toward that same goal at their level, like keeping their room clean, taking care of their pet, offering to help carry out the garbage or any simple thing, but you start teaching them beyond that, and sometimes it's through chores; sometimes it's just asking and hopefully they start to do it but just making them feel like they have a role in the household that they're not just receivers but they're also contributors.

*Errol Marks*

Responsibility is basically taking ownership of whatever it is you take onto yourself to oversee, such as the success of an endeavor as a person. Essentially, parenting is an endeavor. You take the responsibility to raise a contributing member of society. And I've seen many parents fail miserably at that. The result of their endeavor is their offspring and their contribution to society. I have dated many women and have broken up with many women, saying, "Hey, the world already has a lot of assholes, don't give it another one." These parents are giving in to their fears that if they discipline their child, the child will not love them; if they are any way other than nice and comforting to their child, their child would resent them. It's common with single mothers, and it's because they don't have that balance of the disciplinarian father and the nurturing mother. Women are designed to be nurturing, to receive love and to give love. Men are designed to be a little more logical and a little less attached, or a little more detached so they can actually think with less emotion and be more methodical and deliberate in parenting. However, in our modern society, where men are most times not present or not present not only physically but mentally or emotionally, women are outearning the bread and bringing home the bacon. They're too tired when they get home to actually engage their children or their families. They are just so exhausted trying to keep their family fed that they don't engage in an intellectual or unemotional manner, especially with their children.

I was fortunate to have a father who engaged intellectually with me on a regular basis. We had these very simulating conversations, and he was the one who actually encouraged me to chase my dreams and to dream. So I try to do the same for my children, and it's not like I'm just winging it. It's a lot of stuff I learned from my father; that is the way he inspired me as a child to dream and aspire to do thing. Growing up in Guyana, a lot of opportunities were not there at the time, but because of his knowledge, he inspired me. Although he was not college educated, he had so much knowledge and was very intelligent. He read many books. Like I said, as parents you need to inspire your children and try to surround them with people of that caliber. That's why I don't have many friends; it's very difficult to find such people. That's why it's usually just the three of us…myself and my two girls…which is disheartening.

Responsibility is taking it on yourself and taking it personally when things don't go the way you planned. My responsibility is to raise my girls to be responsible, contributing citizens. Their job is to seek responsibility and not just deal with it when it's thrust upon them and to take responsibility of their endeavors. As you know, some parents tell their kids, "If you're going to do something, do it well, do it to the best of your ability." That is the responsibility we take to provide value or add value to whatever we do. I find it a most fulfilling attitude, and it's a new attitude I've adopted, especially in my work and my relationships. Now, I'm still new to it however. I think if you put your energies into your relationships as well as your work, the reward is far more bountiful and far more immediate than you actually realize. Life is relationships even with your boss, your coworkers, your children, your family, your friends, and your lovers. It's all relationships and how you manage those relationships has a strong effect on how your life turns out.

From that perspective, I put the onus on my kids to say, "Well, maybe I should act responsibly and be more responsive." I remember as a child I wanted more responsibility thrust upon me and appreciated being not being treated like… "Oh, you're just a child, you can't do this," or "Don't worry about this, you're just a child." I don't do that with my kids. I give them the responsibility to put themselves to bed and make them do their own hair because they do a much better job than I, brush their teeth, get ready for bed. You can ask one hundred parents how difficult it is to get their children to bed. For me, I set bedtime for them, and whatever they are doing in regard to video games, playing music watching TV, when I say it's time for bed, they're in bed in less than two minutes. I put the responsibility on them. I say, "If you go to bed late, you're not going to wake up early. So it's on you to get more rest. You know I get up early, so think about it." I let them fail a couple of times, and then they learn the lesson. I've never had to spank my child except for one case when she lied, and they know that's a hard and fast rule for me. You get me.

Please don't lie to me, because I don't want to hit you. This is one of the things I actually learned in the academy learning to be a corrections officer. If you give an ultimatum, make a promise, or make a threat, you make sure you follow through. So I try not to make any threats.

*Maxine Maloney*

Oh boy, that's always a challenge, because again that's role-modeling the notion of responsibility. It is very important for me as an adult, as a parent, that I role model what responsibility is and then articulate it to Zaria. I think it goes back to when she was an infant, a toddler, and a preschooler, really honing in very early on that value of responsibility and just role modeling it for her and being able to follow through on requests or on tasks. One of the ways that she learned responsibility very early on as a preschooler was having chores at home and responsibilities of picking up her toys and I'd tell her, "If you don't pick up your toys and you trip over your toys or Mommy trips over your toys, someone may get hurt." I think also having her put away her coat or put away her shoes when she was very young was really a part of teaching that responsibility, and as she's gotten older, that notion of being responsible for herself, being responsible for her things that we have at home, and being responsible for things that she needs to do for school like her homework or clubs that she joins. She needed to think about if she could take on the responsibility of being a member of a club at school, because it's not just joining because you want to join and have friends, but that there is some responsibility in being part of a club. So as she gets older, it's important that she recognizes the different ways of thinking about responsibility, because responsibility is not just fulfilling tasks; it's also a responsibility to the environment, to people and family, our friends, and responsibility for our home, and then also responsibility for each other.

*Virgil McDonald*

Well, this is feedback from my sons. First of all, where their mother was concerned, they recognized that she was a responsible person and everything that she got involved with that it was going to be done thoroughly and to the best of her ability. They admit that they never had to worry whether dinner would be ready when they got home from school or for that matter that breakfast would not be ready before they left for school. They have a great deal of respect for the way that she ran our household, and they realized that she was a responsible person. They noted that, as the breadwinner, there was no question that their dad was going to get for work every day, and without a doubt, at the end of the day that dad would come home—full of energy and ready to do fun things with them. So I am a proponent of the philosophy that you definitely have to be there for your children and they learn responsibility by your behavior. I don't think there was ever a conversation in our family about responsibility except to make it abundant clear what their chores and responsibilities were. Our children learned responsibility by example from us.

In terms of parents being role models for their children, we don't like that term "role model." We were just being ourselves. By being ourselves, if our children wanted to model themselves after us, then fine, but we had no thought in our minds that we would be their role models. It seems that there are persons who are self-proclaimed role models. I don't think that's quite the way it happens. I've found that in many aspects of my life, I model myself after other people, and they don't know it, neither do they know me.

There are legendary stories in our family which made us realize our children had learned the lessons we were trying to teach them.

We always notified each other if we were running late or our schedule changed. We insisted that our children do the same. Our daughter, Adrienne, was in college in Chicago, and we had tried repeatedly to reach her to tell her we were going to Georgia. (This was before cell phones.) She was so busy in her world that we didn't hear from her and we had to leave without telling her. A little girl from across the street agreed to take care of our pets while we were away. After we left, Adrienne called, and Christie answered the phone. Afraid that something had happened to us, Adrienne immediately asked her, "Why are you answering our telephone?" Christie told her that she was a caretaker while we were away. Adrienne tracked us down, and she treated us like we were her children, saying, "How dare you leave home without letting me know!" We said, "Well, Adrienne has grown up."

Our son Clark actually saved a little girl from drowning when he was seven or eight years old. She had wandered out in the deep water and was struggling. Clark was not a great swimmer, but he realized that she was in trouble, and he risked his life to save her. The cool and calm way he went about doing so was unbelievable. We saw a side of him that we did not know existed. I said to Kelley, "If ever I am in trouble, I want Clark on my side."

When our son Jeffrey was, I guess, four or five years old, we were at a picnic, and all the kids asked to go to the playground area. They had to traverse a wooded area to go and return. When they returned, Jeffrey was not with them. We asked, "Where's Jeffrey?" You can only imagine the fear that came over us. We notified the park police, and our friends joined in the search for him. When we found him, he was sitting on a bench out in the open. He said, "I know that you love me and if I sat here in the open, you would come to find me." His words still bring tears to my eyes. Rather than wandering, he had the good sense to stay in one place. I thought, "This guy's going to be all right."

As parents, there are times like these that you realize that your children have learned the lessons you have been trying to teach them.

*Jacqueline Rose*

Listen, watch, and observe when your child is ready and/or asking for responsibility, even at a young age. You have to know your child. They'll let you know when they are ready. Readiness begins with small, everyday activities like setting the table, loading and unloading the dishwasher, helping with laundry, sweeping the floor, picking up toys, etc. Self-esteem is built by feeling good about myself when I contribute to my own self-care and care for others at any age. Responsibility in this way guides the very young throughout their development and path to being contributing citizens in their future families, communities, country, and this world. As for restraint, I see too many parents restraining their children by imposing logical rules and/or emotional and reactionary controls on them from the outside. They display strong emotional reactions to their children's behavior. Restraint comes from within. I have to practice self-restraint in order to expect it from my child. It's a matter of heart. You have to care enough about your child to turn to your heart. I care about my child, so I need to speak, but I need to turn to my heart before I speak in order to receive the answer to what my child needs, then I have to be willing to say it and follow through. I don't believe in punishment. I believe in guidance, communication, self-reflection, and self-discipline.

*Joseph Shields*

On the topic of responsibility, the first thing I probably hear, like most men do, is about my financial obligations and duties, making sure my children and my wife are well provided for and taking care of my family. Sometimes that's really hard. Other times it's not, but that's the immediate value I probably associated with it, or my perception, rightly or wrongly. Obviously, there's much more to it. But you know, when financial responsibility is not being addressed, it makes a lot of all the other parts of responsibility much harder. I think about responsibility in a proactive way, as opposed to just reacting to circumstances around it. I teach my kids to think about responsibility in this same way. So having a plan, whether it's with your finances, or with your family or friends, how you want to act and then be prepared around family. I think my wife is better at having a plan around a value system as opposed to the way I could be at times.

My wife and I would like our kids to be responsible up to the top level. We try to imbue in both our kids a sense of adventure and of taking responsible risks. We travel a bit, and when we do, it's partly about giving them an eye to the world that's bigger than their backyard or their neighborhood. We have a racially diverse family, obviously, and people live in different types of neighborhoods and different communities, so I think that it's partly our responsibility to share that with our kids so that it's hopefully engendered within them and it's something that they want to continue to facilitate and focus on. I think it's a way to soften the lessons and to think about the world in a responsible way and what they want to learn from it.

Engaging in other cultures and communities is on top of what they do from day to day in terms of being willing to adapt and explore. This is about them being responsible for creating an environment where people can actively learn, not just take away from books and education, which is also work. Both my kids are honor roll students and are doing very well in school. As parents, we're pretty disciplined about that, monitoring the grades and making sure things that are important to them like gymnastics or extracurricular activities do not interfere with their schoolwork. Their responsibility has more to do, a lot of times, with making sure they have a plan and prepare for, on the academic side, challenges that may arise. Sometimes the hardest part is not that they don't want to make the effort; it's actually being prepared in ways we should have anticipated. So my wife, Yasmeen, and I try hard to point out the things that they may be facing, because they're going to have to face them and navigate through them as opposed to us fixing it for them when they're faced with it. We're trying to do both, but ideally, it's preparing them as opposed to just being a fixer for them.

*Halima Thorne*

As a parent, education is very important, so I make sure Carter is acclimated with reading by reading to him in the evening or morning and any time we have some downtime. I always make sure I read him a book or two or even have him touch a book. My responsibility as a parent is to make sure that I educate him first, also to make sure his basic needs are met. I don't feel I need to give him flashy things.

As a value, responsibility is very important. How are you going to survive in this world if you don't have a sense of responsibility? I look at the kids in my neighborhood who are younger than I am, and I don't see them taking responsibility for their lives. Other people are taking care of them, so they may feel they don't need to get up and work or even get a life. There's no ambition, no goal. For instance, there's a twenty-three- or twenty-four-year-old guy in my neighborhood whose mom is taking care of him. Is this why he may not feel that he needs to take responsibility for his life?

And whose responsibility is it to make sure he takes responsibility for his life? And by the way, he's not the only one. He's an example of what's going on, and a lot of that is going on.

*Barbara Van Dyke*

Responsibility as it relates to a child from a parent's perspective is ensuring that my child's needs are addressed by me, the parent. That I am diligent with meeting those needs, that I'm a provider as I'm required to be. My responsibility is to love, protect, care for, and provide resources for a child to grow and develop in the way they should, and I'm responsible for that, and I think it's important for me to show my child that I am doing what I need to do to uphold that responsibility—not for them to have to understand why I can't and when I can't. That's my belief. I'm also responsible for ensuring that they get a well-rounded view of life and are prepared for adulthood—not to be raised in a cocoon without being exposed because I'm not the only teacher and can't be the only teacher, but I'm also responsible for making sure that there are opportunities beyond the home or our life for the child to grow and to mature into who he or she is capable of becoming. I think the other part of the question is responsibility, not just as a parent, but how do I see responsibility…

It is absolutely important for a child to develop responsibility because to be a productive citizen, to be an adult who is successful in one's career and personal life, it is important to understand responsibility in terms of what you need to take care of and what you're supposed to own in your life. As an adult, no one will take responsibility for those things that you're to take responsibility for.

The concept of responsibility for a single parent is different because there's no shared responsibility in a typical single-parent household, as there is only one parent and the result of that often leads to the perception of that one parent being a control freak because they're doing everything, truly trying to control everything. But he or she is taking responsibility for the things that need to be done in raising a child and taking care of the home. Unless you are within the household and understand the needs of the household and the family, you won't understand why that parent has to do so much. The burden should not be on the child for the things for which the parent is responsible.

# Ten Things about Responsibility

- Living in a household together requires everyone to have responsibilities to ensure efficient running of the household. Responsible behavior requires you at times doing something even when you don't feel like doing it. This teaches children they are part of a family partnership and must do their part as members of a family.

- The responsibilities of parenthood include leading by example in order to teach your children what are acceptable and unacceptable behaviors. This should result in the children learning and practicing responsible behavior. Leading by example includes setting and acting on priorities, honoring your word and commitments, providing for your family and making sure they have everything they need to sustain them at home and at school. These needs include providing a clean, comfortable, orderly home, appropriate routines and structure within the home, and a quality education.

- Parental responsibilities are endless and must include teaching children respectful behavior and making sure they are in the care and company of respectful individuals when away from home, such as childcare providers, teachers, church leaders, club and activities leaders, to name a few.

- It is also of utmost importance for parents to attend to children's nutritional and health care needs in a timely manner.

- Make your home a stress-free zone for the entire family. Children need a safe haven, a refuge from the chaos and confusion of the world outside their home. As such, parents should discard the things in their lives that no longer work for them and adopt the things that will improve their lives and the lives of their children.

- Teach children to develop a sense of responsibility for and to self, family, school, and community. Children can be taught to be responsible for tasks within the home, such as self-care, the care of pets and plants, assisting with the laundry, putting out the trash, dishwashing, and other chores. Children should be contributors and not only receivers within the home. They will then be able to carry over these habits to other settings as they grow older and live on their own as adults.

- Being responsible is the key to success for every individual, as a sense of responsibility goes hand in hand with a positive self-esteem.

- Although some parents may not consider themselves as role models for their children, it is encouraging to hear them acknowledge that children learn to be responsible by experiencing their parents' responsible behavior.

- For fathers, responsibility goes beyond financial obligations. It encompasses creating an environment in which they can learn thrive and grow. It is also important that you expose your children to the world at large and help them create a plan to survive in the world.

- When parents do everything for their children, they create a situation in which children do not learn to be responsible for themselves as they grow into adulthood.

# CHAPTER 4

# Parents Share Their Views on the Value Reciprocity

## Reciprocity

*Do to Others as You Would Want Them to Do to You*

In the context of this book, "reciprocity" is defined as "the Golden Rule"—that is, "the principle of treating others as one would wish to be treated. It is a maxim that is found in many religions and cultures. For example, Christianity states, "Whatever you wish that others would do to you, do also to them, for this is the law and the Prophets" (Holy Bible). Confucianism states, "Do not do to others what you do not want them to do to you" (Analects 15:23). Hinduism states, "This is the sum of duty: Do not do to others what would cause pain if done to you" (Mahabharata 5:1517). Buddhism states, "Hurt not others in ways that you yourself would find hurtful" (Udanavarga 5:18) (gotquestions.org, What is the Golden Rule?).

Parents have used the Golden Rule over several generations of parenting. My own grandparents used this maxim with their children and grandchildren, and no doubt, it was used by generations of parents before them. The Golden Rule has been passed on to present-day parents, and children and parents make reference to this rule in their relationships with their children and children reference it in their relationships with peers.

This pervasive use of the Golden Rule is possibly due to its religious underpinnings across major world religions. I remember also learning and practicing the Golden Rule throughout school, from elementary to secondary classrooms, and present-day teachers are very much focused on helping children learn the value of reciprocity. My conversations with young adults in Section 2 illustrate how they have internalized the value of reciprocity, having acquired it, more than likely, in their relationships with parents, other family members, and teachers.

Child development literature is replete with information about the importance of reciprocity, particularly in the domain of social emotional development. The literature informs and reminds parents, professionals, and all of us that reciprocal behavior begins at birth and the back-and-forth exchanges between young children, their parents, and others set the stage for children learning and practicing acceptable social behaviors.

As a parent, how do you define the concept of reciprocity, or "the Golden Rule"?

How do you model reciprocity as a parent?

*Marguerite Anderson*

I touched on reciprocity a bit when I talked about responsibility. One thing George has been doing lately is that he's been hitting me a little bit or biting me to get attention when he wants something. He has to understand that sometimes he can't get what he wants immediately. And if you bite people in order to get what you want, it's not going well, because someone may bite you back. So I think that the most important thing that we have been teaching him lately is, well, not the most important thing, but one of the many important things is to be kind, to be understanding—maybe Mommy cannot come to you immediately, George. He also has been trying specifically to turn me around whenever I say something. It's just an interesting thing that he started doing about a week ago. We're trying to model the right behavior for him. Reciprocity is a bit more advanced than the others at this age.

Getting back to the concept of kindness and caring, Sean and I are very respectful of each other in our relationship. We take a moment—whenever if we have a disagreement, we make sure to pause before we get into our disagreements. Because even though everyone is going to have a disagreement when you're in a relationship—that's just how it is, but I think it's how you treat each other when you're at your angriest that shows who you truly are. So I think it's very important to take a moment, to pause, to consider the other person's feelings before you react. And I really believe George is internalizing that. From what I understand how he plays with other children, he is very considerate and he is considering how they feel about things. He likes to share his food. He likes to share his toys. Unfortunately, he doesn't understand that not everyone likes to share their toys yet, so he does occasionally take a toy away, but one thing the teacher told us is that he always gives something if he takes a toy, so he may take a toy, but he will give you something back. So I think that he's learning to be generous and to be kind. And another thing is a simple act like if Sean and I hug each other and either of us hugs, then sometimes, without anybody asking, George comes over and hugs us. We see those things go together. He understands that if he hugs us, we'll hug him back. It's a stage—again, he's at a very, very early stage of development, but I think he is discovering that something as simple as saying "hello." He understands that if he says "hi" back, we get very excited. He's very good at "goodbye."

*Christopher Blanchard*

As a parent, you have to show the children that everyone is equal no matter man or woman and you have to treat everyone you come across with the same kind of respect that you would like to be treated. That's leading by example.

One thing that's going on now is that Blair is in a biting stage, and sometimes she bites for no reason; she may be tired, or it can be a number of things. We tell her teeth are not for biting. The biggest thing is instilling in her right from wrong and to treat others the way she wants to be treated. Those are very strong values for us, and we instill them in our daughter. We are working with her on sharing so when she goes to school she will not be forceful toward other children. I know it's difficult at this stage for children to share, but sharing is an important value that we definitely would like her to do when she goes to school, also because not doing so may lead to problems.

*Robert Bovell*

When it comes to reciprocity in the upbringing of children, I try to teach the kids how to balance the information they transfer, as well as their behavior. There must be balance in behavior and information that is transferred between parent and child. We have to understand that life comes with what I call results behavior—if you do something the same way every time, you can decide to change it, but you risk losing certain components in the process. But if you consistently do something, the chances of becoming successful or being accelerated to a higher level is greater, because in addition to developing a comfort zone, you'll also develop a system of doing something that works and that benefits you and benefits others. That's how we respond to one another. If I always tell my aunt that her hair always looks beautiful, that could have been eight years ago, but she knows, "When I get around this nephew, he compliments me about my hair." She will never want me to catch her out of that zone or element. That's the same thing with raising children—you teach them that consistently doing positive things in life will give them better results.

If children are used to doing things a certain way all the time, in terms of reciprocity, it will take both the parent and the child consistently doing and repeating behaviors the parent wants the child to learn. A child is not going to process new information the very first time—not unless they're processing a piece of candy is sweet, or I don't want this piece of candy. But when it comes to behaviors and responsibilities, when it comes to being respectful, we have to interject these behaviors on a consistent basis in order for children to carry these behaviors over from two- to three- to four-year-olds. Consistency! That's how we get results from children.

*Marlon Bovell*

When my children were younger, they did more acts of kindness that showed more reciprocity. For instance, when their mother and I would come home from work, they would run to hug us and kiss us and would do the same before going to sleep at night; now they just say good night and go to bed. They don't show us that give and take as much anymore. They don't show us as much love as they used to as they get older. But we also know that we should do so as well. Now they're going on their own and are more interested in their friends.

We've had several conversations with the kids about other kids, particularly at their school, having feelings too, and they should respect other kids the same way they want to be respected. Our daughter has had small things happen to her at school, not bullying, but she's had little things happen to her. Then there is this kid that she says nobody likes at the school because he always messes around with people and he's so rambunctious and full of energy. She always says she doesn't like this kid. I try to explain to her that that's not good because what if nobody likes her, how would she feel? I asked her to make sure she treats him fairly and not leave him out when they play games even though nobody wants to pick him, because that's not fair. What if you are the guy that nobody wants to pick? I stress that she shouldn't follow along with the crowd.

And then, also with her brother, they're at the age where they do a lot of bickering and she does little things too. She says that her brother is annoying. But all he wants to do is come and talk to her or look over her shoulder—although sometimes he may do things to annoy her—you know, little-brother stuff—but then she may not want to share with him because of something that happened earlier. We tell her, "You know he loves you, he's just playing with you, don't take it so seriously. You shouldn't not want to share with your brother because of a small thing that he did yesterday or something he did the other day." We try to tell her not to hold grudges against people, especially against her brother for little things. We try to model reciprocity. I try to be an example. I feel that I do, because I always try to treat them fairly, meaning that I give them the same respect and response that I would want from them. That goes back to what I said earlier. I feel the kids won't respect me if I don't show them respect.

*Shanice Bovell*

Reciprocity is giving back what you've received. To this day, I give my children plenty of love, and in turn I get it back. They are respectful and mindful of other people's feelings. I have been told many times that I have raised generous and respectful young men, and this compliment comes from older adults. To me, that means I've done a good job. They give back what they've received and put it back into the universe, and that has always been important to me.

*Holly Blum*

Reciprocity in adult-child interactions also has a connection to respect. It's the give-and-take that goes on in human relationships and it starts in that give-and-take that you do with an infant. That's really when it begins. You know, I'm getting something from the infant, and I'm giving something to the infant. We communicate with touch, we communicate with eye contact, and we communicate with our facial expressions. We teach reciprocity indirectly; we use the many teachable moments.

Reciprocity is like there are two sides to every coin and you have to use restraint while you take some responsibility for looking at both sides whether you're talking about restraint or reciprocity. You don't want to minimize when you know your child feels really hurt. Well, we all know turning away and saying, oh, we shouldn't feel hurt. We know how that feels when somebody implies that to us as an adult and when you say that to a child. And I'm not sure that I balanced that well because I know I've had conversations with Jordan over the years about the fact that there were times where she felt as if I was not empathetic enough. Parents don't always understand the need to look at situations from some other perspective. That's a little bit of what reciprocity is about; it's being able to consider another person's point of view. If you have a point of view, then that person must have one too. It's not all about you. We may disagree because we are different people, we've had different upbringings, and we have different temperaments. We don't always have to see eye to eye.

Then we have to think about what's developmentally appropriate. I work in schools. It's the second week of school, and they're having a whole conversation with the kids about sharing. And the kids just wait. It's their first time in school. Do they want to share? If I were to teach in a classroom, especially two- and three-year-olds, for example, I would give each kid their own basket of blocks during the beginning of school and gradually encourage reciprocity—sharing.

Reciprocity is about the give-and-take of a relationship, sharing, and a desire to connect with others. Reciprocity is related to helping your child appreciate others, their efforts, and demonstrating appreciation: one kindness deserves another. Although I think that thank-you notes are a form of reciprocity, Jordan always found them burdensome; she is now an adult who writes thank-you notes and often receives appreciation from the recipient for the gesture.

### Dorel Campbell-Adams

Reciprocity is giving and receiving, the same as doing to others as you would want them to do to you. I tell the kids, "Charity begins at home. If you want your friends to exert kindness to you, then you exert kindness to them and you start at home by being respectful with your brother and sister. Your behavior is like a cycle in the house so if you know that your brother was mean to you yesterday and you're mean to him today, it's going to continue. Someone's going to have to break that cycle. So if you're aware that something is wrong, then you need to encourage good behavior." I tell this to Nevin a lot because he's the oldest and the others tend to pick on him because they're younger. So they want to gang up and tease him about stuff. I told him, "If you let them know that they're getting to you, they'll continue doing it. You need to surprise them with kind words and it'll change." When Nyron started a new school just last week, and didn't know anyone, I said to him, "Well, you know what the strategy is. When you see somebody, give them a compliment, 'Hey, nice shoes,' or 'I like your bag,' 'Nice haircut.' Send out kind words and you'll get kind words back. Do the same thing at home." It's a constant battle, but Nyron knows exactly everything that I would say in every situation because he likes to mock me. Just today he asked me a question and responded in my voice exactly what I was going to say, and I said, "You know exactly what you should and should not do because you've heard it enough so you just need to do those things and you'll be fine." Whatever you send out into the universe, it comes back to you tenfold.

My younger son experiences bullying at school, and his father feels he should defend himself if he's disrespected. I have a different perspective. I feel it's just wasted energy and he doesn't need to prove himself on this unless he thinks that he's in a corner. But the first time that something happens and he's not comfortable with it, he has people that he can go to, and if they don't help him, then he has to come to me. He needs to come to me, and I will address it. It does not make you a coward if you don't put your fist up, because you know that when you do, you'll be suspended.

Social media is another area of concern. Certain situations are direct, and others are subtle or indirect. I tell the kids to think before they do things with social media; you do something on there and it's there forever and you can't take it back. Some of their classmates are noncompliant in terms of their social behavior at school. That could be due to their upbringing or a result of them wanting to be popular in school and in doing the things they see on TV.

My kids are having a new experience going to public schools; I think the need to fit was so strong for my younger son, that he became friends with the kids who gravitated toward him, the ones who are in the group you do not necessarily want your son to latch on to. But it is what it is. Maybe for him when there's a larger group of troublemakers, he feels safer in that crowd. He says he now knows that if he wants to play football, he has to get good grades, and in order to get good grades, he has to pay attention in class. But if there are kids around him that he feels are disrupting him, he feels a lot of pressure because he feels he has to pay attention in class. But these kids are around him and he's fighting to not be himself by being the natural class clown. So it's like a constant push and pull for him. My older son has had no problem navigating through school.

He's in high school and has had no issues with other kids. He either ignores them or he just doesn't interact with them. They are two totally different boys, and reciprocity feels and looks differently for each of them. It's different for every child. We have five fingers on each hand, and every finger is different. My husband and I have three children; they were raised under the same roof, and they have three different personalities. We cannot treat them the same. For instance, Nyron plays football, and his father is there every single trip, every single game, and every single practice. And he's out there yelling for Nyron and supporting him. If that's the only way that he can get the encouragement from his father, he's going to latch on to that as long as he can. That's why he's holding football so high on his priority list, because that's the only way he feels valued and the only way he thinks that he's doing something really well. And they get the attention naturally as they are the center of everybody's attention for those two hours of the game.

*Desiree DeFlorimonte*

Reciprocity means to give and take. I think when a mother and her child respond to each other in the same way, they are demonstrating reciprocal behavior. The Golden Rule comes to mind—"Do unto others as you would have them do unto you." First and foremost, the love between me and my child was reciprocated from birth, and even before birth, in the womb. This love is demonstrated through acts of kindness for when a parent or adult is loving to a child, then the child, in turn, is usually loving to the parent. An important virtue I learned from my mother is that my positive actions will usually cause positive reactions.

As you demonstrate positive behaviors to your child, your child reciprocates these behaviors to you and then transfers these same behaviors to her relationships with others. This is true because you'll find when parents are abusive and speak negatively to a child, inevitably, that child's response is abusive and negative. The role of a parent is to model, mold, and nurture the child in order that she may grow up to be a good, positive, compassionate, and self-confident person. Simple things like teaching etiquette or manners as the parent says,

"Please," "Thank you," "May I" to the child, then she learns to do the same. In school, church, and the larger community, these mannerly behaviors will be demonstrated.

There were occasions, as a single parent, when out of frustration my expectations for my young child might have been unrealistic and her responsive behavior demonstrated her aggravation. For example, when my body language and tone of voice demanded that clothes should be on hangers rather than on the floor or dirty dishes should be washed after use, Angel's response might be to cry, pout, or do such a poor job that I would end up doing the cleaning myself. I learned that through the years—being loving but firm with rules or directives caused a more positive response. Especially during my daughter's teenage years and later as a young adult, my actions and words be they positive or negative, definitely influenced her behavior. I observed more defiant behavior when I was harsh and showed lack of empathy about her emotional and mental health. Our relationship strengthened when we were able to communicate, listen to each other, and mutually agree on the reasons and benefits for rules and the values I taught her.

*Ryan Dickson*

What I'm doing as a parent is attempting to articulate the space that I come in. I parent from the space of teams and teamwork. When you're encountering anybody, they are potential teammates. If you play any sports, your teammates are your comrades, they're your compatriots, they are the ones who go into battle whatever the battle is, or whatever game you're playing. There is no *I* in team, so there's no *I* would do this for somebody else. No, we have a mission so I can give 100 percent, and if you give 0 percent, that is irrelevant. I'm here to win the mission and anything that you add is in addition, so that's the space that I come from.

For me there is no reciprocity, no tit for tat. I mean, if a situation is not working, what are you creating in that situation? Going back to being one hundred percent responsible for how you show up, the questions become, "What am I generating in this situation such that there's no trust here?" "What space am I holding such that this person doesn't feel safe speaking to me?" "What can I give up?" "How can I listen in a different way so I can figure out what this person needs or wants in this particular situation?" It also reverses you from being out in front, like, "What am I getting?" It reverses you on the inside to feel, like, "Well, what can I give to this team?" That's a different sense of fulfillment. You can get fulfillment in both ways—there's fulfillment when you give, and there's fulfillment when you get as well. I teach my son and daughters that they can learn to develop their sense of fulfillment from who they "be" and what you give, then you never lose, you know, and you never end up being a victim as a result of a circumstantial situation, because you get to generate yourself in every situation.

*Richlyn Emanuel*

I think it's important for Giovanni to develop a sense of reciprocity. Teaching about reciprocity is teaching by example, and I didn't realize I was doing this until a teacher said it to me. Giovanni is very giving, and if someone is in need, he'll be the first person to help them out. I remember getting mad at him because he actually bought someone a book because they wanted a book. I got upset, and then I had to catch myself because he has seen me do that. I treat people that way. If I were hungry, I would want someone to but a meal for me, if they could. If I fall down, I want someone to be there to pick me up. And he has watched me do that. So I think, as parents and as adults, in general, we have to be careful what we do, because our actions reflect who we are and our kids watch that. We help folks with their groceries because somewhere down the road we may want people to do that too. We speak kindly to individuals because somewhere down the road we want that to happen. My mom did that too. But the other kid said she went a little bit overboard. She took all these kids and were like, "Oh, what about us?" But you know, I watched it in my mom's life; she could visit anyone, anywhere, and they would let her stay in their home.

So for me it's what I have done, and Giovanni watches that, and he does the same thing.

It's very important to teach them reciprocity and sometimes even more important to teach them to give without expecting to receive and to give from the heart. Sometimes we may want to show off, but I'm shocked that Giovanni doesn't show off; he just does it. Once at a band event I had snacks in my backpack. I walked over to the kids, and I opened up the backpack so everybody could get a snack. His engineering teacher looked at me and said, "That's where he gets it like!" and I said, "What are you talking about?" He said, "Giovanni always feeds the class." He doesn't expect anything in return; he just does it, that's the way he is. He treats people the way he wants to be treated. There are times when anger gets in the way and you lash out; you get angry—I've done it a million times, then I have to stop and go back and apologize, "That was out of anger, it's not my best behavior, and I'm sorry, but this is why it happened."

*Raymond Fisher*

Reciprocity is interesting. My fiancée jokes with me all the time that I like to have reciprocity, or the Golden Rule, in our relationship, where you expect to be treated the way you treat others in the relationship. In a parent-child relationship, you have it from sacrificing and showing respect. I want my kids to understand at an early age and through life that reciprocity is not a given; it's earned by the example I'm setting for them, and I'm doing all this in love. So I expect their appreciation and respect for the sacrifices that I'm making for them once they come to the cognitive point in their growth to realize it.

The funny thing is that a lot of parents, to the detriment of their children, are not confident enough in their parenting to realize if they're doing a good job or not, to realize that they can't take back some of the things they do and to know that reciprocity helps the relationship develop from them. Some of them become more of a dictator or very authoritarian instead of letting their kids, within a controlled situation and environment, make mistakes and have free rein because that's the only way they're going to learn how to think critically and be creative to work themselves out of situations.

So a reciprocal relationship or the reciprocity dynamic in the relationship helps kids to develop to be more critical thinkers, because if they are treated like robots, that's what they'll always be; they won't be able to think for themselves and work through situations. I work with a lot of young kids and young men and women I can't call kids…young adults. I'm the old gray guy in the office now, and I see how some of them are socially inept because their parents were helicopter parent, as they say; they dictated everything to them, and now to be out on their own and in the workforce, they're like, "I never thought about that. I've never done that, because my parents have always… You know, I still live at home with mom and dad." I constantly try to charge my kids the give-and-take to make them understand that we're going through these exercises because there's going to come a day where they're going to be on their own and there's going to come a day when they're going to be a parent. So they need to be able to have these too. I've gone through a lot with my oldest child, my son. Now he's counseling kids, doing stuff, and he told me the other day that he's just telling these kids half of what I told him. As a parent, you behave a certain way to teach your children how to behave in certain circumstances. That's training up your child, being their role model.

*Martine Gordon*

Reciprocity is a harder one for me to define, but the more I think about it, I guess it's not harder for me to define, because as I think through each of these terms, I sort of am thinking about it in terms of reciprocal relationships. So to me reciprocity is that I have a responsibility in a certain way, my daughter has a responsibility, and each of us has a different role in the relationship; we are both there and present in contributing to the relationship. So to me reciprocity is I have my role and she has her role and we're both contributing in the way that's appropriate for our roles, and that's creating reciprocity in the relationship.

When I think about how I interact with my child, how other parents I know interact with their children and the degrees to which children struggle with expectations of them, there is respect in there;

there is responsibility in there, but I think one of the pieces that people may not think of off the bat is the reciprocity piece that's in there and helping children to value what children bring to the table and to the relationship as opposed to constantly viewing as a parent your role as having to always teach them, you know, you're a guide, yes, but your role in the relationship is not the burdened role, and I think that when we're stressed sometimes, we feel like we're giving and giving and giving and the kids are just taking and taking and taking. To some extent, that's going to be true, especially in the personal care area when they're young, but I think for parents to come into parenting and understand that you do get so much back from your child in the way that they can give it. It's really important. Your relationship with your child is very, very important. It's almost everything—everything comes back down to relationships.

*Justin Hampton*

I think my kids are just now coming around to understanding and expressing the concept of fairness. I'm starting to hear that a lot since Victoria is going to school. Before she went to school, we never heard it from her… "That's not fair, it's not fair." In turn, we try to consistently keep fairness in the house to impress upon them, "You wouldn't want somebody doing that to you, and so you shouldn't do that to your brother." I also try to be vulnerable with them when I mess up. So if I say something to April, or if I hurt her feelings, or if I do anything that I shouldn't have done and I recognize it, I apologize to her, and if they were witness to it, I apologize to them as well, "That wasn't right, I should not have done that. I should not have said that to your mother. And we should never do that to each other." We try to impress upon them that if you're bold enough to say that, then you need to be bold enough to apologize.

*Leticia Herrera*

Well, I cannot teach something that I do not practice. Everything that I taught him, I was taught. I was raised by a young mother with a lot of siblings, and our family just didn't pretend. "If you are not going to do something from your heart, don't even try." That's what my mother used to say. If you are being asked to do something, if you're going to start whining and have a bad face, don't even try. And that is something that I've taught him—you must do things in a good way. If you don't do it in a positive way, it's not going to be good. So that is the rule, and it's still the same. It doesn't matter what age, what country, and what time it is; it is the same. If you do something, make sure it is well done. If it's not going to be, don't even try. That's the way I am, and I raised him that way. Do things for others in a good way if that is the way you want to be treated. Yes, that is important in parenting.

*Joseph Kijewski*

Reciprocity is to do unto others what you would want them to do unto you. It's called the Golden Rule for a reason, and it could be the summation of everything I've said so far. It really is you showing by your behavior kinds of persons you want your children to be and helping them to do the same. If you would not want to be treated a certain way, why would you treat someone else that way? Think about how the person that you're acting upon feels. Do you want to feel that way? I certainly was raised with that. I went to a Catholic schools, and the Golden Rule was the number one rule from nine years of kindergarten and grades 1 through 8. You're always taught to put yourself in the shoes of others and think about how they feel. That should be the number one thing when you sit back and say to yourself, "Am I going to do this?" or "Am I going to do that?" That should be your conscience at work, and you know, there's a reason you should follow it because if you treat someone in a way that you don't want to be treated, that you wouldn't want to be treated yourself, you're not going to improve the world or do anything to better yourself. Further, you're pulling things down rather than building things up, which is very important, and it's something I've always stressed.

*Errol Marks*

I think responsibility and respect play into reciprocity because that's along the lines of respect, and I believe respect is earned especially from your children. You have to earn your children's respect; reciprocity is the same thing. You know when you say good night to your kids, and you say "Give me a kiss, I love you," and they feel a sense of obligation to say "I love you too." Well, I'm trying to turn that around. They don't have to say it back to me. They say it when they want to say it. And I kind of had a talk with them about that a while ago. So when I tell them, "Good night, I love you," they don't say anything. At first it was, "What you don't love me?" "Okay, I love you." It was more of a formality versus what they really felt.

The funniest thing happened recently. I took my kids on a weekend trip, and when I dropped them off at their mother's house on Monday morning and they went into the house as they always did, the door closed then reopened, and Narissa ran out and said, "I love you, Daddy, bye." That was that reciprocal behavior, where I didn't say you have to tell me you love me; she just ran out to say, "I just wanted to let you know that I love you," and that is way more meaningful than that "Good night, I love you," and we feed off of that. We are social beings; we feed on the energy of others. This is what they talk about in the Bible, that love comes from God and it flows out and it flows around. If you give out enough of it, some of it is going to come back, and when it comes back, you will feel that. It's kind of like rock stars after a concert; they can just roll over and go to sleep. They are wired for that energy. So the party goes on because they feel so much love and energy from the crowd. Imagine you were on the stage performing over in front of fifty thousand people. You have fifty thousand people loving and adoring you. That energy flowing into you is invigorating. The same thing happens when your child just tells you that she loves you just out of the blue or your child tells you, "Hey, my grades are high," or your other child tells you, "Hey, I got skipped two grades because I was too smart for my grade.'

We poke fun at each other, and I like to make fun of people, and my kids are the same way. I teach them not to take themselves so seriously.

*Maxine Maloney*

As a parent, I think that's hard for parents, but I think reciprocity comes in a lot as children get older and that it's like a dance that we do with children; it's the give-and-take where we have rules and we have expectations and for children and parents to learn when we have responsibilities or we have demands, what are the consequences. As Zaria has gotten older, I've recognized that there's a little bit more give and take—things that I think are rules may not even work for her. They may have worked in my mind, but as we think about the expectations, it's not that I'm giving in or being lenient; it's that now I think about does Zaria understand, or does that make sense? Then I may have to think about it from Zaria's perspective and that may not be in alignment with what she understands or where she is at a specific age. So I see reciprocity as that give-and-take when we're setting boundaries and goals and rules and reciprocity is often when we think about how we parent children, especially from the Caribbean world and the Latino world where there is a "Do as I say thing"—that is not reciprocity. It's not something that we think about when we're parenting, but I find that I think about it because I want Zaria to be flexible in how she thinks and interacts with others and just being able to see other people's views and opinions, not that she will be walked over or stepped on, but recognizing that as a parent, I have rules, but my child is a person too, and that rule or that outlook may not be her reality. I see reciprocity as really a challenge, and I often have to step back and be empathetic to my child and where she is as a human being in order to have that notion of reciprocity.

I see reciprocity as being important for Zaria as she goes out into the world, going to college, and living away from home, and even now as she interacts with her friends and other adults outside of the home, because I'm not with her 100 percent of her time and she is becoming her own person, formulating her own ideas, and I hope that all the work I've done prior to that helped her make really good decisions. But reciprocity helps in listening to her point of view, because she may experience or may have heard something that I don't know about that will influence her decision-making. I think it helps children be able to be more—I don't know if democratic is the word.

Or more empathetic, more open, more flexible, more valuable, but it also helps them be able to stand for what they believe in. If they don't have that flexibility and they're not given that opportunity to express themselves, then I don't think they will be able to withstand peer pressure and the challenges of today's world, because they won't be able to set their own beliefs and will be easily swayed.

*Virgil McDonald*

Reciprocity is very important and is a most valuable lesson to learn in life. Perhaps of the four concepts, reciprocity required the most effort on our part. Understanding and embracing the principle of reciprocity did not come easily. Selfishness is innate. In order to get our children to practice reciprocity, we initiated the practice of celebrating each other's birthdays, achievements, and successes, and that continues until today. Honor each other, share with each other, support each other, console each other are principles we tried to instill in our children. Kelly and I did not tolerate fighting among our children under any circumstance. There were arguments, quite naturally, but we'd never let them get out of hand, and never allowed them to say hurtful things to each other that they would regret later. They learned to respect each other and be reciprocal in the exchange of gratitude and support. The precept we tried to impart was, "The world can be cruel, why make enemies in your own family?"

*Jacqueline Rose*

Reciprocity is about give and take. I see two extremes…parents who are givers, who give their child everything, and parents who are takers, who are so needy they look to their child to fill their own needs. We have to strive for balance, a middle ground focused on the health and well-being of the child and to foster heartful, open communication with my child. I give to my child, and my child also gives to me. When they are babies, it's instinctive; but as they are growing up, it gets more challenging. Our own ideas and expectations of our child make it so.

*Joseph Shields*

I would say reciprocity goes with all the other things I was saying earlier, treating others how you want to be treated—the Golden Rule—a value system the kids are learning from us as their examples. My mother-in-law lives with us, and she has health challenges. I've been noticeably pleased as to the responsibility and reciprocity both my kids have shown her in terms of their interactions with her. She's not difficult, but taking care of somebody older can offer some challenges at times, but I think the kids have been really, really, genuinely kind and really helpful. My wife and I are her caretakers, but we all have responsibilities toward Grandma, so that part of it, just as an example of reciprocity, has been really nice to see. And we get it back when we see how happy she is living with us. Not that she wasn't happy in the past, but there's a level of enjoyment, that peace of mind she gets as a result of the way she's treated in the home, as opposed to being in a place where maybe she wouldn't get that, perhaps in a private facility or another environment.

*Halima Thorne*

I want him to treat people the way I would want people to treat me, in a good way, not try to get over on me or anything like that. But I feel that raising a black boy in this day and age, it's like he automatically has a target on him, so I have to teach him about racism and how to respect others and you to stay away from those type of situations where he can be a target.

I treat people with respect up to a certain point. If you disrespect me, I'm not going to deal with you. I know my take on it is a little different, because we were raised in a different time, and I think that plays a huge part. When we were growing up, everybody was involved. Now you're on your own and you have to figure out and deal with things. So I would like him to respect people, and I would like people to respect him, but I just don't want him to be a pushover; I want him to make right decisions about people. How the world is working right now, there's a change, there's change, there's no value system anymore. That's what I'm trying to say. So I'm going to try my best doing what I think is right, and I know my parents will support me. I know they will check me and put me in line if I'm doing something out of line; that's not going to help Carter for his future.

*Barbara Van Dyke*

As a parent, the first thing that comes to mind about reciprocity in a parent-child relationship, are the things many parents say to our children that probably exemplify or demonstrate reciprocity. We say things such as, "I am sending you to school to learn," "I'm giving you an education—what you need to give me are good grades." Another example is, "I impart these values, and I expect you to demonstrate them." The funny thing about that is that we expect our children to reciprocate here and now, but as a parent, I know you don't see those values as they manifest at the time you're imparting them. You may see them when the child becomes a full-fledged adult with their own family. So you don't always get reciprocity while you're raising your child, but you get it in later years because I see reciprocity as getting the fruits of your labor back—that's how I see that. The biggest gift a child can give the parent—well, at least for me, is just success in the things he or she does and demonstration of upholding the values you're imparting. And the best part is when in addition to our children demonstrating the values we impart, we also hear and see them teaching their peers the same values that you're imparting. That's reciprocity for me. I don't need money or anything that's tangible—I need to see it in how your life has turned out.

As regards to peer relationships in school and outside of school and the guidance I've given my child, two things come to mind. One is when a child responds to you regarding a subject or a behavior that you do not uphold and the response to you is, "Well, that's not how Johnny, and Johnny's mom, and you know, Mary Sue…" And my response or a parent response may be, "I don't raise Johnny, and you don't live in Johnny's house, and Johnny's mom is not your mom. You are raised in my house, and so I expect you to uphold my values—you don't just forget about it when you go over to Johnny's house or you're with Johnny." The other is dealing with conflict which appears in school which I think most parents have had challenges with because society, I believe, teaches our children to respond to conflict in a physical way, and if you don't respond to conflict in a physical way, you're a punk, or you're soft, or you're a sissy or whatever they may call it. And I don't believe or recall that I ever taught that when you're confronted with a conflict, you better fight back, and if you don't fight back, I'm gonna spank you. I've always said when you're confronted with a conflict, be the bigger person, speak to an adult, walk away, and share at home so that you can get advice on how to handle the conflict. Sometimes our children are not equipped to handle the conflicts that come their way. They may be too young and not developed physically or emotionally and need help to handle some conflicts. So I expect that my child will do what I taught him—that is, don't take it into your own hands. But I've learned differently as a parent in regards to what I or other parents teach our children about conflict. I've learned that peer pressure is of such a high degree that children may yield to what their peers do and not reciprocate that value regarding conflict that their parents have taught. I know that's one area that, in terms of reciprocity, I would have a challenge with, because it's you against the world—your values against the world's values or societal values. We see it demonstrated in movies where parents are teaching their children how to fight so that they can go out and fight for themselves. I really have some serious issues with that and always have, and I don't care who says you need to teach your child to fight, send them to boxing lessons, and so on. I still believe that behavior should come from an adult, not from a child, because then when you demonstrate that behavior as an adult, then you're grown enough to deal with the consequences that comes from engaging in physical conflict. Until you become an adult, don't respond to conflict that way.

# Ten Things about Reciprocity

- In relationships, reciprocity is like a dance—lead and follow, back and forth, twists and turns. It also involves giving thought to what others can and cannot do at the moment. At times you have to pause to think things through before you act or react.
- Reciprocity goes hand in hand with respect for both children and adults. If you want to be treated with respect by others, including your children, then you treat others with respect.
- Reciprocity is teamwork, and there is no *I* in teamwork. There must be give and take among team members to make the teamwork, and no one should hold back just because another team member is not giving one hundred percent. Think about giving and not always about getting back.
- It's important for parents to understand that a child's perspective may be different from that of their parents. Children may have their own thoughts and opinions about things and situations. It is not unusual for a child, as he matures into adulthood, to adopt his parents' way of thinking about and doing things.
- Parents may view "sharing" as an important value for their young children. But "sharing" may be a difficult concept for young children to internalize depending on their developmental maturity. Parents should be patient and continue to teach and lead by example.
- Parents may want to respond to all their children in the same manner; however, each child has her own unique temperament and should be responded to and treated in a

manner that is a good match for her behavioral style. The concept of "fairness" is important to young children, and they may not understand why the parental response is not the same for every child. This is a teachable moment relative to the nuances of reciprocity.

- Children put back into the universe what they receive from their parents, grandparents, uncles, aunts, and other family members, and what they put out will return to them tenfold.

- We want our children to be critical thinkers; therefore, we should interact with them in a manner that allows them to think and work through situations for themselves. We don't have to hover over our children and provide them the answers, as this may lead to codependency later on in their lives.

- An example of reciprocal behavior is when a child looks at a parent and spontaneously says, "I love you, Daddy." Think about the number of times this father has said "I love you" to his daughter.

- Reciprocity encompasses exchanging gratitude and support, celebrating each other's accomplishments and consoling each other in times of duress. Reciprocity is also when children return to parents the fruits of the parents' labor by living their best lives and upholding the values they learned from their parents.

# CHAPTER 5

## Parents Share Their Views on the Value Restraint

### Restraint

Restraint, as used in this book, refers to self-control, self-regulation, or self-discipline. Self-control is "the foundation, the prerequisite for so much that is important in life…few things in life are as important as self-control, self-restraint… Some of the different facets where it (they) comes into play are moderation and restraint in regard to the consumption of food and drink; restraint and self-control in the spending of money; restraint in the use of the tongue; restraint in regard to our emotions (e.g., command over anger, hatred, jealousy, etc.; regulation in our behavior toward others) in the form of politeness, honesty, truthfulness, justness, etc.; sexual restraint. Few things in life are as important as self-control." James Miller, Solitary Road.com

Over the fifty years I have worked as an early childhood teacher and administrator and primary school teacher, I have observed child behavior both within and outside of the classroom and have developed a theory that I have applied and continue to apply in both my personal and professional lives—that is, that children need to be intentionally taught how to understand their emotions, specifically anger and frustration, and how to respond or react to these emotions in socially acceptable ways that will not get them in trouble with their peers, parents, teachers, and other authority figures. I am pleased that over the past two decades, child development and human psychology professionals have also focused on this same realization and have provided parents, teachers, and other professionals who work with children volumes of literature and research on relevant topics such as executive functioning and the importance of self-regulation. As parents and teachers become more aware of the importance of social and emotional development to children's cognitive development and school success, they will understand the critical need to teach children self-regulation strategies or how to practice restraint.

As a parent, how do you define the concept or value of restraint? How important is restraint?

Give examples of how you practice restraint when relating to your child/children and other family members.

How important is it for your child to practice restraint—not only within the home as they relate to each other, but outside of the home, when they go to school, and are older and interacting with their peers and others in the community?

How would you like your child to express negative emotions?

*Marguerite Anderson*

I was thinking about something I touched on a little bit earlier—how we deal with a disagreement—and I think this is very, very important. When you are unhappy with yourself, as people become, you know, the most important thing is to try and take a moment, try to pause, try to be mindful of not hurting the other person—show some restraint in dealing with your anger or your frustration. You know, I'm not perfect; Sean's not perfect, so sometimes we don't show as much restraint as we need to in many circumstances. But I think if you try, I think it's something passed on to your child—just calmly approach a disagreement or calmly approach a problem that you're working on. Lately, George has been wanting to do one thing and one thing only, and that is throw a ball—a big ball—up and down the stairs. And he is having a lot of difficulty understanding that's something he can't do all the time. So I've been trying to basically teach him, "Listen, these are the time periods in which we'll do this—we'll do this for about five or ten minutes, and then we'll stop and do something else." I believe it's working—it's really hard to tell. He's gotten a little better in understanding that, you know, we cannot play ball all the time; we cannot necessarily go outside when it's really raining hard. He's learning, but restraint is one of the hardest things to teach a toddler. They don't come by modestly; they want what they want when they want it, and one of the hardest things about being a parent is understanding that you have to do things over and over again before it sinks in. It doesn't happen immediately; it's not day one, it's usually day 21 before he understands that things can't always go your way.

Back to the tantrums—I really think the most important thing when you're dealing with a kid with a tantrum is coming and talk to them. I try to talk to George, and I say—even though he cannot vocalize his actual words what he's feeling—"George, are you upset?" And he says, "NO!" And I ask him, "What upsets you?" And he says, "Blah blah blah." And I say, "I'm sorry that you're upset, you know sometimes things don't go the way we want them to, but we can learn from that." And he seems to calm from that. I don't know for certain, sometimes he doesn't, but we need to let him work through that, give him a big hug, and at least talk to him.

And also there's times when he doesn't get a hug, and you know, I say, "George, this is absolutely unacceptable. This is unacceptable behavior—we do not do this." Then he cries a little bit, and then I think he does—you know, when you're doing something wrong even when you're a baby you know when you're doing something wrong that you're not supposed to be doing. And I think there have to be boundaries—he has to understand that some things are harmful, some things are dangerous, you know, there are consequences to our actions, and it's important to us that he understands that the world is a big, amazing, but yet a beautiful and dangerous place, and George is just a part of that world because he has to understand where his place is in the world.

*Christopher Blanchard*

I would want my child to not be aggressive, mean, or forceful when she's around other children and she's feeling angry or frustrated. We are trying to instill in her that biting, or behaviors like that, is not the way to handle herself or the situation, whatever it might be. We'd like her to have some restraint and not be aggressive and forceful toward other children that she would be around or is having a problem with.

I have to practice restraint around my children. There are times they just want to push your buttons. They may see that you are frustrated or either you're frustrated with them. Taking a deep breath, walking away from the situation or asking for help from your significant other may be helpful, but you definitely do need to show restraint—because showing aggression toward them is not leading by example and is not showing them something good and it's not good for them to see. So restraint is very important whenever necessary.

*Robert Bovell*

I see restraint as a form of removing something from a privileged child, or a child who thinks, "I'm gonna get up every day and watch my show even though I don't clean my room, I don't get good grades, and I don't listen to my parents." What I teach on the flip side is, "I'm gonna restrain you from going outside and riding your bike with your friends and place you in your room by yourself to think about what you've done."

I've never been an advocate of corporal punishment or physical discipline because I don't want to harm a child, but I will restrain them from a lot of their activities or the things they want to do that they got so used to doing and when you take something away from them, you know, you may get a temper tantrum or tears, "why?" As a parent this is when you take time to explain to them how their privileges can be restored and how they should behave in the future if something comes up and they feel the need to voice their opinion or act out, so they don't lose anything. For me, restraint means to remove a child, whether it's a boy or girl, from a situation that could result to physical punishment. That's me, that's just me.

In terms of a child's own self-restraint, children need to learn if they have a situation that may cause them you to act out, whether it's physical or verbal, there are consequences to the action they take, including legal consequences. The law of the land is that punishment for one who acts out without using restraint could be incarceration, it could be jail. When a parent places a child in a room as punishment, there are walls around them and they can look out the window, but just imagine as they get older and are restrained by the police, they put handcuffs on them and place them in a room where there is no window and they can't see the trees and the birds. Now someone is controlling them and restraining their minds and their ability to readapt or go back to what they're accustomed to doing. Once I gave my kids this illustration and I explained it them, they never acted out of impulse. They thought about it.

I restrain myself in my relationships with other people, especially with my kids when I get angry by removing myself from the situation, but I take the cell phone and the social media advantage of communicating with them because I know they're gonna pick their phones up, but you know they're gonna read their computer and I may send them a message about the situation, and I may say, "Daddy started to respond in an angry way," or "Daddy started to respond when he thought he had to physically touch you and I want to take this time for both of us to take a deep breath and kind of reanalyze our situation and see if we can come to better terms without getting verbally or physically combative." That works because you get to read what someone says over and over so you can process it.

I try to illustrate the situation, and I do it in a way where they—if they leave the house and they go half an hour away and they sit somewhere for forty minutes, you know, twenty of those forty minutes they're gonna read what you said two or three times—they might stop at a light and get something to drink and read it again, so by the time they get home, the negative part of that whole situation was reprocessed. One thing about a text is, once you hit Send, you can't change what you said, so you get the opportunity to clean it up and fix it because you want to leave them with something positive.

*Marlon Bovell*

I need to get better at restraining myself because sometimes I get angry if we ask them to do something and they don't do it right away, especially if it's getting late at night. We may say "Davin, do this, do that. You know it's bedtime," and after the third time and maybe the fourth time, at that point I get angry and I may raise my voice. So that's one of those instances when it's the opposite of showing them how to handle the situation, about how to behave. It's hard. That's one of my struggles for sure, having restraint to not get angry, because I've noticed that my daughter handles similar situations the same way with her brother. She raises her voice and gets angry and starts to yell, and I know that is probably from me modeling that behavior.

I need to show more restraint and handle my anger a different way so that they can learn a better way to deal with situations. I don't want them to go out into the world and especially even at school and feel they have to deal with problems by raising their voice. I have to do a better job with not raising my voice at them. I'll have to try to maintain a better tone.

At this point we take away privileges, and they have to earn time to play games on their devices. They cannot play video games until Friday. If they don't listen, I remind them that the Friday privilege will be taken away, and I follow through if I need to, then there's pouting and me getting angry. That's when I remind them that they had a choice and they knew what was going to happen.

*Shanice Bovell*

As a parent, restraint can be hard, especially when they're toddlers because sometimes you just want to drop a lash on their behinds because you're frustrated with their behavior and don't always want to talk things out. Even as teenagers you want to drop a lash because you just want to get your point across quickly, but they won't properly learn that way. No matter how old your child gets, you'll always have to exercise restraint, depending on the situation. I've always wanted to have a good relationship with my children and always wanted them to know they can come to me and I won't "freak out."

I want them to always trust me and feel comfortable enough with me when things get a little uncertain, scary, or if they need advice. Having restraint wasn't always easy, but it's definitely worked for me.

*Holly Blum*

Restraint is something you want children to learn. Restraint has a lot to do with anger management, self-regulation, and self-control. What are acceptable ways of demonstrating anger, frustration, etc.? I also think restraint has to do eventually with, as we become older, being able to slow ourselves down and being more sophisticated in terms of how we express anger, frustration. I call that peaks and valleys at different developmental stages. We need to be able to do some self-analysis about our feelings, such as, "Why are you so upset?" "What are some other ways to express your anger?" I remember the times Jordan slammed the door and I said, "You know there's no slamming doors in this house," etc., and she did raise my awareness to the fact that I am a door slammer…then there was my mother's expression: "Don't do as I do." So even these many years later, I'll say to Jordan, you know that may be the message that you walked away with (i.e., uncontrolled expressions of anger and frustration), but that was not necessarily the message I meant to communicate or model. It's not about not being angry or not being frustrated; it's the demonstration of it. But this bigger picture is somewhat developmental; it's about being able to balance and about finding the respectful, responsible, appropriate behavior.

I didn't talk to Jordan directly about, "Do unto others as you would expect others to do unto you," but when she would come home and say, "Did such and such, and tomorrow I'm going to do such and such," we would have a conversation about being respectful, etc. I do know that I probably had a conversation with her even though I didn't per se necessarily always say the Golden Rule, but I would encourage her to use some restraint, saying things like, "Step back, what's another way you could do that?" "How would that make you feel?"

As a parent, for me the hardest part in terms of restraint was allowing Jordan space, restraining myself from doing the thinking for her to ensure that she was either doing it my way or the path that I think was the most valuable path. Sometimes you have to let kids fail and learn from their own mistakes. I think I probably struggled with that a bit, and she might say even a little bit more than a little bit.

When I think of restraint, I also think of having some awareness of what your impulse is and why it is important to not overassume. Those of us who work with kids tend to overassume at times. If we step back, observe, or listen, we'll probably make a better assessment of the situation. I realize this now, not when I was twenty-five or twenty-six years old, when I first started out teaching, or when I was a first-time parent. I think some of that is when we get older we get theoretically wiser or at least more thoughtful. For parents, this is food for thought. It's that balance between overassuming and restraining yourself from making assumptions and acting on assumptions when you may not even have the information. I think it's important to teach kids how to do that. And then of course, that looks different in four-year-olds than it looks like with fourteen- or thirty-seven-year-olds. I think it's an important skill to have, and I think it goes back to respect. You're doing it on behalf of respect—self-respect and respect for others.

### Dorel Campbell-Adams

You have to be conscious of your behavior; you have to know when you're going onto the wrong path. If I get angry at home and I yell at the kids, I realize that I've gone past where I should be with them, and I acknowledge this and let them know, and I promise that in the future I will not address them in this way. For example, I'll say, "I'm not perfect, and you're the first sixteen-year-old that I've ever had and I'm going to do some things wrong, and I'm going to do right things, and when I do wrong things, I will acknowledge it and let you know."

My husband thinks I talk too much like that to the kids. But they connect with me. My older son feels he gets the respect he deserves and appreciates me telling him that. I tell him he has to practice restraint too. He's has a very calm personality, but then he holds a lot in, and when things get overwhelming for him, he can explain them. We've talked about situations at school, we've talked about anger, and I've told him, "You cannot hold anger for somebody who is still learning about themselves. Think of them as a tornado. A tornado takes everything in its path. So if it's moving from point A to point B and you just happen to be right there that tornado is not going to hear about you. You're going to go from point A to Point B and wherever you fall that's not that's not their business anymore. They don't care about that. So you've got to let go of whatever anger you have. You have gotten in relationships in high school and realized that everybody is growing and you have to let go of that anger. You experience it and move on. It's not always about you." But that's a hard concept for them, even for adults.

I've never had this conversation with my mother at sixteen, but now I'm having it with my sixteen-year-old son. I tell him, "Focus on your schoolwork, that's all I need from you at this point."

*Desiree DeFlorimonte*

Restraint means to have self-control or to hold back your feelings or actions. I think restraint is one of the most difficult parenting skills. It has been my observation that some parents want their children to have what they did not have while growing up, such as a certain educational experiences and material things. Like most parents, it was my desire to always do the best I could for my child. However, there were numerous occasions when I had to show restraint and hold back both my feelings and actions when my child tested my patience with such statements as, "Mommy, why can't we go to McDonald's for dinner? I don't like your food." "My friends have designer clothes, and you don't even have a credit card to K-Mart." "Why can't I spend the night at my friend's house?" "When will I have an allowance?" "I am fourteen years old and don't understand why I can't go on a date."

From a young age, Angel was introduced to eating healthy meals and from that time until her adult years, she objected. I demonstrated restraint by not literally shoveling the vegetables and fruits down her throat but gave in to cooking macaroni and cheese or ordering her favorite pizza or mac-nuggets on rare occasions. When Angel begged for something that another child had, complained about spending time overnight with friends, having an allowance or going on a date at the age of fourteen, I showed restraint by lovingly giving reasons why I could not permit her to have what she wanted… I couldn't afford it, and it wasn't in her best interest. At times her defiance and my lack of restraint caused her to get a good spanking.

Teaching my child how to be patient and show restraint was also not easy. As a parent and role model, holding back from picking up or cleaning after Angel when I observed the messy room or saying "no" to requests was quite a feat. I recognized that just as I learned from my mother, Angel would emulate my behaviors, and so I tried to demonstrate restraint.

*Ryan Dickson*

I err on the side of limited restraint, you know, but getting back to the teamwork and game mentality, if we're on a mission, depending upon the mission that we're on, there are different rules to the game. For instance, if we're going out to eat at a restaurant with multiple people other than just daddy and kids, we're on a different type of mission, and the rule of that game is no singing at the table where. But if we're just dad and kids, in this type of restaurant, maybe there's a little humming. So it's not necessarily restraint; it's more abiding by the rules of the game that you're playing and playing within the context. Other than that, feel free to create within those parameters.

I create context to be powerful. For instance, if my daughter is doing whatever she's doing with her mom and it's something I wouldn't do, I give them space because they have their own program; but when she's with me, my program supersedes all other programs. If, for example, there are children with their parents in a restaurant, and the kids are throwing food around, I just accept that the parents either didn't care that what the kids were doing was interfering with other people's experience and people's livelihood, or they have not discovered a way to parent effectively such that their children understand it's not in their best interest to be doing those things.

When you consider that children live in a world outside of their home as well—they live in a school community, they live in a neighborhood community, they live in a church community, they live in the world at large, you realize they will have experiences with people from all parts of the world because the world has gone global and there are different degrees of sensitivities.

So I mean, it's such a broad umbrella, and you want your child to respond within the context of each situation. A common situation these days is bullying, and for me my child's response should depend on the situation. I mean, if somebody was talking about his shoes, that's one thing; if somebody was saying, I'm going to kill you tomorrow, and they laugh every day when they say that, that's another thing. Is it okay? Bullying is not specific. What is specific is what's your reaction going to be. But I guess it has different levels of somebody talking about my shoes. "Oh, my kids." That's one response, you know. So you know, in terms of creating the space for your child, you know, you want to create a resilient person to where someone's not. Yeah. Shoes. But is there another thing if someone's threatening your life? Yes. So speak to me immediately. Yes. And you might, you know, but it's just various ranges. And you can't control the various ranges of bullying that you might be present to, but you can control how you move through the situations.

*Richlyn Emanuel*

Restraint is holding your tongue, holding in your anger, holding your fist, holding your belt. Sometimes you have to hold it because you're very angry, and it's not good to talk to or discipline anyone when you're very angry, because you can go overboard and that's never good, because then you end up apologizing, but then you could really hurt someone and that's all they remember. They don't remember what led up to the hurt or how it happened. There was a period of time where I actually had to catch myself because I was dealing with challenging behavior from Giovanni, and I couldn't understand what was going on. I remember getting angry and upset; nothing was going right. There were times when I actually sat in the car and talked to Giovanni about, "Okay, this is why it happened. It shouldn't have, it's not an excuse, I'm human and it happened." But how do I restrain that? Yoga? Prayer? It helps to recognize that I'm angry before I lash out. Giovanni has learned that also over time;

because in his total young life, he's had much to be angry about. Last year in his Spanish class, he actually got so angry at the teacher that I told him he had to lash out at home. So he beat up a pillow in my room, and we talked about it.

It's difficult, especially if you're under pressure, and you don't know how to turn off the pressure and you don't know why you're lashing and you haven't been able to pinpoint the cause of your anger. So you're unable to restrain yourself. But when you start to learn yourself, and you know the things that people do that make you angry, you walk away, you pray about it, and over time and…for example, at work there's a woman who just kept pushing and pushing and pushing, and I said to her, "One day I'm going to knock you out, you're going to wake up and realize that I have knocked you out, and I will lose my job. You need to stop doing this. You are a thirty-something-year-old woman, and there is no way that you should be acting worse than my child."

Being with Giovanni's dad, had I not gone through that period of frustration and anger and trials and tribulation, I think I may have knocked her out, but I knew she was purposely pushing my buttons. Sometimes you learn restraint by going through things. Whatever the case is, we go through it and we learn to recognize the things that at push us beyond our limit. Restraint for me is something that you have to learn and you have to understand yourself in order to have restraint.

As a young black man, it's important for Giovanni to exercise restraint. He cannot afford to speak his mind or to lash out, because it may cost him his life. He has to learn at a very early age about himself, and as he grows more into young adulthood, he has to refine who that person is and he has to be focused on who she is and realize the things that can push him beyond that point. He has to learn that, because his life depends on him being able to control his words and his actions, whether it be in school, or wherever he is. He has to learn how to control that, and it's hard to control a young man trying to grow into manhood who is taught that he has to be the one that defends and protects the family, but he has to stay in this box before he loses his life. It's extremely important, and I don't know how he will balance that, and that's not something I can teach him.

*Raymond Fisher*

You have to practice restraint. For example, like I said earlier, from being a helicopter parent, there also has to be a balance. You also have to restrain yourself from giving your kids too much too soon. Restraint is constant through everything that you do as a parent. You have to ask yourself questions, like, "How do I want my child to be? Do I want my child to be financially responsible and understand finances? Do I want my child to be able to converse with anybody from the hood to the top diplomats and people from different countries around the world? How do I mold them not do too much too soon, or do too little too late? How do I walk that walk in strength?" A great example is some people I know give cell phones to their kids at age five and put every toy under the Christmas tree. They give them the latest Jordan's, or whatever, or go to this event, or do this and that. And then I ask them how much they put away for their kids' future.

I also try to show my kids I love them by giving them things, but when I can't provide something, I explain to them why, because I know their feelings get hurt. So coming from the gift too soon and too little, too late aspect, I try to be transparent and explain to them that if I had it, you know I would do it. But right now we can't accomplish that. At times I've said, "Look, this is on you. You need the stuff. You know you're not going to get your driver's license unless you go to work this summer to pay for it. I told you to get good grades, which is your responsibility and you neglected your responsibility." I'm just giving examples of how you have to show restraint and not reward mediocrity, but make it a teaching moment, especially young parents. They just give and give and give. That's not restraint. They need to restrain from giving their kids too much, such as clothes they're going to grow out of, or toys that they're going to play once and throw away. Parents should prepare for a rainy day when they really need the money, whether it's for a health issue, a financial issue, or whatever the case may be.

The other angle is practicing restraint in an extremely difficult situation, the need to keep a calm, level head. There are times when we react emotionally with our kids, times when restraint is needed as a parent to embrace them in a loving way when they make a mistake. That's when you have that calm conversation. All the kids smoke these days, and this is normal. I know the end result because I grew up in DC when it was the drug and murder capital of the universe. So have that conversation when they're mature enough to handle that conversation. Let them know they're not doing anything new under the sun, and that's transparency.

My kids have always seen my level of spiritualism. I don't turn it off. But they have also seen me struggle and curse and fuss. I think it's important, like I said, not to be put on a pedestal, but to be transparent and show them that I'm human, because we are nothing but human. And the beauty of humanity is we are always evolving, and we have to take that in context and build on that, because you know, my daddy told me the day we stop learning is the day we die. You have to make what you learn applicable to your life because everything that you did in the past is preparing you for the moments that you encounter right now and in the future. And then of course, restraint... Everything in moderation, I'm of no delusion that they're not going to, they need to have guidance and be embraced. You can't just say, "You smoking weed, that's wrong." You have to show some restraint, show maturity. The thing is, you always have to be the adult in their lives, even if it's in a joking or laughing way, that's parental psychology. You have to be the adult in their world, helping them understand things like premarital sex or sex at a young age. That's the restraint that we have to tell them about, but a lot of parents don't talk to the kids sincerely like that, they hope for the best, but don't put in the work. Like Kevin Hart said, everybody wants to be famous, nobody wants to put in the work, especially with some of the younger kids we're seeing, that we know are two or three generations of what we have in our community, children raising children. When we put in the work, when we work for results, it comes through. When you look at it, responsibility and restraint are intertwined.

I've told my kids that the greatest reward, I realize, is when they come back and talk to me and say, you're right, and thank you, thank you for being hard on me, thank you for your sacrifice, and thank you for the commitment you made. I realize now that my kids are young adult what it takes, now that my kids are having these conversations. I think that's God's way of showing me that I'm doing something right. Yes, my kids are good people.

*Martine Gordon*

As a parent, you are a person and sometimes you're stressed or you're not necessarily in a place to be totally calm and zen in the moment, and you have to check yourself and say, "Okay, this is not how I'm thinking, or how I might feel like I want to act, and how can I either remove myself from this situation safely so I can calm down or how I can alter my thinking in the moment." And then also, children, young children especially well even you know they say that emotionally people's brains don't fully develop until their midtwenties, so children, we'll just say, you know they don't necessarily have all the coping mechanisms and abilities to restrain themselves in every situation, so how do we as parents demonstrate for them what appropriate restraint is and show them that they can get through it? And how do we have understanding, when especially if very young children are having difficulty demonstrating restraint, because they're not going to get it every time and some situations are very overwhelming, so here again, I think of reciprocity when I think of restraint.

I actually don't feel I'm very good at practicing restraint. My husband is a very patient man, and he is very, very good at practicing restraint. I feel I didn't have a good demonstration of this when I was a child, so it's a lifelong process for me to practice restraint, one of the things we agreed to, is that if one of us, assuming that we're both present, ideally we're both somewhere close by, if one of us needs to take a moment to calm down because we can feel ourselves getting a little worked up that we ask the other to step in, and we can step away and come back. If he is not there, my daughter is old enough now that we've been trying to teach her the terms to express her feelings. She knows the word *frustrated*. I'm still not sure she knows exactly what it means, but I identify my feelings, like "I'm frustrated, because you're doing something that could be unsafe and you're very important to me and I want you to be safe." I try to just clearly and simply state what my emotion is and why I'm feeling that way, and in addition, I think it's helpful for her to understand why Mommy's voice might be getting a little agitated. It also ends up helping me to calm down, to be able to name those feelings and why I'm feeling that way, and it helps me to rethink the situation in the moment, sometimes like, well, maybe I could handle this a little bit differently than what I've been doing. I guess that's one example to just name it and say it out loud.

My daughter doesn't have any developmental delays or she doesn't have any difficulties in identifying emotions for her age group, so we can do those things with her pretty easily and I imagine that it's probably simultaneously more difficult but even more important for children with autism or some other developmental delay. Thankfully, I'm in a position where my daughter will say, "Mommy, are you frustrated?" And I'll say, "Yes, I am frustrated because this is what is happening right now."

*Justin Hampton*

Restraint starts with me being the physical force in the house, the disciplinarian in the house. I could be very overbearing, the dictator in the house. And I think men can fall into the trap of assuming that their needs and wants should be met all the time. But one thing I try to not do, especially with the children, is to respond in anger or emotionally respond to anything, because then I will get in the habit of responding based upon how I feel and not based on the situation. And so even if they've done something to anger me, or if they've done something to one another that requires a response immediately, I try to think through it first, because every interaction is a training experience, and I have to practice restraint with myself and what I say to them. So if it's corrective because we physically discipline our children, but if it's a spanking, and I'm not going to spike in anger, I'm not going to discipline them when I'm upset because that's going to exceed, you know, the forcefulness or whatever where the aggression or you know, whatever the word is, the intensity, I guess, of the responsible will be too much in fact, wearable or anything like that. I just tried to really show restraint in it with them and teaching the same thing they do with each other. When you brother makes you upset, you don't get to just turn around a screamer. Try to control yourself before you try to control some audios.

*Leticia Herrera*

You know, sometimes you may want to yell or scream, but you know that your child is going to be learning from you so you might have to check yourself. I have done a lot of restraining myself. I was working seven days and I never left my son out. Every time I went to work, I got him books, toys and food. Whatever I was doing, I always took time and involved him. As I was working, I was talking to him and watching what he was doing. That's how I became very good at multitasking. I would ask a question about the book, I would ask questions about what he was playing. I would ask questions about the food. So I always keep it on track. I still remember when I was done cleaning in one place, and David went back and opened the piano and started to play the piano. I was very mad and angry because I was rushing to get home. I had been working all day. It was a Sunday, so I yelled at him, and then I took off and I went upstairs. It took me a couple of seconds to think about it that it was not his fault. So I went back downstairs, and I apologized to him. I said I'm so sorry it's really not at all about you. I did realize that that was not fair to him. I decided then to put him in an extended day program. I appreciated this program because it gave me time to get myself together after work before I picked him up. I was drained on the job and felt overwhelmed sometimes, so I learned to come home and take a fifteen-minute nap, get myself together, then go to pick him up. We always talked as we walked home, and it didn't matter how tired I was, I would take his bike downstairs from the third floor where we lived and take him riding.

*Joseph Kijewski*

Well, restraint can come in a number of forms, especially restraint on the parent's part. There are times when you lose it and you want to be physical with the children, you really do. Going back to my own childhood, to a situation where that was the norm, there was no holding back by my father, but you're teaching violence and a lack of self-control. If you don't model restraint for your child, you know, everything in moderation, not flying off the handle when they do something wrong, moderating your own conduct, not drinking too much, not doing crazy things infront of the children, then you are engaging in what you know is not good for you and what you wouldn't want to be doing. You have to show respect for yourself if you want to be a good parent. I guess you have to be putting the well-being of the child ahead of everything else in your life. That really does need to be your first priority.

And the same thing for the the child who throws a tantrum because he didn't get his way and may break something, or the child who breaks something because she didn't get her way, or stomping their feet or punching their siblings. You don't allow that. You teach them from the very beginning, first with gentle restraints. If the child wants to take a tantrum and falls on the floor and is kicking and screaming, you pick the child up and hug the child but you don't want the child to continue doing it. So you hold the child until he sees he's not going get his way and the bad conduct is not getting them anything. Every once in a while, when when one of our little ones misbehaved in church, we took her to the car and put her in her car seat and sat out there with her, and if we had to go back to church later because because we weren't there for the mass, well, you know, the child learns she has to control her behavior and that bad behavior is not going to get her her way. You can't show a lack of restraint; you have to restrain them with love.

*Errol Marks*

I had to work on restraint, and I'm still working on it. I've been working on it for close to seven years—not yelling at my kids, not badgering or barking at them. It's very disheartening, and it breaks your spirit. I remember how I felt. That was one of the contributing factors to why I'm here in the first place, why I'm in this country. It's a mixed bag when it comes to that. My motivation for wanting a better life is because I didn't like the one I had. I didn't feel comfortable in the one I had and wanted to live on my own. I loved living on my own because I never found peace in my home. I think that's wrong. I don't think you should make a child not feel part of the family; you should not break a child's spirit. That's the time to practice restraint and not do things the way your mother did because she might not have a clue about how to do things differently based on the way she was raised. We are intelligent beings enough to step outside ourselves, stop and say not because it's always been done that way means that it should continue to be done that way. Not because you saw your parents do it or saw your elders do it. Take time to stop and to question why.

Some parents have an overtly restrictive, domineering, dominating, and controlling personality and their personality and their method of influence spill over into their parenting and their children don't have the freedom to develop into who they want to be. This may stem from fear. I am overprotective of my children because I do have a fear of my children getting hurt. But being overly protective is bordering on being obsessive. That's where I try to step lightly with my children and put the responsibility on them to practice restraint. Yes, I would send them out to parties. Would I be afraid? Absolutely. I would be terrified, but I'll have to have faith when that time comes. They're girls, they're beautiful, and they're going to go to parties. But you know, I would hope by then I would have taught them to be smart enough to avoid certain negative situations. And I feel that I would have that type of relationship with them that a call will give me early warning, if needed.

In the past, I became easily aggravated, but since my life is more or less stress-free in the last few years, I'm a lot happier. I do practice restraint, so I'm more pleasant and inviting and very encouraging. Having such a tough time growing up and actually through part of my adult life left me with a lot of anger. Most of that anger is gone—not all, I have to work on myself first. You know it's like the safety procedures on an aircraft. You buckle yourself and put on your own mask before you help your child. So when it comes to that, I think to be an effective parent you have to be an effective adult first. You have to be right for yourself first. Same thing with relationships like parenting and parenting is the most important relationship you will have in your life with your child because you will love that child forever. So you may not always love the mother or the father of that child forever, but you will definitely love that child forever. That's the relationship that lasts the rest of your life. Don't you think you should put your best effort into this relationship? This is why I had to do the work on myself for us. I had to work on my anger issues which were many and I had to face them.

There are times I do get stressed, but my kids can sense that and they understand. So as far as the relationship with my kids, as far as restraint they are clued in. They know where I am to the point where they will come rub my shoulders and say, "Okay, Daddy, is everything fine? I want you to be happy. What's bothering you?" And I say, "I'm fine. But thank you for caring." It's come to that point, and it seems like it happened overnight, but in reality, it happened over the course of years. Everything takes time, and anything worth having is worth sticking to.

*Maxine Maloney*

As parents, we know children have to deal with restraint, but we also know that as parents, sometimes we want to say something but have hold back. I know I've said some things that I really regret, and I think restraint is often where we are most challenged. As a single parent, I'm hit in every direction with every single thing, and I don't have an outlet, and so somedays I really have to practice restraint. I think restraint requires practice—that's something that is not innate, and it's not easy—it requires a lot of practice. When we work with toddlers and they're learning their self-help skills, and they're learning their words and expressing emotions, I think that's an area for growth in parenting, but just as adults, there's so much pressure. But then it's worse for children as they're growing, being able to have restraint. I'll catch Zaria in moments where I will say, "I know you are angry, and I know you were agitated, but maybe that was not the right thing to say at that time. I didn't really like how you said it." Or sometimes she'll come home and tell me about something that happened at school and her reaction and I will ask her, "Do you think that was the best reaction or the best approach?" But restraint is a challenge because I'm always having to bite my tongue when I want to say something or I want to say you should do it this way, or I think you should, or you know, I bite my tongue and not give too much advice or response. For example, my daughter Zaria is telling me about her day, and I want to say something or give my opinion, and I'll have to bite my tongue because really letting her speak and tell how she feels is probably the best approach.

Zaria is good at exercising restraint—that's one of her areas, but recognizing when she has reached her peak—when she's emotionally heightened and recognizing when she's getting ready to say something that may not be appropriate—having her recognize those feelings, and those buttons is important. Sometimes we work on "You're gonna have to breathe or even have to step back," especially as she gets older, especially as she's challenged by varied personalities and other adults. She is recognizing where her hot buttons are, and she knows if she says this to someone, or she looks at someone a certain way, she can pull herself back. I think that's kind of like two-year-old stuff, where you're coping, self-soothing kind of stuff.

I think this is my soapbox—this is why society is so out of control, and there's a lot of anger, and there's a lot of violence and a lot of outbursts is because restraint has not been properly taught. I even think of restraint when it comes to food and to different activities or actions. I just don't think we spend a lot of time talking about restraint. We're very impulsive as a society, and I try really hard to support Zaria in this area, so she recognizes she doesn't have to do everything. She doesn't have to be on the phone all the time; there are times to relax, and there are times when we listen to what people say, and they may say something we don't like, but we don't need to respond.

I realize how important it is that she learns restraint from me, her parent. This is transparency. I have even from last year learning restraint from going to counseling because last year she was struggling with some interactions at school, and I could not fully support, so I said, "You know what, let's go to counseling, and let's get a third party to help us deal with a response." That's because my response was not favorable, and I knew I was not going to do well, and so that helped both of us. I don't think parents should be afraid of that.

## Virgil McDonald

Restraint is not saying or doing the first thing that comes to mind. In talking with our sons, they consider people who exclaim, "I say what's on my mind," as people who are lacking in restraint. Saying or doing whatever you like without regard of how it makes the other person feel is nothing to be proud of doing. They do not subscribe to the practice of speaking before thinking or considering how their words and actions will be received. They subscribe to the practice of engaging your brain before you opening your mouth. Think first about the other person's feelings and in a tactful way try to communicate in a manner that is not hateful or destructive. Our children give us credit even for exercising restraint with them and with our grandchildren. They say that they recognize when we are showing restraint. Now that they are adults and have children, they are careful not to say or do things that are hurtful to their children. Kelly is very good at using stories to get her point across. I have heard them ask the question after one of her poignant stories, "Mom, are you talking about me?" I'm not giving you academic answers—I'm giving you examples. I am simply saying that our offspring recognize when we are showing restraint, and they understand why we are doing it.

## Jacqueline Rose

I see too many parents restraining their children by imposing logical rules and/or emotional and reactionary controls on them from the outside. They display strong emotional reactions to their children's behavior. Restraint comes from within. I have to practice self-restraint in order to expect it from my child. It's a matter of heart. You have to care enough about your child to turn to your heart. I care about my child, so I need to speak, but I need to turn to my heart before I speak in order to receive the answer to what my child needs, then I have to be willing to say it and follow through. I don't believe in punishment. I believe in guidance, communication, self-reflection, and self-discipline.

*Joseph Shields*

The thought that "restraint" triggers for me is probably as I alluded to earlier, something that you have to adapt to as a parent of guiding your children and not fixing everything for them. So the restraint factor would be there, I can do the math homework for my kids all the time, or their English assignments, or whatever it may be. But they're not learning a lesson as a result of that nor anticipating when they have a test how much preparation they have to put into it. So to the extent to which I have to show some restraint and myself but not assert myself in the situation and let them be challenged, I think is an important value for parents to learn, because at some level restraint is part and parcel with trust, and *trust* is another word for strength. Strength is not mitigating the risk per se, as much as letting them navigate around adventure as long as they don't put themselves too much in jeopardy. So it's a balancing act. I think everybody deals with the fact that they never want to see their kids' arms hurt. But I think you've got to make value judgments along the way as to how much you're going to fix because you want them to learn lessons.

This goes to the nature-nurture argument, a framework I was talking earlier, if it were that kids were purely about years to make and shape and years to nurture, and there wasn't DNA or RNA, then restraint would almost be an academic topic. You would feel very little restraint, because they come out of the womb as God's own creation with your personality and you would have no assurance from the get go to show restraint. Despite what your instincts are, you really have to figure out a way to nurture back on your own the restraint value. That becomes a positive value system as opposed to something that you regret.

In terms of challenges outside the home, we were just talking to Chris about this two days ago, not really anything he was dealing with, but rather about another child he knew who was going through some bullying and everything else. We told him he could be a leader and set an example by how he treated the child. I think, particularly with Christopher, he's still in the minority, and it's importing for him to articulate and assert himself around those types of issues. I keep referring to my son because, I think, as a teenager, he's probably dealing with issues more acutely than my daughter is because he is a teenager, and it's really about being willing to articulate his own value system and not just being a bystander, being a positive influence by asserting something as simple as a simple sentence, such as, "Jon Jon's okay with me," or "Hey, guys, this isn't cool," or whatever it may be. But knowing when and where to do that, kids don't always understand the significance of peer influence on their own friends and their own network, most of it is by example. And the kids that do figure it out really learn a way to lead in different ways and capacities.

My daughter, on the other hand, is much more assertive in terms of her personality. She has a bigger personality than my son. She's somebody who's running for office in school and knows a bunch of kids and isn't afraid to fail in a public setting in a way that I would say is different, distinguished from the way Christopher is with a smaller peer group. I think, again, it's kind of where you want to be, where and when you want to engage with people and things, and hopefully define them for other people that may be in that situation or may be abusing a situation.

*Halima Thorne*

Restraint is having self-control. I feel that I demonstrate restraint with Carter all the time, but I know my breaking point, and if I can't handle it I will call my village—my mom, my sister, my dad—and I will call for help. It's not necessarily him that he's doing it on purpose, he's a baby, he doesn't know how to use the words, and he's trying to discover things, to figure things out, just like I am. I know at a certain point, I will call mom or dad or my sister, but right now I have self-control when it comes to him. When he gets older, I think he's really going to test me, but right now he's new, and I don't always know what's going on, but I just have to be prepared for that.

*Barbara Van Dyke*

As a parent you need to demonstrate restraint, because the behaviors of a child can often lead you to behave in ways that you have taught your child not to behave. For example, you teach your child to communicate with respect, never raise his voice, engage in a conversation, use right messages, not point the finger, but the moment your child does something wrong, you want to lay into them, and you do exactly what you tell them not to do and sometimes you just want to go after them, but you have to exercise restraint because then you do exactly what you told them not to do in handling conflict. Sometimes they drive you to anger because they didn't demonstrate the value you taught them—not to be aggressive, not to fight, not to be a bully, not to hit younger children. You're the adult, they're the children—you're teaching them all those things, but then, I don't know if it's instinctive, but to address them breaking a rule or not, upholding a value, sometimes you feel pushed, or I don't know what it is—your adrenaline flows and you feel that you should respond to them physically—spank, push against the wall, you know use a paddle or cane—whatever it is, but when you do that as a parent, you are giving vent to your own feelings—you're not fixing the behavior. You are putting fear in the child with the hope that the fear is gonna prevent them from breaking that rule or whatever bad behavior it was, committing that act or whatever, but it's the fear that probably gives the response that you're looking for. Over a long period of time, you still haven't reinforced or continued to teach the value that you want them to demonstrate. I was spanked many times, but I still don't think you get the best bang for your buck when you spank. When you spank, it's because of a feeling inside you, it's nothing about what the child did, it's about that feeling of disappointment or lack of reciprocity in regards to the behavior that they demonstrate that leads you to feel, "I've done all this, I have spoken to you a hundred times. I've taken care of you, I give you what you want to eat, and this is how you're gonna behave?" And you spank. It's about the parent's feelings more so than the issue at hand.

We vent, but think about how you feel after you spank. I clearly remember, after realizing that I was raising my voice or just being totally different, unlike who I am and how I behave, that my feelings were such that I needed to remove myself. So I learned to become very quiet and go off and distract myself. And later, I may say, "I'm never to see that kind of behavior again." Or we talk about it. I had one experience that actually I think set the course how I respond to issues. And I'm not saying that I've never gotten angry and very upset to the point where I have to check myself, but I knew to check myself. I did self-reflection almost immediately. So Elon might have been three and a half or four, and he had a responsibility in the morning. We were living in Oxon Hill; he had the responsibility to feed the fish before he went off to school, and I guess I chose to do too many things in the timeframe in the morning like I usually do before leaving the house, so I'm rushing around and rushing him around, "Get your..." "Why didn't you do this..." And so when we got to the point we are now going to pick our things up to go through the door, he's now hustling with the fish food, and trying to put the fish food in the tank and he still has to pick up his book bag, and I lost it. And I said, "If you don't move, why didn't you feed the fish. I told you to feed the fish—now we're rushing and what's wrong with you?" Elon turned to me and said, "Mommy, why are you angry?" The tears started flowing, and I said, "Oh, Father God, what is happening to me?" I immediately went into self-reflection, and immediately I said, "Let's go, come on let's go because we're going to be late." And it made me think that he didn't cause me to have to rush him. I am rushing him because I didn't have a good enough plan for us getting out of there given the time that we had.

I shouldn't rush him because I see that we're gonna be late. It's my responsibility to time things and have the activities set up so that we both can get them done within the time we have before we leave home. That's one example that taught me restraint. The other example is restraint in providing what your child needs more so than what your child wants or what you think—it's three parts—what your child needs, what your child wants, and what you think your child should have. I have a girlfriend, her son is a couple years older than my son. We were best friends when I was younger, and we talked about raising our children. Some issues came up around what our children expect from us, and sometimes what they expect from us is grand and unrealistic, but they don't see it as such, and she said that her child did not make the best use of all that he was provided as she raised him, and she came to the conclusion that our generation, my generation, somehow provided our children with more than what we should provide them and sent them the wrong message that fostered in them a sense of entitlement. I agreed, but I made a mental note that I am gonna do everything I possibly can not to foster this feeling of entitlement because it's something that plays in our society today across all colors, ethnicity, social, and economic groups—that sense of entitlement that impacts personal responsibility, restraint, and all the things I aforementioned.

# Ten Things about Restraint

- Restraint is about managing negative emotions such as anger, fear, and frustration. Parents and teachers can teach children to recognize, label, name, and understand their emotions and to express these emotions in socially acceptable ways.
- Exercising restraint can be challenging for some parents. In fact, it is probably one of the most difficult parenting skills.
- Know the situations that push your emotional buttons and trigger your anger, fear, and frustration. Recognize your feelings and decide on ways of handling these feelings that work for you, such as positive self-talk, thinking about positive solutions, walking away, prayer, physical activity, reading, and taking a nap, to name a few.
- For both adults and children, when things don't go your way, as they sometimes do, take time to calmly think about it before you act on it.
- The saying "Engage your brain before you open your mouth" is excellent advice for parents, children, and all of us. Think before you speak and always before you act. Also consult your heart and consider the feelings of others. This is exercising restraint, and it comes from within.
- Expect ups and downs during the teaching and learning processes, but maintain consistency and children will in time internalize these behaviors. Young children's brains are developing, and they don't have all the coping mechanisms and ability to restrain themselves in emotionally charged situations. Don't give up talking with your child. Problem-solve together, talk about alternative ways of expressing

144

feelings of anger, fear, and frustration, and then you behave in those same ways when you experience those feelings.

- Behaving aggressively toward your children is not leading by example. Instead, teach them that there are consequences for unacceptable behavior, then follow through with the consequences whenever they indulge in the unacceptable behavior.

- It's important for African American children and youth to practice restraint, especially boys and young men. Their freedom and their lives depend on their ability to be restrained in emotionally volatile situations.

- Fathers are often viewed as the physical force in the home, the enforcer. However, fathers can seize opportunities to turn this expectation around by modeling restraint in the ways they discipline their children. For example, they can refrain from aggression and discuss alternative, acceptable behavior, and following through with consequences; they can restrain in a loving manner. For both parents, yelling at, badgering, and barking at children break their spirit.

- Bullying is a common behavior nowadays, and children need to be taught to react to bullies in ways that will not be harmful for them. Bullies need to be taught alternative ways of expressing their needs, fears, hurts, low self-esteem, and other emotions that contribute to their bullying.

# CHAPTER 6

## Parents Give Parenting Advice to Twenty-First-Century Parents

What practical parenting advice do you have for twenty-first-century parents? These must be things parents can actually do.

*Marguerite Anderson*

Create a shared family calendar. It's really important to create a shared family calendar, even a calendar that has separate family members, if possible. I can't stress this enough. It makes our lives so much easier; we actually see a break in a relationship breaking down because it's ultimately a communication issue, right? Having a structured calendar, a structured environment of sorts is substantial. It is key to understanding where your partner is during the day. Sometimes it's as simple as knowing that Sean has a doctor's appointment or a haircut on that day, or we can't schedule this family outing, or knowing that George's appointments are this time. It's so easy for us to just look at our calendar and know exactly what's going on in our family. And not everything gets added to it, but we're doing pretty well, and it's really incredibly helpful.

One thing that we've done with George is deciding to limit the screen time that he has. We're not really a big television-watching family. Sean barely watches TV, I watch a couple of shows on my own occasionally, and we can see that George is interacting with things in the world in ways that some of his peers are not. He's definitely more engaged with reading—he loves to read, and he's a very physical child, he enjoys playing with his ball, he enjoys playing. He enjoys music, and I think a lot of that comes from the fact that he's not distracted, and I can see the way that children are distracted with technology today, and it's interesting and I get it—I get why parents use technology. It's a way for you to sometimes cook dinner or to just decompress from a busy day, but there are consequences to it. Anything that's easy that you can just pick up and pull out of your pocket; anything that comes that easy has to have a consequence. So I would say, "Try to limit the screen time if you can." Look, the people who invent this stuff, they are also limiting the screen time for their children. A lot of the people in Silicon Valley don't let their children use the technology that they have created, so keep that in mind as a parent; that's really important.

I think it's important to schedule time for you and your partner to be together. Before I got married, I knew that I was not going to settle for a relationship where I felt that I was the only person in the relationship, or if we were living separate lives. We definitely try to make time to spend together. At night, we have dinner together. If you can, sit down and eat dinner, or lunch, or breakfast—whatever the meal is a few times a week. We try to do every meal; it's very rare that we don't sit down as a family at the table and eat together.

It's easy to run out of time because there's so much to do all the time, so there's plenty of Mommy and George time, plenty of Daddy and George time, there's plenty of whole family time, but the thing that's tougher is Mommy and Daddy time, so that needs to be on the calendar. In order to nurture your family, you have to nurture the first two members of the family. The parents are the fundamental foundation of the family and a lot of parents forget that, so we take at least once a week we go out for date nigh; we try, we try, and we do. And George is on a sleep schedule, which is very important. George eats dinner and lunch and breakfast at a certain time, and he also takes a nap at the same time every day; he also goes to sleep at the same time every day. We have a bedtime routine where he gets a bath, we read to him, he lies down, he drinks his milk, we brush his teeth, and then he goes to sleep. And this is by 7:00 p.m. and after

7:00 p.m. is Mommy and Daddy time and we spend the evening together or doing dishes and cleaning the house, taking out the garbage, but we spend time together. We decompress from our day, and sometimes we spend time together apart. There are times when Sean is reading, and sometimes I'm doing something else, but we do take the time to nurture our time for ourselves and have a life apart from George. It wasn't that easy at the beginning, but certainly, we found a routine, and it's important to us. Having a routine has been very beneficial for our young family.

### Christopher Blanchard

To my generation, I would say that parenting is something you really never is hundred-percent prepared for. You just take it a day at a time and learn as you go, because, you know, every day you learn, just like in life, every day, you learn something new and something that you can use to be better. So just do do whatever you feel the situation at the time is right. And you know, always be the person that's going to show your children a lot of love and care toward them. But there are going to be situations that come up all the time that you never really are prepared for, but you learn as you go along.

Parenting can be challenging, but it's very, very rewarding. I know in the future you'll look back on these times and say you're very proud of your children for the persons they have become and the persons that they become is going to be because of you and the people close to you and your family who helped shape and mold the children. So the biggest thing is just taking a day at a time, learn from your mistakes, and remember what it is that you can do better to better yourself and your children to be good adults in the future, because you want them to be responsible adults and do the right things. Now, what you need to do is show them right from wrong and just be good parents (in my case, a good father), someone that they look up to and know they can always count on and come to with their questions and for advice or anything that they need. It's very important that they know that they can look up to you and you will always be an essential part of their lives going forward.

Seek help when you need need it, because like I said earlier, you don't come programmed to be parents, you learn it when you're in it. Ask for advice in certain situations; it will definitely make things a little bit easier. There are plenty of times when I would ask my wife or my mom for advice about what to do in a situation, like when the baby is doing something, and I just don't know what to do. So definitely seek advice from others. It's nothing to be ashamed of. It's important because you can read all the manuals or all the books, but until you actually experience it on your own, you really just don't know. You learn as you go, and you get better. It's like a job, you get better at your job by doing it constantly, and you work at it and get better over time.

*Robert Bovell*

When giving advice to anyone, your own behavior must reflect the advice you are giving. So parents must be consistent in their own behaviors, making sure they do what's respectful, what's responsible, and what reflects the values of the family. The best advice that I can give is to be consistent. Do what you say. You don't want to give advice to anyone, whether it's to a child or another adult when you're constantly looked at or known for negative behaviors like cussing, and being disrespectful, even though you hold a professional position. You could be the vice president of a company, but talk to people ignorantly. How can you give me advice when you can't follow your own advice? Live the advice you're trying to give people. If you want your children to do something, you do it too. Keep your home clean, eat vegetables with them. You have to be the example in life for your children, for parenting, for just in the household all together. Parents, you know one parent is clean and the other parent isn't clean, so what you do, you talk to the parent that isn't clean, and you say, listen, let's clean something together. So they will get the respect and the result from a completed area or project that took two people and you both benefit or reap the rewards of it.

Parenting requires the respect and responsibility of both parents—mother and father. So if one parent lives in one place and the other parent lives in another place, it is up to those two parents to come together collectively in the upbringing of the child in order for there to be consistency in raising the child. As they develop, children learn to take advantage of inconsistencies between parents. For example, a child may choose to stay with dad on Saturday because dad lets him stay in bed until noon, while mom gets him up at 10:00 a.m. A child will play one parent against the other, so that's where we, as parents have to be on the same page.

*Marlon Bovell*

Spend time with your kids. I think my wife and I are doing a good job with this. We spend a lot of time with our kids, not just taking them places, but also when we're at home. It's something that I learned as a child. Just about every single night of the week we sit at the table and eat dinner. We put the phones away, no phones come to the table, we sit at the table, and we eat dinner and we look each other in the face and we have a conversation. You know, sometimes the kids may bring previous anger to the table and we've got to calm that down, but we always sit at the table as a family. So parents make spending time with your kids a priority.

Limit their use of devices. Let them shut it off at a certain time during school days. In the summertime you can give them more flexibility. We use apps so we don't even have to say put the phone down. We automatically lock the phone at a certain time. I don't know if it's helping them or hindering them from becoming more responsible, because before we used the parental control apps, we would tell them to put down their phones, but it wouldn't be as quickly as we wanted them to. Going back to the respect concept, it's like, if I told you to put it down at nine o'clock, you put it down right away and not fifteen minutes later, I don't want to ask you to do it again. Definitely limit their time on the devices.

Make sure that they read at home. This is important. Also, make sure that they're in social situations with other kids, because young kids just aren't as social as we were when I was growing up. Back then it was about being together, and now it seems like everybody is in their own little world, on their phones, to themselves and their interaction with other people is over the Internet.

I would say, definitely make sure that you put your kids in social situations, and you take them out to a birthday party or to a park with some other kids to play and to get outdoors. Teach them to be mindful of their surroundings, because as a child we would go on our bikes and be outside for hours and hours riding our bikes and not really having a care in the world. But nowadays, I don't know if it's because there's more reporting of it and because we have worldwide information that it seems to be happening more, but it seems like so many kids are being taken away. I think kids may not be fully mindful of their surroundings or their situations because their head is down in a phone and they end up not paying attention to what's going on around them. So I tell our kids when they get out of a car to put their phone down when walking on the street. And I always tell them to look both ways because they may be with an adult who's looking at their phone and walk out into traffic so they shouldn't rely on the adult to be the only responsible crossing the street.

Teach respect and responsibility by being the person that you want your children to be. Self-respect and responsible behavior are just as important nowadays, especially with the instant gratification of videoing and posting everything online. We see this more now because everybody has a video recorder. People seem to be so hateful toward one another now, and I don't know why.

*Shanice Bovell*

Your child is not your friend. Parenting never stops. Your child will always learn from you and will always need you. The early years are the most important years because your child will need you the most. Just because they're teens doesn't mean the learning stops. It's a continuous cycle. Parenting is forever. It's the most important, serious, rewarding, and loving jobs you'll ever have.

*Holly Blum*

Put down the phone. Have fun with your kids. Spend time with your kids. Have an attitude of playfulness and joy. Be intentional and take pleasure and pride in growing a human being that is compassionate, generous, and socially responsible. Our children are coming into a world that is less familiar to us; acknowledge that it is different and demonstrate sincere interest learning about it.

It's a responsibility to have a child, and I suggest that you spend some time thinking about what and who you want your child to be when they're fifteen, eighteen, or twenty-five years old. How you can help them to become that person, while being respectful and appreciative of their uniqueness? Those are things that you need to think about. Being a parent is a wonderful lifetime commitment and relationship.

*Dorel Campbell-Adams*

My childhood was a very modest but happy one, and it didn't take a lot of material things to create happiest in our family. That's why I'm convinced that it wouldn't take a lot in this new millennium either to create happiness in our families. Sometimes just going back to basics is all we need to find our peace.

Every parent wants to give their children everything they couldn't have, and I feel the same way, but I also want to instill a good sense of value and appreciation.

I am very careful how often I shower my kids with gifts because the abundance of "things" creates the impression of entitlement and I think this can create more challenges as they become adults. I want my kids to understand that great things are earned through hard work and not only by request. Their father encourages them to work for what they want. He tells them, "Keep up your grades and what-ever you ask for you'll get from me." On the contrary, I feel that good grades are their responsibility, and we shouldn't be paying them for good grades.

Get away from your devices. That's a struggle. I am struggling with that now because I am at a stage in my life where I want to change certain things to make more time for family. I've even told the family we're going to have a "no device Sunday." We're going to do what we did before our obsession with devices. One thing we did was sit around in a circle (this would usually come when things are a little tense in the house), and each of us would say one good, positive thing about the others until we ran out of compliments. That really helped, because it forced each of us to talk to each other and that was a good exercise we all loved.

Find time to do things that don't involve devices. I don't go to movies, and I don't take the kids to watch movies anymore. I think that's a waste of money. Of course, they get to see everything at home anyway on their devices, so we don't miss going to the movies. When the weather is good, we go biking together, and do other physical activities that force us to not use our devices.

*Desiree DeFlorimonte*

Parenting in these times is so much more challenging. In this age of technology when children are exposed to so much negativity and disturbing behaviors on television and social media, bullying in schools and the community, sexual abuse, gun violence, and lack of morals or values; it is imperative that parenting be proactive. Good old values are just as needed today as they were they were taught in years gone by. The following are some nuggets for twenty-first-century parents:

Be intentional in laying a firm foundation for your child. Start in early childhood which will lead to building character and having high standards and morals. If that foundation is laid, then the child will exhibit responsible behavior at home, school, and in the world at large.

Teach your child to be a good person by demonstrating respectable behaviors yourself. In other words, practice what you preach.

Accept your child for who s/he is.

Read daily to and with your child while limiting hours of TV viewing for yourself and your youngster.

Be consistent and not send conflicting messages to your child. Most importantly, maintain good communication.

Discuss with your child safety rules, which can be deterrents from some of the pitfalls leading to verbal, physical, or sexual abuse and drugs or alcohol consumption.

The fundamentals of money should be taught to your child while s/he is young and long before the college years. In this way many of the choices made while the student is in college and after graduation will not leave her/him decades of financial debt.

Teach your child to be respectful, responsible, and to demonstrate reciprocity and restraint.

*Ryan Dickson*

For young fathers I would advise some personal development courses like in empathy and listening, and setting aside their own thoughts feelings and emotions and being able to be with people, because they're not going to be able to give anybody oxygen if they can't get it for themselves. So whatever underlying insecurities, frailties, or whatever they never dealt with as a child will come up and be dealt with in any kind of situation, even if they're married, in a committed relationship, or if they're not. The main thing is, to make anyone better, you have to make yourself better first. It's like being conditioned and this is how I parent my kids. So to single dads, I say, "You don't need certain circumstances to be whole, you're already whole. You don't need a condition of satisfaction to give love. You know you love this person, and you understand that they're going through whatever it is they're going through." That's my advice— take courses to develop themselves and loving themselves so that they don't need that from external sources, because people are going to go through what they go through.

To all present-day parents, my advice is also to take self-development courses—yearly or one or two-day workshops, whether it's gender specific, whether it's co-parenting specific, or whether it's with the child and the parents together. There's always time to discover where you are as a person, where your co-parent is as a person, and where your children are as people. Sometimes we overlook that and we hold them in a space of, they aren't who they were last year, but we're not who we were last year.

That means you continual hold a space of discovery of your co-parent and your child and yourself so that you can keep honest communication flowing and you can also listen for what the child or parent or co-parent particularly needs in a circumstance, so that you can be of service to the unit that you are with the children, stepchildren, adopted children, your co-parent, your co-parents' new relationship and all that, which is all part of your circle.

As you know, relationships determine the quality of your life, and you can discover a new way of listening and speaking such that you own the space to everybody else's elevation and communication. You've learned parenting from your parents and all the other stimuli that you have. Now is the opportunity to be intentional with creating a space and discovering how to communicate better with each other.

*Richlyn Emanuel*

I advise parents to create a village. Not just a village of your own peers. Create a village of elders and those older than you and those younger than you—those that are in your immediate circle and those who are farfetched.

Instill some value in your child, whatever they may be, because everyone is different and everybody has their own thing. Provide consistency. Kids need consistency.

Always tell your children how much you value them, regardless of what they do or don't do, regardless of how angry you get at them, let them know that you love them and hold them a lot regardless of how old they are, just grab them and hold them, because sometimes they pretend they don't want you touching them, but they really do, so you love them and you hug them. You have a village for support.

Give them the opportunity to experience any and everything, because they need to know that the world isn't small. It's huge; it may seem small beause we can connect so easily. They need to see the world, and they don't think that they're privileged. They need to see what real poverty is. They need to experience the world.

*Raymond Fisher*

I would advise them to take the kids outside, teach them agriculture, teach them to use their hands, teach them to be tactile. Whether it's planting a garden or some other outdoor activity, get them from in front of the computer. Let them appreciate the outdoors. I remember when I would get my kids outdoors in my old neighborhood in Glendale. The way that everything was set up in that community, the sun, the trees, the ecosystem, the animals, the birds, the lakes, and all that stuff. I would wake my kids up and have morning devotion on the porch and say, "Let's just sit here for a minute, I want you to experience God's creations." I encourage parents to take the time to take their kids outside to enjoy the sunrise. No noise, no talking, just experiencing the symphony of seeing the sun come up and hearing the birds sing, the frogs croak, enjoy the start of a new day, and the motion of creation.

I advise parents to give their kids a spiritual foundation. Sacrifice—take them to church, Sunday school, Sabbath school, the mosque, temple, or your place of worship. Make that sacrifice. Give them that spiritual foundation. Teach them to question it and pose it against others not in a fanatical way but in a learning way because faith is nothing if not tested. Building a spiritual foundation is spending quality time with your kids. In my divorce, I chose, for a reason, to have my kids from Thursday to Monday. In the hustle and bustle in which we exist, parents don't see their kids or interact with them in a quality way Monday through Friday, except helping with schoolwork. You have to yell at them to do their homework and then you collapse, because you drove fifty minutes one way from work, or whatever the case may be. But to me as a Seventh Day Adventist, I bring the Sabbath home and teach my kids vespers and then go to church and interact in church and they see me active in church and in the activities that we do on the weekend, going camping or hiking.

Do everything that you can do, teach them the different music forms (I remember sitting with both of my kids and teaching them classical music), bake pies, experiment with things, put models together. It's important because every moment is an opportunity to give them a creative or critical thinking learning experience. My daughter is a great artist because of the nurturing and encouragement I gave her. I showed her examples of her grandfather's paintings. He was an accomplished artist, and she developed the drive and desire to honor him, and now she's a phenomenal artist. That's going to lead her into different things. But if I didn't put that time in, sacrificing to nurture the gifts that both she and my son have, it may not have been so good for them. My son's talents in basketball, music, leadership, and other different areas, if I hadn't nurtured those things then it would be in vain, it would be a waste.

So I would tell young twenty-first-century parents to compartmentalize and prioritize and make their kids the most important priority in their lives.

*Martine Gordon*

Put your phone down—that's my advice for parents. I think millennials, especially younger folks, are very attached to their devices. I think a lot of parents will say, you know, "Well, I don't let my kids watch TV," but while your kid's playing, even if they're playing by themselves, are you on your phone? Are you looking at a screen? It's something my family struggles with quite a bit. Parents are really used to spending a lot of time on their devices, either they're playing a game, or they're reading an article or something on their phone, and their kid doesn't know that they're reading, or they don't understand that yet at a certain age, so I think it shifts their attention. I've seen with my daughter; she is much more engaged and ready to handle shifts in the day if she feels that I'm present with her. And I think the biggest distraction we have on a daily basis is our phones.

I think it's hard for some parents. They may think, well, you know my six-year-old is watching a show, and I'm just going to sit next to him and read my book or whatever on my device. The kid's show may not be fun for parents, but parents could watch the show with them and ask them questions about the show. I think there are moments for parents to have their own time and there are moments for parents and children to have time together. Take the time, find the time, talk with your child. That's my biggest pet peeve—people say, well, we're in the same room—well, you're not talking.

*Justin Hampton*

I think, just be conscious of the imbalances in your own thinking. I personally feel like we tend to overcorrect for what we feel were the inefficiencies or the weaknesses in how we were parented. So we may say, "I didn't get to do this, I wish my mom would have done this, I wish they would have talked to me about certain things, or

I wish they would have let me participate in more activities, I wish they wouldn't have done this." So I'm looking for every opportunity to be in every single thing. My mom never let me say anything back to her. So I'm going to let my children express how they feel. Or my mom never let me have this, so I'm going to let my children have it all. I think we can swing the pendulum way too far sometimes by bringing in the things that were done with us that may not be applicable as much today. So I think it's just recognizing that whatever I'm trying to do with the kids, I may not have it all the way together in this way. And I've got to be open; people should be open to learning about their child and to creating the best environment for the kid to thrive in. It doesn't have to be based on what was good for you. So my practical advice would be to just be flexible and recognize the holes in your own thinking.

*Leticia Herrera*

I am very happy and excited with the technology. But parents need to stop and think about the children and take time to give them attention when they are in the car with the children and when they take the babies for a walk in the stroller. These are good times to talk to your child, even the baby because they can see the babies now with the modern strollers that have them facing the adult. Just talk. At mealtime talk, at bedtime talk. Put the phone down and talk with your child. I remember turning the radio on in my car and singing "Jingle Bells" with David, and he loved it. He sang along with me and was so happy. These times will not come back. This generation of parents spend too much time on the cell phone. This needs to stop. These precious moments to give attention to the children will not come back. We must remember to tell our children I love you. Have a good day. I always remember.

When David was in kindergarten or first grade, there was a massacre in one of the European countries, and a lot of little ones were killed. It stuck in my mind what one of the parents said…

"No matter what I do, I'm not going to bring my daughter back. But one thing does hurt me that I didn't tell her that I love her and have a good day." That's what we need to keep doing. Every day after that happened I would say, "David, I love you. Have a good day." And when I see him at the end of his school day, I was always ready to say, "How was your day?" Children will remember this when they grow up. They have a tremendous memory. They remember everything and will do it with their children.

Parents also buy cell phones and other devices for their children. They're the ones who put the TVs in the car or they have their babies to have a cell phone. The technology is important, but we can't let it overwhelm us. So parents must set limits for themselves and their children for how they will use the technology in the home. Children also get to use the technology at school. It's not going to be easy, but parents must try harder to have a better balance.

*Joseph Kijewski*

I think you need to spend as much time with your children as you can. I think you need to give them as much attention as you can. I realize parents have to work. My wife and I both work, and there were years when one child or another went to daycare for part of the day, we couldn't avoid that, but the time that they had with us was really undivided time that was devoted to them. We didn't use TV as a babysitter. We read books with them, and we played games with them.

We went on walks them. Even if you don't have money, look for things that you can do with your children such as visiting venues for entertainment, visiting museums and shows and things that are free or for very little cost. That's what we did with our time on the weekend. We also went to the children's free concerts or out in the woods here in Virginia.

We chose to spend time with our children, and now that they are in their twenties, we're rewarded by the time they choose to spend with us. They actually do come over to spend time with us and just hang out with us because you know, I think it's what they grew up doing and enjoying and loving. So parents, be close to your children, be involved with your hildren practice listening to music that they're interested in, even if you don't like it because you want to have a relationship with them and that opens the door for all the other good influences that you want to bring in. Now it's spending time, it's making sure they know they're loved, and it's making sure you're there for them when they need you to be.

*Errol Marks*

Well, regardless of age, I think parents should have a relationship with your child. Coming from my experience—I think I'm generation X—not many parents had direct, engaging relationships with their children. I had a relationship with my father, my father engaged me, and that's what inspired me to live to be as good a father as he was. My father wasn't a great father because he did these magnanimous and huge feats. It's the simple things in life that he did. He was always there, he was never out late drinking with his buddies, he never had a whole bunch of people over making a bunch of noise. He didn't do a lot of guys stuff. He played tennis, came home, and spent time with his family. He talked to us, we had conversations where there were both parents in place, and he did do some great stuff. He built me a kite when I was seven years old. We spent a week building it together, and the first day we went out to let it out the twine broke. It was so disappointing at the time. But I'm forty-two years old, and I never forgot it. It meant the world to me. It was not about flying the kite. It was the time we spent closely every day to build that kite. This is the most prominent memory in my mind of my father. He showed such dedication, and I sat there with him every minute as he made that kite. I would hand him the scissors, I would hand him the twine, I would hand him the glue. Being a father now, and having a demanding job, I understand what it took for him to do that.

Parents should not look at parenting as a job but as as the best relationship they'll have. Don't look at it to get something out of it because if you go into it for that reason you'll never see the value of what it is. But the rewards are great only when you go into it with a pure heart knowing that your children grow and they will leave you. And even though they may hate you, you'll still be proud of what they've become. You may have disagreements you may have differences of opinion. You may have arguments, but I tell my kids when you grow up, and you have your own family don't feel that your responsibility is to me. You go live your life.

The next piece of advice is to live in the current moment. Be present when you're sitting having a meal with your kids, engage them, make eye contact. Talk to them, tell them stories, listen to their stories. Engage kids with high quality questions a lot of open-ended questions ask their opinion about something that they may not even have. You may not think that they have a perspective, but you'd be surprised. Ask questions such as, "What do you think about this?" "How do you feel about how this country is progressing?" "How do you feel about the political climate of this country?" They may ask you what do you mean by political comment, and then that's for another conversation in itself. But you'd be surprised how quickly they absorb things. My child surprises me. She's eleven years old, and I asked her that very same question and she didn't ask me what political climate. So I went on to try to explain what political climate means she said I know what it means

Don't think about what happened in the past or about what you are going to do tomorrow. Live in that moment. It should apply to everything in your life. If you're in a meeting at your job to be in that moment, understand what is going on. That's a lot easier said than done because our minds tend to wander so easily. If you're dating someone it's usually taboo to take people you date around your kids. I don't believe in that nonsense. I say take them the first thing they come around because your kids will tell you the truth immediately. But you've got to be careful of the type of person. If you know your kids will not like this person why are you there with the person in the first place? Why even bother? So use a little common sense as well.

Encourage your children's fantasies, tell them to share their dreams no matter how outlandish and how ridiculous they will want to tell you about it. Treat it as if it were something real. Encourage them and spark their imagination. In that way your kids won't feel self-conscious about sharing their dreams. It helps to help them be more expressive and more outgoing. You know most of us are taught and trained not to rock the boat and not to stand out too much. I think children have a great value to contribute. It all falls in the vein of me doing the opposite of what conventional wisdom says in helping my kids be just fine, and I'm enjoying the results. My kids are far more stimulating, intelligent, and articulate than a lot of the women I dated. It's amazing. So I look forward every day to Thursdays when I get them. So yeah, parenting is awesome if you do it right.

*Maxine Maloney*

The first thing for me is there's a problem with technology. My daughter didn't get a phone until she was in junior high school, but she could call nobody but me. And when she got to high school, she was able to get a call outside of that, but here's the thing with the phone—she has a phone that I have a tracker on my phone, right? I see who she calls, when she calls, and every week I go through her phone, and I check all her texts, I check all her voice mails because I tell her it's my phone. Sometimes she doesn't even know that, and as for like e-mail, she didn't get an e-mail account until she was in eighth grade. It was my e-mail. I created an e-mail that was appropriate for her. She couldn't give that e-mail address out to anybody. That was for Mommy, and her school because her school uses a lot of technology. I need to control that technology, right? And that technology includes TV and computer. Zaria was not allowed to watch TV until she was four. When she watches TV, she only watches TV on Saturday and Sunday, and that's it. And she's sixteen, and she only watches TV Friday evenings, Saturday all day whenever we're home which we're not home and Sunday until seven o'clock. After seven o'clock, the TV goes off.

My concerns about technology—computer, cell phone, television—are that they provide access to information, and people that may not be aligned with the family values. See, we set family values, and they're on paper and we have a contract that she writes, including the consequences for breaking the contract. She can't watch regular TV because there are commercials, the commercials, many of them are not aligned with our family values, and they don't represent what I would like her to see of the world. So in our home TV channels with commercials don't work. We have always had streaming, because commercials don't represent for us what I'd like her to see. They allow access to people and things that are just not age-appropriate. And it's funny because this week she asked me if I could change the parent control on the streaming device because the parent control on the streaming device is still at PG, and she said she'd really like to watch PG-13 because she's sixteen now. I mean that literally, and before she was in ninth grade, when we went to the library, she couldn't check out any book unless I read the book, looked up the author, and the contents of the book. And just last year she got released off of that because now she makes the decisions on the books that she is reading because she already got set in her mind these are the kinds of books that I am comfortable reading and my mom is comfortable with me reading so it's books, it's magazines, it's websites—after a while I've given her more room, but she can't be on her cell phone after 7:30 p.m. She can't be on her computer after 7:30 p.m. And the school— I've had to call them because they now send them texts or things at nighttime, and I had to go to that school and tell them you can't do that. I will not accept that in my household. If you cannot stop that, then we are gonna have a problem because you're not teaching them good ethics and also limitations, because you know, I believe that technology impacts children's brain development, and so I really limit her exposure, and as she's gotten older she's gotten more leeway. I mean she still goes to bed at 8:30 p.m.—there are no choices in my house. There's a requirement that she sleep nine hours a night.

I think the technology is really good, but I think in the twenty-first century, building a relationship with children, asking them and getting into the habit from the time they can talk, "How was your day? What was the best thing that happened? What was the worst thing that happened?" Because now my daughter is sixteen and comes home and tells me everything—even things that she doesn't realize she probably shouldn't tell me about, but she doesn't see anything wrong, and just the other day she was having a telephone conversation with a friend downstairs in the living room, and I heard her say something, and I said, "Zaria, I'm not really sure that was the proper way to express that. You should try to express that in a more positive manner." And so her friend said, "Why did your mom say that?" She said, "Well, my mom was just saying probably that wasn't a good way for me to say that." And then the young lady says, "Do you tell your mom everything?" And she says, "Of course, because she's my mom." I was glad to hear her say that.

I think parents need to talk to their children and be optimally involved in setting family values and sticking to them, setting aside what I call floor time—you know how we used to sit with babies on the floor, we've got to do that, when it doesn't become floor time, it becomes table time or couch time, devoting that time to our kids. Kids are being bombarded with so much, and if parents don't give children that time to talk and don't just listen, we're going to miss out.

I think twenty-first-century children have so many negative things against them right now that parents must create a safe space, because you don't want your child's safe space to be somewhere else. Their safe space should be where their parents are and a place where they know they can come to and say and express how they're truly feeling with no consequence and know that their parents won't judge them and that they will be cared for, and when they do something wrong, their parents will be there to stand by them.

*Virgil McDonald*

That is the most difficult question for me—maybe because I try not to give advice. Just give me a moment to think about that. Parents' working together is very, very important. Children are astute enough to recognize dissension. Parents need to show a united front as much as possible. You arrive at that point by privately discussing matters that relate to your family and children. Try to avoid contradicting each other in the presence of your children. If there is a difference of opinion, tactfully tell the children, "Mom and Dad need to discuss this a little more, and we'll get back to you." So I guess the baseline for me is that parents must work together.

Whether a person is a single parent because of a lack of the benefit of matrimony, divorce, or death, single parents must make themselves available to their children as much as possible. Parents, single, or couples must not let the demands of making a living rob them totally of meaningful time with their children. There is nothing more important to a child than the assurance that their parent(s) will show up, and they can rely upon them. If a single parent has less time to spend with the children because of the demands of making a living, let the children know that they are important to you and that you're going to be diligent about carrying out your responsibilities to them. The parents' behavior will help to develop structure in the child's life. Children in a single-parent household may be required to take on responsibilities at an early age—preparing meals, cleaning the house, caring for the younger children, or a job to help ends meet. Many people who have had to take on responsibilities as children say that it helped them to build character. More than anything else, whether you are a single parent or parenting with a mate, you must establish guidelines for your children and insist that they respect them.

*Jacqueline Rose*

A parent's job is to help guide a child according to their own individual "beingness," to assist them in self-realization, to know themselves, and to be true to themselves. Be engaged with your child from the very beginning—birth. Engage your child and stay engaged with your child. Establish a relationship built on "namaste" and stay heartfully connected. Every moment and very small thing matter and can make a difference in how your child learns to respond to themselves, you, and others.

*Joseph Shields*

First of all, parenting is both more exciting than it looks and harder than it looks. I was anxious as a dad when we first had our son as to whether or not I was going to know what I was doing. And you don't learn the ability to parent in books. Books are not written on all the intricacies of parenting, and there are lessons out there that you're going to have to execute. You have to be confident yourself, but also open yourself to adapt to the changes. And you know, whether it's as simple as you know, between my daughter and my son we learned the importance of routines as a lesson so that kids adapted to their environment in a meaningful way. My son, we, when we put him to bed at night, we probably didn't put him in as rigorous routine as we did with our daughter. But with my daughter, we learned if we did that she slept better. So it was peace of mind for us. So you learn as a parent, and you take notes of that, as a parent, probably in every situation.

We need to acknowledge that the difference is, in the twenty-first century it's a kind of an external world in which relationships are, to certain extent, peer to peer; it's not like they lack depth, but we've moved around a little bit, but kids have access to social media. I was pretty concerned as we moved from Texas, to Virginia, about the kind of social relationships my kids would have. With the way the world works now they have a bigger world out there, at least online. In the digital landscape, that's less of an issue. That being said, it's much more quantity, because it's not just what's coming into your home, but who you're sitting with, interacting with online and the digital social media you're using. Kids coming into adolescence is certainly going to be a game changer, probably for most families.

Technology is a game changer, but it's also your capacity to adapt and being mindful of where you've learned lessons so that you can set appropriate routines for the kids to support their learning. That's probably one of the bigger lessons that I have learned as a parent, and how good that is.

*Halima Thorne*

Ask for help. They have to ask for help when they need it and don't try to do it alone. From nighttime feeding to breast feeding and pumping you don't have to do it alone. When your mind starts playing tricks, call a friend. No one ever tells you about post partum depression, what that looks like, everybody is different so it shows up differently. hey just said that they have it and they just want to be left alone, they don't want to take care of the baby. But you know everybody is different, so it shows up differently. For me, I just knew something didn't feel right with me, and I didn't know what it was. I saw the doctor, but the one thing about doctors is, they're so quick to give you medication, and sometimes you don't need medication, you just need help. That's what you're going to need as a new parent, help, so do not be afraid to ask for help. Push your pride to the side; throw it away because you're going to definitely need help.

Get used to eating cold food. I warm up my food and get ready to eat, then he either starts crying or he's hungry and my food is already warmed up in the microwave or on the stove, and by the time I'm ready to eat again, it's cold. I either have to reheat it or eat it cold.

Then there's breastfeeding. I had trouble with breastfeeding the first couple of weeks, so just be patient with that. Your baby will latch when he or she is ready. Just get your breast pump and start pumping your milk. You've got formula, so be patient with the whole breastfeeding experience because it's important for your child; it's cheaper, but it takes a toll on your body. Sometimes you lose sleep and it may feel like he's sucking all the energy from you, but he's not.

Motherhood and raising children is no joke. It's serious. That's a huge life lesson I've learned. It is serious. I am a single parent, and my advice for single moms apart from getting help is to always say your prayers and thank God that you can do it on your own. Some people don't have the village to help them. I have a girlfriend who really didn't have a village to help. I would tell her if she needed help I would go over and help her, but she always denied that she needed help. She's very prideful and thought she could do everything on her own; everything was on her, but she's still surviving. Her child is two years old now, and she's doing well. We haven't discussed if she had postpartum depression, but I know every woman experiences that.

My son's dad helps financially, and he comes over and spends time with him. But I'm the primary caregiver; he's with me all the time, and that brings me to another thing. You do need to take a break from your child. It's okay. Go to the movies, get your nails done, get your hair done, do something to make you feel good about yourself. Do it. You'll be okay. Your child will be fine without you for two hours. It's not going to hurt him or her.

*Barbara Van Dyke*

Be sure that your child is raised with a world view of things. That is, exposure, general knowledge. When we do standardized assessments, we don't only assess the student in reading, writing, and arithmetic, as we say, but we assess our children's knowledge, ability, and skills in areas such as social studies, humanities, general knowledge, and the first teacher of those things is the parent, and the family—not a classroom teacher. Such a beginning can prepare your child for a successful instructional experience, as they will bring context to the teaching-learning experience. My life experience taught me to parent that way—traveling, being exposed to different ethnicities, being able to conform to rules and routines in different settings not just with your peers, but with adults at church and at social events.

Expose your children to the things that they will need to learn and how to deal with things as they get older. They're not going to read everything in a book. They're going to be expected to visualize and think about things and identify the context of what's being shared with them. To give a quick example, in terms of understanding analogies, I asked a child to complete this analogy—is to—as bow is to stern. This was not a child from the city, so when the child said, "What's a bow and what's a stern?" it stopped me dead in my tracks because I assumed that because the child lived in the country and got on a boat almost every day, or had some experience getting on a boat, he would know about the bow and stern of a boat. Children need to be exposed to a variety of experiences both inside and outside their communities, including learning about the world through reading, watching a variety of shows on television and asking and answering questions. These experiences will help them put things in context.

The other thing is the other colloquial words that they use in the country for bow and stern. I didn't even stop to think language is an issue here. I was stunned, and it brought a lull over the lesson because I thought, "Oops, I didn't prepare." As the teacher, I had to stop, rethink, and replan, but the lesson that taught me was that because children live in a community where there are many objects, artifacts, buildings, etc., they don't learn facts about those things automatically or by osmosis, they need the exposure and they need to be taught. Years later, now teaching in the United States I experience the same phenomenon. I see children not being successful because they don't come with a backpack of experiences that allows them to frame what's being taught, therefore learning is difficult for them and academic success is going to be even more difficult. It's also going to impact how the child sees him or herself and their peer relations. They just didn't get that input at the beginning.

My advice to twenty-first-century parents is to take the opportunities that are there to truly provide your child with the learning opportunities and experiences that will be a foundational platform for them to springboard from when they are provided formal academic instruction and have to conform to certain settings and situations. That's not because I'm an educator, but because I also had an opportunity to get very good exposure as a child. If I were to identify what was the best part of my life or from my mom, I would say the exposure I was given; the well-rounded opportunities from early childhood. I saw how it benefited me, because when others saw that I had a solid knowledge base, it was a good thing, and it made me feel good. So once a child has had an opportunity to experience success—once they taste that, all they want is success. When a child gets an A the worst thing is for them to get a B after that, so it is important to give them the opportunities to get As. That's my perspective.

# Section 2

## CONVERSATIONS WITH YOUNG ADULTS

In this section, young adults respond to the following questions:

- Will you parent your children the way you were parented? If yes, explain why, and if no, explain why not.
- Do you think the values of respect, responsibility, reciprocity, and restraint are important in today's world?
- Talk about having a sense of personal responsibility.
- Tell me how you feel about reciprocity. Is that important in today's world?
- Is restraint important in today's world?
- What are some of the things children and youth can do in the present day to demonstrate to others that they have learned the values of respect, responsibility, reciprocity, and restraint?
- When I walk through my neighborhood, I see young adults who attend the community college on my street litter my street. I also see both young and older adults walking their dogs, and if the dogs poop, they don't pick it up. That makes me think they lack a sense of personal responsibility. Tell me what you think.

# CHAPTER 1

# Young Adults Discuss
# Being Future Parents

Will you parent your children the way you were parented? If yes, explain why and if no, explain why not.

*Sarah Bacchus*

I say yes and no. I say yes, because my mother taught me about having pride in myself and being accountable for myself. She taught me so many values—about self-love, about self-respect, about wanting to improve myself, not just going long to get along, but being my own person. I want my child to have those value systems. It is so important for me to teach my child that legacy that my mother taught me. I always say to myself, I feel like my mother was a little bit ahead of her time as far as her family, because she was never one to encourage me to just get married and have kids. She always wanted me to go to school, she always wanted me to, find out what makes me happy, and to go for it. She was so big on that, and she always said, "That stuff will come, but you should take care of yourself first." I want my child to have that legacy. It's so important for me to have a child and to teach them some or all the values that my mother taught me. I feel like if I don't teach them that I would take away from their experience. I will take away from their foundation; their foundation won't be strong without that value system that my mother taught me. When I think about certain things that I do, or

173

have done, a lot of times I hear my mother, and I do pause and think, "I know better." And I wouldn't be able to say that to myself had she not taught me that. So yes, absolutely. I will raise my child the way my mother raised me.

Now, I say no, because I feel like there were certain things that she didn't communicate with me about. I don't know why, but maybe that's how she was raised, that it was not appropriate to have certain conversations with your child. But there was a lack of conversation about sex and sexuality when I asked her. I remember when my body was changing as I was going through puberty, and I asked her questions, I could tell she was uncomfortable and by the end of that week, she got me a book that said, "What's happening to your body." So I read the book, and I did ask her questions, but I could tell she wasn't comfortable with the conversation, and I knew I never felt comfortable going to her about sex. I never felt comfortable going to her about relationships, and I also didn't really feel comfortable going to her about money issues, finances. So I think that because I never had that knowledge, I had to go out and find out on my own. In fact, I hope and pray that when my time comes to parent, that I will be comfortable enough and strong enough and self-controlled enough to talk to my child about sex and sexuality and money and finances and that I'm able to do so openly and honestly so I can give my child the knowledge.

Just like how my mother gave me the knowledge of self-respect and of self-pride and being accountable for my behavior and not just going off and getting myself in trouble, I think had she done the same with me in regards to relationships and sex. I think I wouldn't have experimented as much as I did. Because I would have known better, because I knew better with other stuff. I knew better with my own body, with my behavior, but yet I didn't know better about the one foundation she never went over with me. It was always, "Read a book," you know, so that's why I say yes and no. I will parent like she did, but I will not parent like she did in certain aspects, because I don't want my child to have to go out to find out about money, investments, finances, sex, and relationships from the outside, because it's just going to be a mess.

*Alexis Braswell*

I would not parent my children the way I was raised. Don't get me wrong; my mother is a great mother. She did a great job, but I believe that my mother parented out of fear rather than trust. She sheltered me more so than allowing me to make mistakes and learn from them. So I feel as though I'm somewhat behind as a young adult, with experiences that I wish I would have been able to have without my mother sort of sheltering me, or wanting to do things for me, just allowing me to experience the things I should experience.

Growing up, my mom was the ideal child; she got tremendous grades. She did a lot of things, like being involved in her community and doing things of that nature. She was just your perfect child. And I think she wanted that for me, and she didn't allow me to be myself. So I think, as a parent, I would allow my children to express themselves more and be more accepting of their differences. I think that would help them in building experiences and learning from them, learning from their mistakes, things of that nature. My dad was more so for allowing experiences, but my mother was the one in charge, so whatever she said goes.

*Damon Braxton*

I think I will parent my kids the way I was parented because I turned out fine. I feel like I wanted to be a good son and a good person. I feel like I am a good person. I treat my parents well, and I treat other people well, so I will probably get the foundation of my parenting from my parents. By foundation, I mean things like sharing, respect, what to tolerate from other people and what not to tolerate. Another lesson I want to teach my kids is the value of the dollar and what it takes to get it. I want them to understand that nothing is handed to you in life. You must work for what you want.

*Anastasia Foster*

I would say both yes and no. There are some things that I like that they did, and then there are other things that I just feel I wouldn't want to do to my kids. For instance, sometimes they can be a little overprotective, and I've always felt that in order to be prepared for the world; you can't always have that veil around you, to protect you, so to speak. As for things that I liked, I liked that in the house; at least, they'd have us experiment with different things, and so I didn't feel like going out into the world, I wouldn't know what was going on. So those are the things that made me say both yes and no.

There are experiences that I wish I was able to have were my parents not so protective.

I didn't have my first sleep over until I was, I think, in high school, and I didn't go on my first date until I was in my twenties. So I mean things like going out with friends, going to parties, those are all things that I didn't really get experience doing in high school like most kids. I did them really late in life, and it's just not what I was hoping for myself, I guess.

On the positive side, my parents are very open to conversation. I can talk to them about things that other people's kids cannot talk to their parents about, like sex and drugs and things like that, and I mean in detail. That's something that I really liked and admired. Because I know it can be an uncomfortable conversation to have depending on what it's about. But it's something that I've always felt helped to keep me grounded, so I was never out and about doing those things, and that's something that I would definitely want to have with my own kids, being able to have an open conversation about things where they know they can tell me anything, and I'm not going to want to run away or say, "No, I don't want to hear that." I know everybody doesn't get to have their questions answered by their parents; they have to go to other people outside of the home, which isn't always the best thing to have to do.

*Amina Jason*

I would say yes and no. I think regarding the basic fundamentals, I would raise my children the way I was raised. My mom is very meticulous as far as our scheduling goes and our chores and us making sure that we were doing our homework and things like that. I think what I would change is that I would want my kids to be able to express themselves more. I would want my kids to be able to express their emotions without me telling them that what they're feeling is wrong. I would rather like an understanding versus it being a child has to be a child and stay in a child's place. Because I do feel that children who are able to express themselves with their parents are more likely to be more socially well-rounded as they grow older and go into the world. As far as my parenting style, I think I would be a little less strict, not for my kids to do whatever they want to do, but just less strict and more trusting. Because it's almost like they didn't trust us in a way. So I think that's pretty much what I would do differently as far as their parenting and how I would parent my future children.

Although I can agree that what I saw as a lack of trust could be concern for our safety and things like that, I feel a lot of it was a little overboard in a way, like simple things I didn't really experience until I was much older, that I think, in a sense kind of stunted me a little bit. Because as I grew older and was able to venture out into the world, I was naive about a lot of things. I didn't know how to react to certain things, I didn't know things like that actually happened, because I was so sheltered. So I think that I would want to expose my children to more things and let them find things out on their own and let them know it's okay to have certain feelings, and it's okay to sometimes be misunderstood.

When I say it's okay to feel certain feelings, I'm referring to my parents being raised in a different country and in a different culture than I am raised. I was born and raised in America, so there's a kind of barrier in a way, because back in their home country children weren't allowed to raise their voice, children weren't allowed to speak out of turn, talking back is rude. But sometimes it's good for children to express themselves instead of just shutting them up.

I work with kids currently, so I can see where there's a point where they're disrespectful, and there's a point where they want their opinions to be heard. It's important for parents to notice that so that their children are being heard, and the children feel their parents are interested in them, and they can talk to their parents about anything without feeling like they're being judged or that what they're feeling is wrong.

*Nyeim Risien*

I'm a little split on the question of whether or not I will parent my children the way I was raised. Yes. I will raise them how I was raised because I turned out to be a pretty good kid, and I do good things. But times have definitely changed, and when I'm going to be raising my child, I will do some things differently. Like, if I were to give my child a spanking in public, I'll have to worry about the risk of someone calling the police or Child Protective Services. That's because some people view that as child abuse. When I was raised, if my mom spanked me in public people would think it wasn't a big issue. But I think I will raise my child with the same values you are writing about in this book—always show respect for others and always put your best foot and best self forward.

# Ten Things Young Adults Have Expressed about Being Future Parents

The majority (four) of young adults interviewed stated they both will and will not parent their own children the way they were parented. The remaining two young adults stated they will not adopt their parents' parenting style. Below are reasons given for the positive and negative responses:

- They will because they grew up to be fine adults, encompassing the values espoused by this book—respect, responsibility, reciprocity, and restraint.
- They will because they relished the open communication they had with their parents while growing up. They enjoyed the freedom to go to their parents with their questions and to get responses from their parents.
- Their parents taught them to make the best use of their time.
- Their parents taught them to be responsible by giving them household chores and making sure they did their homework.
- They were taught about having self-pride, taking responsibility for themselves and striving to be the best person they can be.
- They will not because they consider their parents' parenting style overly strict and rigid.

- Communication with their parents was closed and some topics, for example, sex was off the table.
- They were not allowed to freely express themselves without parents being judgmental and nontrusting.
- They were not allowed to have typical childhood experiences such as sleepovers.
- Times have changed, and with changing times come changing requirements and expectations. For example, physical punishment is now considered child abuse with serious consequences for the abusive parent. Also, with past generations, children were expected to be seen and not heard; today children are expected to both be seen and heard.

# CHAPTER 2

## Young Adults Discuss the Four Rs

Do you think the values of respect, responsibility, reciprocity, and restraint are important in today's world? Begin with respect, including self-respect.

## Respect

*Sarah Bacchus*

Absolutely—especially respect because respect is how you treat people, it's how people see you and treat you. It's how you carry yourself and how you talk to people; it's all about how you want to be treated and how you want that to be returned. Respect is so important in today's world, especially because we use technology to communicate and we no longer have the face-to-face communication that we once had. We use that only for work, and even then, sometimes we use technology to communicate what we can. I think because we have become so dependent on technology, when it comes time for us to meet people and to deal with people we don't know how to, because we don't respect boundaries; there is no respect, there's just—well, this is what I think, this is what I say, either deal with it or don't. I mean, gosh, just look at our politics. We have a leader who just does not always show respect for others and no one holds him accountable. He's not even accountable to the people who put him in office, because there's no respect, there's no foundation, and he doesn't have to be.

In this day and age, you have to be respectful, not because you can send something in an e-mail, that doesn't excuse you from still having to do your part when it comes to respect, you still have to stand for yourself, you still have to make sure people speak to you properly, and you have to speak to people properly. How you look, how you present yourself, that's the whole package of respect. And I think people in this day and age, we're sensitive. We want to be our own person. We don't want anyone to tell us anything, but yet, we want to tell other people what they should and should not do. So it's like, well, where's the respect? You want the respect, but where's your respect? There's just not enough respect in this day and age. The more we become dependent on technology, the more we become dependent on outside, external forces to live our lives, the less we're going to really value respect, but I think it's extremely important that we have and show respect in this day and age.

*Damon Braxton*

I think self-respect is always going to be an important value to have. If you don't respect yourself, then other people will feel they don't have to respect you. Respect for others is important too. If you don't show respect for other people, they won't want to interact, talk, or deal with you and it's going to make them lose the respect they may have had for you in the beginning.

*Alexis Braswell*

I do believe all four of those are very important. As far as respect, you have to learn to allow others to express themselves, to be themselves, and be very accepting, understanding, and empathetic. I think things go way smoother when we don't have a closed mind-set, have a more open mind-set, and are aware of other people's boundaries, standards and values. As far as self-respect, you have to set a standard for yourself so people don't take advantage of you, so they don't belittle you and minimize your feelings, your ideas, and your thoughts. I do think those four values are very important.

*Anastasia Foster*

I think that's super important. I think it's something that you have to learn from a young age because when you go out there and you socialize with anyone, you can't make friends. Like my mom always says, you can't make friends without being a friend. In order to be a friend, you have to be respectful to them, and you have to be able to respect yourself, because if you can't respect yourself, there's no way anyone can expect you to respect anyone else. So respect to me is not just placing someone in authority and just following what they say or what they do, or what they tell you to do. It's more like understanding that you have to be nice to them, you have to work with them, and they're there to help you, you're there to help them or help the situation whatever the case may be. That's kind of what you have to be for yourself. When you respect yourself, you don't hurt yourself or beat yourself up because of something that maybe you did wrong. You have to understand yourself and come to terms with yourself on it and work with yourself.

*Amina Jason*

I think that respect is number one. I think a lot of people have lost that these days because people are so in tune with social media and children are so in tune with their tablets in a virtual world that they don't even know how to interact with people and that could come off as them being disrespectful. If they're not making constant communication with other people that aren't their parents, their siblings or their family, they can come off as a child that doesn't have manners. I see it every day. I work with children who are four to ten years old, so I see that there's a disconnect with just common courtesy. For example, you help a child tie their shoe and they just walk away; they don't even say thank you. In the snack program, I hand out the snack and don't allow them to just grab it, but they snatch it and go. Some of them say thank you. Some of them will make eye contact, because that's a nonverbal way of saying thank you sometimes. I do think respect is big, but I think it's dwindling as the generations progress, and I think that people need to take a step back and look at how they're raising their children and what they're instilling in them.

I think a lot of parents these days forget that their children have to respect themselves in order to be respected by other people. When I grew up my parents always made sure that we were dressed appropriately and took pride in the way we looked, that our teeth were clean and our clothes were nice and pressed and that we carried ourselves in a manner where people won't take advantage of us or misinterpret how we were and who we were. I think that it's important for children to know that within themselves; they come first as far as how people perceive them.

*Nyeim Risien*

Yes, they're still important, especially when you're raising a kid, because nowadays you wouldn't be able to tell because kids nowadays are pretty disrespectful, especially when they're in school, but I really think these values are still important. Respect is probably the most important of these four values. When I come across kids, younger than I am, teens who are still in school, they behave like somebody owes them something. They act as though they don't have to treat you with respect, but you have to respect them. I can respect them, but they might want to show me some respect as well. I think that with younger kids, teens, it really shows when it comes to authority, like teachers and persons older than they are. I see this when I come across videos online, like on social media.

Self-respect is also important. I don't want to raise a kid who doesn't have self-respect; they may want to believe everything someone says about them. I definitely don't want to have a strong minded child. I always remember what my mom told me, "Put your best foot forward."

# Personal Responsibility

*Sarah Bacchus*

Personal responsibility, that's big. That's something that my mother was very adamant about teaching me, that is, to be responsible for my actions. That's something else that's just so lacking today. No one's accountable. People want to treat others any way they want to, but as soon as they get it back, it's like, oh my god, no. How did this happen? Why did this happen? But wait a minute. Be responsible, be accountable, it's a short, little thing.

I remember one holiday shortly after my mother passed away, I went to New York, and my cousin and I were talking about my mother, and my cousin said, "One thing that your mother always did, that I never appreciated until I got on my own, was that she held me accountable. All she ever wanted me to do was be accountable for my actions. If I were more accountable for my actions, I would be further along in my life than I am now. But my mother did not hold me accountable. I could do whatever I wanted and she never said anything. But your mother always held me accountable" I think that's what a lot of people are missing in their lives. People are missing responsibility, they're missing somebody telling them this is your responsibility, this is what you did, this is what you chose to do, so you have to hold the bag, nobody's going to hold your bag for you. Even if you made a choice with ill information, you still made the choice. So you have to hold the bag, you have to be responsible. Nobody takes responsibility for anything nowadays, I guess it's a lack of maturity, or lack of patience, because in order to be responsible for yourself, or responsible for your choices, you have to own it and take time with it and go through it. But nobody does that nowadays. That is something that in this day and age is so needed; responsibility is so needed, but nobody wants to do it. Because it's easier to pass the buck, it's easier to place the blame, easier to just not worry about it or to deal with it another time, but the longer you wait and the longer you don't deal with it, the more it festers, it gets bigger and bigger and bigger. So yes, definitely, in this day and age a sense of personal responsibility is up there, because nobody does it.

*Alexis Braswell*

Responsibility, I think, keeps the world moving in the right direction. When you don't set standards for yourself, this can coincide with self-respect. I think when you're responsible, when you handle your business, you can prevent things from being bad versus them being well and going in your favor. You know, if you don't handle your business there are negative consequences, there are positive consequences and positive reinforcement, things of that nature. So if you don't want yourself in a pickle, it's better to handle your responsibilities in and out of the home

*Damon Braxton*

Being responsible—period—is very important. You've got to be responsible. If you're not responsible, the things you need to take care of won't get done won't get done through the narrowest possible things you need to take care of. I feel there are some things that you see as priorities for your life that you have to be responsible for. You will want these priorities to be in order. Some priorities for me are taking care of my little brothers and my mom when she needs me to be there for her. Since I was young, I've been saving money just in case my brothers, my mom, or my father may need it.

*Amina Jason*

A sense of personal responsibility is something that's important, especially when you're able to give back to people and not only take care of your personal responsibilities, like your bills and everything, but I think another sense of responsibility is that you're being a progressive member of society, and you're actually helping someone in some way You have to have a purpose. I always feel that way regardless of what I'm doing. It's good to have a purpose and be responsible for how you treat people and how you carry out your tasks throughout your day and making sure that you're getting things done.

In terms of my own life, one of my main responsibilities is to make sure that I'm successful, that I'm able to support myself. I also want to give my parents what I feel they deserve, and I want to be in the position to make them proud. That's one of my number one responsibilities, because they sacrifice so much for me, and I always want to make sure that I'm able to show them that I appreciate that, and I'm being fruitful with what they planted here in us for future generations.

*Anastasia Foster*

I think that's also very important, because I feel that some people will say that it doesn't matter, but it is important because there is a sense of responsibility that you have in every situation you're in. It doesn't really matter if you are at fault or not. It just matters more that when you're responsible for something or you're taking care of something, or you're in charge of something that you hold to it and you stay true to it. That's all that truly matters to me, because responsibility for me goes hand in hand with honesty, and I just know that if I'm responsible for something I'm going to feel a burning inside if I'm not taking good care of it. It becomes important, because whether it's a thing or another human being, I can affect other people's lives.

My current responsibilities are probably just making sure that I attend school, passing my exams, my career, and making sure that I'm also taking good care of myself, because I'm responsible for myself. That means being healthy and fit. And the last is staying in safe situations, knowing there are situations which are really difficult in this world, believe it or not, that makes it hard to travel. If I want to travel, I have to think about if everything is safe over there, and if I'm going to be okay, whatever the case may be.

*Nyeim Risien*

Personal responsibility to me is taking care of things I'm supposed to take care of. One example for me is buying my own car. I chose to purchase a vehicle so I have to be responsible enough to take care of it, earn the money to pay the bills on time. It's a good idea to teach your kids to be responsible, so they will behave responsibly when they are older.

# Reciprocity

Is reciprocity (the Golden Rule) important in today's world?

*Sarah Bacchus*

Oh yes, reciprocity is so important in today's world. I still hold responsibility at a higher level than reciprocity, but reciprocity is important, because to me, reciprocity is where the boundaries come in, you know, do unto others as you would have them do unto you. If you don't do that, where are your boundaries? That goes back to our saying, "You can't just be all over the place and not be held accountable."

If you want people to treat you well, you're going to treat them well. But then, if you're the type of person, if someone rejects you, and you can't handle that rejection, are you going to go treat the next person just as bad as you've been treated? Then you'll be starting a cycle where it just keeps going and going, because you don't know how to understand that. While it's important to treat people the way you want them to treat you, they're not going to always do that. So how do you counter that? So many people carry a lot of baggage, and they treat others in a negative way, they take advantage of other people.

Again, reciprocity is where the rules and boundaries come in. It's important in relationships, but I don't think people understand why it's important. I don't think I understand why it's important. We're taught reciprocity in school; our parents teach us that it's in the Bible. These are things we know, but we're kind of flippant with it. But I think we really don't understand and appreciate it until we've seen it or until we've been on the receiving end of people treating of us good, or if we're treating someone good, but they're treating us bad.

*Alexis Braswell*

I do not see reciprocity being practiced in today's world, and I think a lot of people ignore that factor. When you think that you can speak to anyone in any way, handle anyone or deal with anyone without self-respect, you can't expect it back. If you're disrespectful to someone you shouldn't think that they'll be respectful to you. But this is where the restraint comes in. For example the customer is always right. When you're working in customer service, you shouldn't allow people to take you out of your character if you know that you're very respectable. You can control your emotions and things of that nature. That's where restraint comes in I believe, and I think it's just better to be safe than sorry so you have to control your emotions.

I tend to steer away from conflict. I'm not very good with it, so I think the best way to do that is to always put your best foot forward at any time dealing with anyone and anything business related or persona. Again, if you're disrespectful to others, they have no right to be respectful to you. People don't owe you respect. You should always somewhat demand it or imply that you would like respect. But when you give respect people pick up on that and give respect back to you. That's good for us when it comes back.

*Damon Braxton*

Treating people the way you want to be treated is definitely important. For example, if you deal with someone who is sarcastic to you all the time, you may get tired of dealing with that person, or a person who has an attitude with you all the time, after a while you won't want to deal with that person. I do treat people the way I want to be treated. That's one of the things my parents told me when I was younger. It's like when you're a little kid in school; there might be this one kid who is always stepping on your shoes. So now you don't want to be around him because he's always stepping on your shoes. Or maybe there's a girl in class; she may like you, but she hits you instead of telling you that she likes you. So now you don't like her because every time you see her, she's always hitting on you.

*Anastasia Foster*

That's really important, because like my mom said, you can't make a friend without being a friend. So if you're mean to someone they can be mean to you. What's stopping them? Personally, I do treat people the way that I want to be treated, but at the same time, I will also treat people that way, even if they're not treating me the same way. What I mean by that is somebody could be really super mean to me, and they could be cursing me out or bullying me or whatever it is, but I never reciprocate that behavior to them. I stay true to myself, and I'll treat them as nice as I possibly can, which can be very difficult. So yes, I definitely do treat people the way I want to be treated. But I also treat them the same if their own behavior doesn't change, and they're continuing to treat me very badly and negatively.

*Amina Jason*

It's tricky with my generation. There are two opposite ends of the spectrum. There are the ones that are have manners and know how to operate, they know how to carry themselves, and they know how to be professional and how to be productive and actually add value to the world. Then there's the other end where they're selfish and wrapped up in themselves and what they have going on or what they don't have going on. That gives us a bad name. I know so many people who are so shocked at how old I am. They're like, "Wow! You're running a program when most of your generation is doing whatever?" There're so many people I went to school with that just are not doing anything with their lives. They're not producing they're not out in the world helping. I'm not saying that everyone has to be that way, but to any extent you know, adding value.

As far as reciprocity goes, I think that there are people that are just so wrapped up in themselves, just maintaining and trying to stay afloat that they forget that they have to actually give respect to get respect, and they're so wrapped up in, "How am I going to pay my car note? How am I going to finish school? How am I going to…" It's just so stressful because times are different and people lose sight of how they treat people when they're wrapped up in trying to maintain themselves. I can't really say that I blame them, but at the same time you have to take a step back some time to say, "Okay, I'm human. I'm still here at the moment." You're thinking about your future, but in the moment you can't forget how to treat people while you're getting to the level where you want to be.

I think the two different ways of behaving among my peer group has a lot to do with how they were raised. It always goes back to how they were raised and a lot of it comes to—people who know better do better, yet a lot of a lot of times, in my age group it's my age, then it's my race and then my sex and each level has different factors. That determines how they are today. It's tricky, because you can compare me to a twenty-three-year-old white female, and you'll get completely different answers. It has a lot to do with their background, what they see as having value or what are their ethics or morals. A lot of them just don't know, they're just so lost and not in touch. As an example, I was with a friend and his sister has a boyfriend, and you can tell he was raised differently than how we were raised. It's like when you go around someone you never met, you always want to introduce yourself since it's the first time, or at least reintroduce yourself just so you can become more acquainted. But nobody said, "Okay, let me introduce you." Little things like that.

I could tell by how some in my generation treat older people— the elders, that they don't know the value of the wisdom of someone who is older than they are, that there's so much to learn from someone who's been here so much longer. I don't think grasp the aspect of just cherishing and building a relationship with their elders. Some people don't have grandparents, but there's always an elder somewhere, you can volunteer at a nursing home or at a senior daycare or something, just so that you can have that experience. I think that's important, and it's sad because I've learned so much as I've been fortunate to have both my maternal and paternal grandmothers heavily involved in my life. So I know what it is to have conversations with them, and I know what it is to learn from them and to pass these things down to my children. I think this is very beneficial.

*Nyeim Risien*

We want to treat others the way we want to be treated. My mom told me that was important. I guess that goes back to the respect value. We can't disrespect people and expect them to be respectful to us. We respect others no matter who it is, no matter what the situation, they may be younger than you or older than you, we want to treat everybody with the same level of respect. I see very little of this reciprocity among the young people today. This goes back to what I said earlier about what I see on social media—students disrespecting the teachers when they are in school. It was like that when I went to school, when I was in high school only three years ago. It definitely was there. The students treated each other based on the image they portrayed. There were the jocks, the pretty girls, the nerds, and stuff like that. If you weren't wearing a pair of designer shoes, or you didn't have a certain style coat, then all the kids made fun of you. Would they want to be treated like that?

# Restraint

How important is restraint in today's world?

*Sarah Bacchus*

Restraint is something I have probably only just gotten on the other side of. I say that because I've always grown up with a very bad temper, a quick temper, I should say. I think that because of that, I've always been, kind of like, "Oh, I'm going to do what I want to do," or "I'm mad, I'm mad."

I feel we don't place enough emphasis on restraint. You have to have self-control, you have to restrain yourself, or else there are dire consequences to you not behaving. Although you do know that, I feel that knowledge is really not driven home until you have suffered the dire consequence of not practicing restraint. For me, it took joining the army, because as much as my mother would drive home the offensiveness of my behavior saying, "You don't have to cut and carry on. You don't have to do that." It was when I got in the Army, and I started to see certain things. I started to learn very quickly that that behavior is just not going to fly in this institution, and so the type of punishments that would go along with me blurting out something, as I think back on it sometimes, it makes me say, "Oh my gosh, I can't believe some of the things I would say." But I think that restraint is just something that people do not truly do until they have seen someone close to them, or until they themselves have experienced the real consequence of not being disciplined, not being restrained in their behavior.

For instance, I was in the Army, and we were in formation, and I was fussing with this guy, and I can't even remember why, I just remember I was fussing with this guy. When you're in formation you're supposed to stand there and be quiet until you receive the block of instruction. But I was just carrying on and I didn't see the drill sergeant making his way to the back of the formation because he heard something, but he wasn't sure, so he was walking back there. I thought I had enough time to tell this guy off. All of a sudden, I felt this tension on my back, and it was the drill sergeant. I was just like, "Oh god, I'm going to die." And he said to me, "Get down in the front leaner rest and stay there until I tell you to move." This is the big thing about restraint. People are watching you, but you don't always know that. I was caught off guard and was so embarrassed. So yes. Restraint is important, but unfortunately, it's just not driven home until you feel the extreme consequence of it.

*Alexis Braswell*

Yes. Restraint is very important. I've learned as a young black woman growing up in this society that restraint is one thing that separates you from being alive and not being alive. Just as far as dealing with law enforcement, dealing with people on your job. In this society we aren't expected to thrive. We're not treated as equals. So I think restraint should really be instilled in children and especially young black men, and I say this all the time, you just have to learn that some things are better left unsaid. Some battles just aren't worth fighting, so you really have to practice self-control or restraint.

*Damon Braxton*

Not having restraint can get you in a lot trouble and can get you hurt, get your feelings hurt, and you can wind up in jail. You definitely need to practice restraint, especially restraining your anger. You don't want to act on emotion like me when I was younger. I felt I got mad very quickly and acted out my anger. Now I'm older and know better, and I don't act out my anger in the same way, and that keeps me out of trouble. Do whatever works for you. It depends on the person. For me, I have a punching bag and that helps me. Ever since then I've felt a lot calmer. Some people walk away, some talk it out, some need breathing exercises. It all depends on the person. Do what works for you. These values are important in today's world. They will always be important

*Anastasia Foster*

Well, that kind of goes hand in hand with reciprocity, but it's important that sometimes you're going to break down, because sometimes people can't help themselves, and it's hard to restrain their behaviors and attitudes. But something that helps me keep everything under control is when somebody is saying negative things to me or has an attitude with me. I consider that they may have something entirely different going on in their lives. That's true for the most part, and you find out later on in the middle of it that it has nothing to do with you. The behavior they direct at you may the result of issues with a project or some other situation. That's definitely important because we don't want it to actually get worse for that person. And although it can be difficult, it's really important to get your feelings under control. I definitely don't think you should bottle things up, but you should straighten them out, like my mom says, "You don't want your left hand to know what your right hand has got."

In terms of some other ways that I handle your own anger and frustration, I was really lucky my parents got me a cat when I was younger. He was my best friend. I would talk to him about everything when I couldn't talk to my mom right away, in that my mom would be the person I would go to first. Sometimes I would call her, but if I couldn't call her because she was at work, then I would go to my cat and even though he probably couldn't understand what I'm saying, I felt really confident that I had someone to talk to about these issues, and I would get it all out, I would tell him what I really feel about the situation, what I couldn't talk about with anybody else, but I could talk about with great confidence with my cat. Another great way of letting those feelings out in a safe and controlled environment is by punching a pillow and also shouting in the bathroom. People may think that's crazy, but I'm just trying to get through life.

*Amina Jason*

I think that restraint really helps. It's always good to be in control of your emotions because you don't want people to think that you can't function while you're upset or sad or are experiencing a mix of emotions. So I think that just being able to take control of yourself is very important. Because people won't take you seriously if you can't control your emotions. It's a level of maturity that people have to reach to be that in control where they don't retaliate. It's good to know to pick your battles. I'm not saying you can't be transparent, but not everyone needs to know that you're angry, not everyone needs to know that you're sad. You know there's time and place for everything. If someone makes you upset, you don't have to respond. If you have a relationship with that person, I've learned within the last few years it's best to just give it some time and then respond, because you might regret what you say when you're upset. I think that's really important

In terms of the bullying and lack of respect for teachers by students that are reported in the media, I think this is so interesting, because I see bullying a lot, and I think that in today's society they're overdoing it with the bullying. I think the media portrays bullying to be this out-of-control thing that people that schools can't get a hold of and can't contain. But I honestly feel it starts in the home, because there's not only bullying that's happening, cyber bullying is also happening. If the parents were more involved with their children as far as social media goes, I think a lot of it would be under control. I think a lot of it also has to do with certain parents allowing their children to do certain things like wear acrylic nails and name brand clothes, while there are some kids whose parents don't allow them to paint their fingernails, wear certain hairstyles or wear certain clothes. So there's a discrepancy, and children aren't being taught how to express themselves in an efficient manner. They don't know how to handle confrontation, and I think if children learn how to handle confrontation and be grounded in that, then they wouldn't have to take that on, they wouldn't have to take on that emotion from the person who is putting it on them.

*Nyeim Risien*

It is important to show restraint. People often want to act out of their emotions, and sometimes that doesn't have a good outcome, especially being a young black man, because now people will call a cop like it's nothing. I guess in certain situations like that, it's good to have restraint, because one false move, and it could be your life. When I'm angry or frustrated, I try my best to pause for a moment and try not to act out of emotion. I try to restrain myself because I know I will get the best outcome if I stay calm. My mom always told me not to get upset about things I have no control over. Let it be. It is what it is.

# Ten Things Young Adults Have Said about Respect

- The four *R*s are important in today's world. The common courtesies are still important, and it is important to put your best foot forward.
- The widespread use of technology has affected the way young people communicate and consequently the way they treat others.
- Respect for others include accepting people the way they are and being empathetic toward others.
- Children and young adults can at times be disrespectful to others, including their teachers and older adults. Respect appears to "be dwindling" in today's world.
- Self-respect means setting standards for oneself and not doing hurtful things to oneself. This is a super-important value.
- Self-respect includes being dressed appropriately and taking pride in your appearance. This communicates to others who you are and influences how others will perceive you.
- Parents should communicate to their children that people will respect them if they show that they respect themselves.
- Parents from different countries and cultures who are raising children in the United States should be aware of any negative impact of their parenting on their children's emotional development.
- Parents need to seriously think about how they are raising their children and the values they are teaching them.

# Ten Things Young Adults Have Said about Responsibility, Reciprocity, and Restraint

- Children, young adults, and people in general need to be held accountable for the things they do and don't do, and they should accept responsibility for their behavior.
- The lack of personal responsibility can lead to negative consequences for the individual.
- Young people should set priorities for their lives and follow through to bring them to fruition. This demonstrates they are living out an important value their parents taught them.
- Personal responsibility includes paying your own bills on time for the things you purchase.
- Children are taught reciprocity at home and in school, but they may not understand what it means until they have their own experiences with the way reciprocity works in their own relationships.
- There isn't much evidence that reciprocity is practiced by children, youth, and young adults nowadays, as they tend to be disrespectful toward each other.
- When people don't treat you the way you want to be treated, you lose interest in them and no longer want to be around them. You have to be a friend in order to have a friend.
- It's important to be in control of your emotions, and there are times you have to take control of your emotions. You have to know how to pick your battles.

- In today's world, it's important for young, African American men to show restraint in emotionally charged situations. A lack of self-control can result in negative consequences for them, including life-and-death outcomes.
- Children, youth, young adults, and people in general need to learn and know what works for them in calming their feelings of anger, fear, frustration, and other negative emotions. Some people walk away, breathe, and take time to calm down, others use punching bags or do other physical activities, others talk to their pets or trusted family members or friends. Learn a calming strategy if you do not yet have one.

# CHAPTER 3

# Young Adults Discuss How Children and Youth Can Demonstrate the Four Rs

Tell me some of the things children and youth can do in the present day to demonstrate they have learned the values of respect, responsibility, reciprocity, and restraint.

*Sarah Bacchus*

The first thing that comes to my mind is watch how you talk to people, watch your tone, and how you address others. Don't feel because you're an adult that every adult is your peer and you can talk to them every which way. I think that what children and young adults can do is to show that they have restraint by addressing people who are older than they are properly. Once you're over eighteen, yes, you're considered an adult, but you're not an adult, you're not a peer to every adult. I think what young people today sometimes fail to realize is that although they are grown and feel they can talk to anybody in any way, they need to have respect and understanding of social hierarchy in the presence of the people who have come before them.

Another thing the kids of today need to know is someone can look at them and know they were raised right if when they walk into a room they have common courtesy, present themselves properly, carry themselves well, have their clothes fit properly. The young ladies can be sexy and yet leave some things to the imagination. You know, they don't have to have everything exposed and hanging and dripping. There's a time and place for that. When we see a lot of young ladies exposing themselves, they want the attention, and it looks like they don't have any type of upbringing, but that's probably not it. But you wouldn't be able to tell because they're just so out there with the hair and the clothes and stuff like that. There's nothing wrong with having your own personal style, but restrain it. Have some respect behind it. You can be sexy, appealing, and attractive and not have to show body parts. You can let them figure out what they want to get from and you let them earn it. Let them respect you, make them have some self-control. So when they look at you, they don't have to already think they know what they're going to do to you.

The young men nowadays, the way they carry themselves is either one extreme or another. They either carry themselves like they're dirty, or they carry themselves like they have a whole bunch of money, and they don't. Their pants are down; their hair is not groomed. Where's the respect in that? I'm pretty sure their parents taught them how to pull up their pants and put on their shoes and clothes properly. So why would they leave the house like that?

Young people nowadays don't feel they need to be respected by older people. They feel, "I'm me, I'm gonna do what I want to do. I don't care if you don't respect me, you're not part of my crew cleric," or whatever they call it. But that's not true. It's not only about wanting someone to like you or approve of your behavior; it's also that you want to be a reflection of those who carry your DNA, your legacy, your blood. When you leave your house, you're not just representing you, you're representing more than what people see. But I think people young people nowadays don't care about that. They just want to represent what they like, or who they are in that moment, at that second. So if they look a certain way, it's "That's who I am. That's what I am." If their hair is a certain way, or they look a certain way, they don't think, "Oh, well, I'm representing my mom or my grandma who raised me, or my aunt who raised me after my mom passed away, or my dad who was a single father." They don't think of it like that. They're thinking, "I'm stepping out, I'm looking fresh. I'm gonna get this girl and get this guy, and I'm gonna look like Cardi B." They don't care about behind it.

It always goes back to your value system, your foundation, how you were raised. Yes, it's good to be individual and have your own pad, your own sense of style, and look a certain way, but you're still a representation of so many people that have come before you, that had their hands on you to help raise you, whether it was through their prayers, or literally through having their hand on you to raise you. I guess that comes with time and maturity. But understand you can be your own person and still represent your legacy and still have pride. You don't have to go with the latest trend if that trend goes against your value system.

I'd like to see children and young adults show respect for people older than they are. I can say this because It's come with my maturity because if you had asked me this question ten or fifteen years ago, I would have said, "They just have to say yes sir, yes ma'am," and so on and so forth, but I'm at a different generation now, and I understand the importance of certain values such as respect for my elders. Although I'm an adult, it doesn't mean that I can address you as "Carmen." That's crazy. My mother always instilled in me, "No matter what, they are your elders. They are not your peers. They are not people you will hang out with. These are people who are my peers." I will always remember that."

My other advice to children and young adults is that they don't have to react to everything. If an adult is asking them something, just answer the question, and show restraint in how they communicate in tense situations. To me, the highest form of restraint is being able to remove yourself from a situation without damaging the situation. Further, I think a young person can show restraint by walking away from a situation that can possibly turn verbally or physically violent. I think that is probably the number one way that they can show restraint and learn how to think twice think beyond the situation. We usually think in the moment, because we are very triggered when we're young; we're arrogant, everything is boom, boom, boom in that moment, but I think if a young person can think twice, think beyond that moment, think of the consequence and beyond the consequence, they'll be much better off. Yes, think beyond the moment.

*Alexis Braswell*

You have to always keep in mind what your parents have taught you. I believe that when parents raise their children they do want to protect their children and instill in them values that will protect them when they go out into the real world. So when you're at home just remember your mother wants you to keep your room clean. So maybe when you move into your own place you'll keep it clean, or if your mother tells you to say thank you after being given something, or please, when you ask for something. It just shows respect. When we go into the real world, I think we have to keep a lot of those values in the back of our minds and when we practice them they become habit. Never question yourself when it comes to displaying those values or showing them to other individuals so they will become second nature. It takes a lot of practice.

I would say, with responsibility, that's where you practice in your home, and the real world is your test. So when you're at home and you know your parents are telling you your responsibility is to take out the trash, once you practice those responsibilities, out in the real world when you have responsibilities for bills, for work assignments and things of that nature, it's going to be second nature. Then as far as treating others how you want to be treated you would never disrespect your mom, so why disrespect another woman? You would never disrespect your father if he told you to do something, so why disrespect your boss if he asks you to do something? These are things you keep in the back of your mind.

As far as restraint with bullying and being disrespectful, you just have to think about the outcome of things like what your mom would do in the situation. How would she react? What has she taught you? How would your father react? How would he want you to act in this situation? You just have to think of everything that you've learned and just apply it to the situation. A lot of learning happens in the home. My mother has taught me to be respectful of others, their space, their values, and their beliefs, and I believe that parents have the responsibility for teaching their kids these values. My mother tells me if I want someone to do the same thing, then I should reciprocate. I would never want anyone to disrespect me for no reason, but some people do, and you can't stop those people. But you can't be ignorant. You know what's right, and you know what's wrong, so always do the right do the right thing.

Going back to bullying and violence in our schools, as well as student disrespect of teachers, I think that some teachers do their jobs very well, but some teachers aren't passionate about the work they do. I've noticed, for example, I go to a predominantly white institution, and I see professors that are very invested in their students and their well-being and the success of their students. Then I'll encounter professors who are just there for their check. I find it easier, and I'm more willing to respect the individual who respects me rather than the one who doesn't, the one who's just here. I think with teachers it's just a matter of whether you want to do something or you don't. Because I've seen plenty in my years of being in high school and middle school. I've seen plenty of bad disruptive children in the classroom, and I've noticed professors and teachers who take the time to say, "Hey, what's wrong? Why are you acting out? Is there anything I can do to help?" Those students tend to not suppress their anger and disrespect by saying, "This person is on my side, maybe I should show more respect," or things of that nature... Again, I think it starts at home with children, and I think for teachers it's a matter of passion or just being there for a paycheck.

As far as bullying, I think that starts at home as well. I believe that children who have built-up anger from things that happened in their household, or who have traumas in their life, I think that's where bullying starts. Because I've noticed a lot of bullies have parental problems, or they're being abused at home or they have mental illnesses. I know a young girl in one of my classes in college, a drug class, who told me how her father was an alcoholic, and when she would go home her father would hit her. Then when she went to school, she took that anger from home to school, and she would hit on other girls or she would be very disrespectful. She said school was her outlet, and bullying was her outlet until she grew older and realized that wasn't the right thing to do. So she got help. I really think you have to talk to people; you have to understand you can't always blame somebody else. It's just a matter of asking for help.

*Damon Braxton*

They should act like they know the four *R*s. When they greet people, they should say hello and talk to people the way they want to be talked to—say hello, thank you, sorry, excuse me, you're welcome. I don't like bad manners. Talk to people in the manner they want to be talked to. Treat people the way they want to be treated, the four *R*s basically.

In terms of personal responsibility, I think once you get to a certain age, you should start applying for jobs on your own, use your own initiative in going to school, helping your parents out with things you can do, like help paying bills, taking the trash out, washing dishes, looking after your younger siblings. Help in any way you can, do anything you can. Take care of yourself by making money. Get a job or go to school.

You can show restraint by not letting certain things get to you, like road rage, for example, when people cut you off on the road or something like that, you may want to pull up to their car, roll down your window, and talk trash to the person. It's restraint when you don't do that, and that's a strength.

*Anastasia Foster*

Well, in order to show respect, starting with that, I think that it will go a long way for them to show that they if they can be humble. Much of the time they act like they think they're above some people. They show respect for older people, which is great, but they also need to have that same respect for younger people and people they think are not on their level. But we also have to show respect for people that are on the same level as we are, as well as those we think are not necessarily on our level. Whatever way they look at it, they can start by doing that. I know it's really difficult, but that's definitely something they could do to show respect, not necessarily to look at where you sit with them, but also knowing that you're a person and you deserve the same respect.

As for responsibility, I think that there are a lot of things that millennials are responsible for right now, and it's not necessarily more difficult than when the other generation was growing up, but it is a different sort of responsibility that they're looking out for right now. I think that the way that they can show that they're responsible is by being able to play the cards they are dealt, no matter what they may be, whether it's having to work three jobs to get by, or having children at a very young age, or whatever they are responsible for. They should be able to work with it and know that it's going to be unique for every person, so they shouldn't point fingers or compare or complain, but to just take their time and not take things for granted.

Reciprocity is a hard one, but the best way for them to be able to do this is not to fight with people. I know we see these videos about people fighting with each other about different issues and different topics. While the issues may be very important and I don't think they should minimize them, but at the same time they definitely should be able to have a conversation and key in that respect, while also being able to treat the other person the way that they would want to be treated if they were on the other side. So when you want to talk to someone about an issue that they're perpetuating or whatever it is, you should be able to have a conversation with them that's not aggressive, and it's not going to turn into a fist fight, something like that. I think that happens around political issues that they should be able to just have a conversation about, and if the other person is not willing to listen, give it a break, because no matter how much fighting you do, they're not going to listen, and that's something that you can work on later on. But it's not worth a fight or anything like that, because the bottom line is still showing people how you want the world to be. If you show them aggression or negative control, that's what they'll take from it.

I think we have a lot of anxiety, and that may come from how our parents dealt with their problems. I know that a lot of people don't seek counseling because of the negative stigma that's attached to it, but counseling may help. They can also scream in their bathroom and punch their pillow to let out their anxiety in a safe and controlled environment, and then they can go out and continue to be positive.

*Amina Jason*

I think they should go about it in their daily lives—how they treat people, how they interact, how they carry themselves, how they function. It's as simple as saying, "Good afternoon," or "Good morning, how are you doing?" Just being genuine. That has a lot to do with it. There comes a time in a young adult's life when they're about to be a parent; that's the most important thing—to raise a child who is a member of society, a child who reflects you. I know people my age who are parents and by now their children are about two years old and it's just like the children are out of control. So it's important to make sure that your child knows respect and they know how to carry themselves… It starts in the home and it has to do with structure. I realize that structure from a young age is very, very, very important. I can't even stress how important it is. It molds the kids, and everything falls into place after they know their structure. They know that they have a schedule, and they know that they say please and thank you when they receive things, or when they want something they say excuse me. That comes along with responsibility in a young adult's life when they're called on to be parents. It has a lasting impression throughout that child's life and their schooling, and so on and that is important. A lot of these parents are young, and they just want their kids to look cute, so they dress them in all the name brand clothes. I've never understood that, and I still I don't understand them bragging about what they can provide for their children, because that's their job. They go on Facebook, and they say, "I bought my baby this and I bought my baby that," but that's their job.

It just baffles me how children are so overly stimulated by these things. But what are their values? I have conversations with kids who have everything, and I have chats with kids who have nothing, and it's two different types of conversation, and you can tell where their heads are and what they are exposed to and how they handle certain situations based on how they're being raised and what they're being exposed to and how they're so stimulated over just their daily lives. Overstimulation is huge. For example, you go to the restaurant, and you see little kids there watching something on their tablet. When I was a kid, I used to color; they used to bring out the crayons, and you color your menu and talk to your parents and your siblings. Now there's no conversation, and the kids are so engulfed in watching their screens. It's sad, and that's where a lot of things are being lost.

My advice is that parents should limit the use of these devices by their children. I'm not saying that they don't allow them to use the devices, because obviously, technology is growing, and they have to know how to use technology. I'm not saying to just completely take away all those devices. But parents need to be able to limit their use. Kids still need to be able to pick up a book and turn the pages. They need to be able to touch paper and color with a crayon instead of downloading an app and using your finger to color it on a touch screen. What young parents call "old school" should still be present in children's lives. I had a parent the other day who was upset because her child wasn't able to use his tablet. I said to the parent, "I'm sorry, but I don't allow that. He has to go outside and play and be able to play with some toys and socially interact with his peers instead of sitting there on his tablet." I don't allow it, but that's what some parents do at home; that's what the kids are used to. Parents need to have them disconnect and get into some conversation.

I really appreciate that my parents always conversed. They always spoke to each other with respect. I've never heard my dad call my mother out of her name, or my mom call my dad out of his name; they literally shaped me into how I treat people and how I interact with others, even when I'm upset.

*Nyeim Risien*

Children and young adults can show respect in the way they talk to people, the way they talk to their elders and strangers—people they don't know. They should imagine the people they're talking to could be their parents or grandparents and ask themselves how they would want people to talk to them. In terms of how children and teens treat their teachers, here again they should put themselves in the teachers' shoes. Suppose their parents or grandparents were teachers, would they want anybody to talk to them any kind of way? So they should treat their teachers with respect; it's not going to hurt them.

Teens and young adults should also consider how they look when they go out in public. I'm not saying they need to wear brand name clothes, but they should pay attention to how they put it together before leaving home, not to look like they just threw stuff on, but to put some effort into looking nice.

They should also consider situations they might get into when they're out in public and how they should respond. For instance, if they're walking in the mall and someone bumps into them and the person says, "I'm sorry," they should accept the apology and not escalate the situation.

When they're at a restaurant and are served by a messy waiter who spills something on the table, they should point out the spill to the waiter and give him a chance to clean it up. There's no need to make a scene about the spill. They should put themselves in the waiter's shoes and consider how he might look at it.

# CHAPTER 4

# Young Adults Comment on Personal Responsibility

When I walk through my neighborhood, I see young adults who attend the community college on my street litter my street. I also see both young and older adults walking their dogs, and if the dogs poop, they don't pick it up. That makes me think they lack a sense of personal responsibility. What do you think?

*Sarah Bacchus*

I totally agree. In my neighborhood we have little stands with the plastic poop bags, so when your dog poops, you have the bags to pick it up. It drives me nuts how people just let their dogs poop down the neighborhood and they don't take any responsibility. It's like they don't care because I guess they know someone is going to eventually pick it up.

It's also about a lack of restraint because there are no consequences, and there is no personal responsibility, because eventually, someone else is going to take care of it. They don't have to be responsible if no one is making them do it. It doesn't even make sense, but in their minds, that's what they're thinking. I'd rather not pick up poop; that's gross, but I assumed that responsibility once I decided to own a pet.

I think littering and not cleaning up after your pet is laziness and disregard for authority. It goes back to reciprocity. It's like, "Would you want someone to throw stuff in your yard and not pick up after themselves? Do you want to attend school or go to work in an area that's nasty? So if you if you want places where you go to be clean, why can't you clean up after yourself?" Some will respond that it's already dirty, so what's the big deal? If I put another trash bag right here what's the big deal? If I throw another piece of tissue out the window, it already has ten other pieces of tissue out the window, so what's the big deal? Who's going to tell me anything?

Maybe they really don't know, because maybe there are some people out that were not raised to clean up after themselves, or to have a clean area or to be responsible for the mess they make. That's something that needs to be taken into consideration. Whether it was because of entitlement privilege, lack of discipline, lack of structure, or something else, they were not raised to keep it clean.

I say that to say that there are people who do it just because they can, and no one is going to tell them otherwise, and there are people who do it just because they were never taught that if you do something, you fix it, you clean it, you correct it, you put it away. If you take out something, you put it away. There are rich people who don't have to pick up after themselves or their pets because they have people to do that for them. So I think that while we do have people who just want to buck the system and do whatever they want to do, we also have to take into account that there are people who just don't know any better.

*Alexis Braswell*

I think it's disrespect intertwined with laziness. It doesn't take too much to put something in the trash can. But also people don't really care about things of that nature. They don't seem as important to them. Some people just think, "Hey, I can do this on the ground, nothing's going to happen to me, it doesn't affect me so I can do whatever I want." People don't really take things into consideration unless it's affecting them, or unless somebody stresses to them like, "Hey, this bothers me."

With the younger generation, you may have to explain things more to them and enforce the consequences of the decisions they make that aren't beneficial to them. For example, with littering, either you throw your trash in the trash can and you have no problems you can go about your day, or you throw your trash on the ground and a police officer may see you and fine you for littering, and things of that nature. I think when you weigh the consequences of things and you explain that more to a child they'll understand it better, and it also reinforces positive behavior, while negative behavior will consequent negative reinforcement. I think my mother did that with me. If I did things bad, I got a spanking or was told, I couldn't play games or watch TV. If I did positive things, I would get a treat, or my mom would buy me something new. I think those reinforcements sort of helps with instilling values, thinking that, okay if I do something right, then good will come out of it, and if I do something wrong, bad will come out of it.

*Damon Braxton*

When kids litter, it may be because they're not in their own house, and they may not feel responsible for keeping the street clean. Some people may do it because they don't care. But everybody is not throwing trash on the street. I have friends who walk around and pick up trash in the neighborhood. I've seen them a couple times. The people who throw trash on the street, out their cars... I can't say why they do, other than they don't care. But that's not acceptable because a dirty neighborhood brings down the value of the properties.

*Anastasia Foster*

I was also thinking that's a matter of personal responsibility and also having respect not just for the environment, which is a big thing, but also having respect for the people that live in the community. I don't think that comes from parenting, because there are people who do things differently from what they learned in their families. For some people it's not really that important in their households, or it may come from a lack of understanding about what responsibility is and what it requires. For a lot of people, they just come from a family with mixed views on the whole thing. I think we need to have conversations about these issues. Although there's a fine for littering, I personally wouldn't report my neighbors, they may get angry, or they may pay the fine and not change their ways. I prefer to have a conversation with my neighbors that's informational, like sharing what I do when I walk my dog, and what I do to keep my neighborhood clean, instead of coming across like it's what you want them to do. I feel it's more effective if you talk about it, as opposed to having them pay a fine because that may come off as offensive or passive aggressive and then that would be productive at all.

*Amina Jason*

It think they're lazy and they don't take pride in their environment because they don't care; they don't care, they don't have pride, and they're lazy. That's really what it comes down to, because you can be raised to be clean and keep your place tidy and all that, and all the projects that they teach you in elementary school—there's the recycling club and litter bug and the other things they teach you in elementary school. At that age kids are so wrapped up in these activities, then they become young adults, and it seems they just don't care. Personally, I can't do it. I can't bring myself to throw something on the ground because I just think that's filthy, but some young adults don't take pride in their planet; they don't take pride in the environment. The thing about it is that it doesn't directly affect them, and they don't have an incentive to not litter. There shouldn't have to be an incentive, but that's how their brain is processing the situation, "I'm not getting anything out of it. Someone else has to pick it up. That's their job, that's not my job" type of thing.

I even see adults throw trash out their car window. They also don't care, and it's sad. Is that the example they're setting for their kids? It's terrible. Honestly, it really is, and that's one of the qualities I look at in life. My friends who I choose to be around, I see them just carelessly just drop trash on the ground or on the parking lot, I can't be around that. I think it's a generational thing. They're taking more time to teach young children how to recycle, for example, not only putting plastic in the recycling bin, but also how and why they do it, like the plastic straws they're getting rid of and are now using the metal straws. Children are into that now. Some kids carry their little metal straws in their lunchboxes, I see the younger kids do that, even the preschool kids. All of a sudden, when they get to a certain age, they think that nothing applies to them. They think that's for babies. All it takes is one time for them to litter, and they see that nothing happened and they think they could do that all the time, unless they get a ticket which, of course, is rare for them to actually get a ticket for being caught in the act of littering. Police officers have other things to do instead of trying to catch someone littering.

*Nyeim Risien*

When it comes to throwing trash in the street and having messy neighborhoods, I honestly think that's being lazy. I mean, it only takes two seconds to use a plastic bag and pick up your dog's waste. And you can take your trash from eating in your car to your trash can in your home. You wouldn't want somebody to bring their dog into your yard and have them use the bathroom or you don't want smelly trash in your yard, so please try to keep your yard and neighborhood clean. You live there. Be responsible enough to figure out ways or pick up the trash, it only takes five seconds to do that.

Learning how to behave starts in the home. If you grew up in a violent home or in a violent environment, that's all you know, because that's all you saw. I feel if children get some type of guidance in the right direction, they will act right. I didn't grow up in the best neighborhood, but I had the right people at home. So again, if kids get the right guidance, I feel the upcoming generation will be all right.

# Section 3

## CONVERSATIONS WITH ELDERS

In this section, elders respond to the following questions:

- What are your thoughts about parenting?
- Thinking of the values of respect, responsibility, restraint, and reciprocity, how can parents raise children to develop these values? Start with respect, including self-respect, and then we'll move to the others.
- Is it important for children to practice restraint or have boundaries for their own behavior, especially outside of the home?
- Do you see in today's world, anything in the areas of respect, responsibility, restraint, and reciprocity that cause you any concern?
- What practical parenting advice do you have for a modern twenty-first-century parents?
- How can parents get the support they need in raising their children?
- Do you think the church should help parents internalize these values and pass them on to their children?

# Chapter 1

# Elders Express Their Thoughts About Parenting

What are your thoughts about parenting?

*Herman Bostick*

I think parenting is one of the most important things that a family can do that determines what the next generation will be like. It starts in the home and is very, very significant. My estimates are that it cannot be minimized and it cannot be fixed by anything. Parenting has to be done by parents at the beginning, so I think it has an important place in a youngster's life.

*Derek Broomes*

My thoughts on parenting are that it's one of the greatest responsibilities of life. You receive life from your mother and father, and you bring that life into one, and that's basically procreation. Then, whatever demands are placed on you as mother and father, you want that offspring to represent you, be like you in every way, whether your ways are pristine or not, you want that child to take after you, take after the mother, or take after some other person in your extended family. But that child does not come with a "how to" book—how to raise a child, how to be a mother, how to be a father, and so here comes the responsibility. If you had the nurturing of a caring family, mother, father or another person, and if there is open communication within the household, and everyone is very civilized and nobody gets angry to the point that they cannot control themselves, abusive words are not used, then you really have a complete, and the greatest thing that kids need. Between the ages of birth to three to six, children assimilate both good and bad things, right? They don't have a deciphering mechanism to know what's good and what's bad and most things pile on them and accumulate. By the age of eight—seven, eight, nine, ten—they start to process things that are acceptable. But how do they know what's acceptable either in school or at home, on the street, or with their friends? That's where the parenting comes in, and that's the simple reason that you are the parent.

Sometimes, as a parent, you may not have even been exposed to some things your children experience. It may be you are a millennial parent, and the generation that you grew up in isn't your generation, or you become a grandparent in which the whole platitude, the whole drawing board is quite different. And what ascends from that is the belief in something—we believe that there is a consequence if you sin, and then there are the Ten Commandments. We grew up within the church. Just like the black family over here—it is the church that really gives African Americans the whim to bear and to honor certain severe punishment such as slavery, because they all believe that there is a God, and he knows right from wrong and wrong from right.

*Gloria Clanton*

I would say that it is very important to me as we are preparing our children to live good lives for themselves, for their community and for others, we need to communicate with our children. Let them know that we love them so that they will show that love to folks that they come in contact with.

*Rachel DeFour*

I feel that to become a parent is a gift from God. Once I became a parent, it took precedence over everything in my life. My children became a part of my life—I didn't stop living, but they were a priority. Their care, their nurturing were very important to me. As a parent, I don't believe I can say one thing and do another thing. I feel as though children learn by example. I can't say one time it's okay, and then the next time, in the same situation, it's not okay. I really believe that communicating with my children from the day of birth they understand when you're talking to them. I was one to explain my actions—if I had something I was very passionate about, and they were resisting of it, I explained why I was passionate about it and why I thought that way, and I allowed them to speak to me once they were able to speak. Of course, as an infant, anything that I basically did was their care, and their love and their nurturing, and I was very particular about what I put into their bodies. I was really concerned; I was very concerned about nursing and my frame of mind when nursing. From the point of conception, I talked to the child in my belly, and I worked on my disposition because I believe that the vibrations that I had through pregnancy that I am relating that to my fetus.

*Linda Hampton*

I think parenting is probably the most difficult job that you could have, also the most rewarding. For me, it was a life-changing experience. The birth of my first child totally introduced me to what parenting was all about. Although I had good role models around parenting in terms of what I saw happening in my own family, I had never had the responsibility of caring for children, guiding their development and just trying to figure out what parenting is all about. So it's a wonderful experience, and I would say that if there's an opportunity to be a parent, no one should ever pass it up. I think about people who don't have biological children but are still able to be good parents who are interested in the care of children. To me, that speaks volumes about who they are their caring nature and their understanding of good parenting.

On the challenging aspects of parenting, it's almost a little scary for someone who takes parenting responsibilities seriously, because that means that you have to really be focused as an individual to figure out what's best for each individual child, to make it to the spiritual side of it, to want to do it right. But you're not always sure that it is being done right. So I guess the challenge might be to really define what good parenting is, that you want children who are empathetic, who grow up to have good self-esteem and who are happy and motivated. But no one tells us how to do that. So it's a matter of finding out through trial and error, or through increasing your knowledge about what you perceive it to be, and then putting it into action. Sometimes it's not always something you can do on your own, because it certainly takes a village and oftentimes the challenge might be environmental, it might be a matter of socioeconomic concerns that you have no control over, but to work toward making things better for yourself, and your child can be a challenge.

The rewarding aspects of parenting, for me, is seeing it all come to fruition outside of myself; it's like you see yourself in your children. And when you have a good idea of who you are as a person, and you start to see those characteristics in your children, or you get the kind of support from others around you that you need to raise your children based on what your definition of good parenting is, it is so rewarding.

Your relationship with your child often reflects what you do and how you act so that it's almost reciprocal, you know, that you have to ask yourself—are you listening? Are you ignoring? Sometimes when they do things it doesn't always mean that you will respond in that way. But it's developing self-control while sharing the love and being adaptable and creating guidelines for your children. It forces you to be very disciplined in terms of the consistency that you want to provide, not only in your relationship with your children, but in your environment. You have to have conversations about expectations, and why. So that forces you to raise the level of your own expectations, because you can't expect someone to do something that you're not willing to do, especially in a respectful way, and that can be so rewarding. I think being a parent is the best thing that ever happened to me, and I'm so grateful I had children.

*Gretel James*
Parenting is a full-time responsibility to be taken seriously because you guide the life of a child, establishing values, patterns of

behavior, and those things that we embrace to enhance the quality of life. These include the values addressed in this book, such as, respect, respect for self first, respect for others, and respect for authority. Parents have to set examples for their children and be firm. Being firm is very important, this includes parents saying what they mean and meaning what they say, also doing what they say. That's because children watch their parents' actions more than they listen to their words. Parents should establish authority early in their child's life, with love, because a child needs to know that they are loved and a part of love is setting boundaries. If you love a child, you don't let them just do anything, say anything, and behave in an unbecoming manner. It's important for parents to establish a firm belief in God, our Creator, and raise their children with some knowledge of God and His laws for our lives. God set out laws for us to live by, and it can make our lives so much better. Not that we won't experience trouble, but it can prepare us to deal with the vicissitudes of life, which will come. It won't always be easy, but God has laid out for us how we can avoid some of the pitfalls we experience in life.

*Brenda Jones*

Parenting is a multifaceted and challenging undertaking. Rearing children involves identifying parenting skills which help children to be responsible, capable, independent, and socially competent. There is no one-size-fits-all set of strategies when it comes to parenting. Children have unique needs, skills, and abilities. It is incumbent upon parents to establish a healthy balance between parent expectations and the child's natural capabilities and proclivities. Parenting is a two-way street that requires mutual respect in the parent-child relationship.

*Rev. Jeanie Martinez-Jantz*

I think parenting is the hardest thing you can do. It demands the best of you even when you're feeling your worst, and there is never a time when you're off, even when you are away, when you leave your kids with someone, they're still there in your mind, and they're still there in your heart and you worry about them, you wonder, and no matter what, you can't walk away. So it's really intense, it's really hard, it's also an amazing journey. But you have to approach it as a journey.

The worst thing I think people can do is parent by accident. I think children are so important that the best you can give them is to be very intentional about being a parent. It's a life's work. When I decided to have kids, I decided one of the big things I wanted to do with my life was to raise two decent human beings. And I think people that don't think about that just say, "Oh well, oops, I'm pregnant." That's not a good reason to bring a child into this world. And when you bring them into this world it's on you to care for them. So you need to be intentional about doing that and taking it responsibly, not do it by accident.

*Lyngrid Smith Rawlings*

Parenting is the most honorable thing that a person can do. It takes a lot of time, effort, and thought, but it's so important because parents are the children's first teacher. Children have nothing else to do in their lives when they're young but watch everything you do and figure out the best way to get what they want from you, because children want what they want and so how do you help them grow and feel good about themselves, take responsibility for their lives, and be a part of the integral relationship that makes the family work. It's important that each child understands their role and responsibility so that the household functions. Of all the tasks that adults have, I think parenting is the most challenging, yet the most rewarding. Parenting is something that I take very seriously, maybe too seriously. I tried to raise my five children in a way that they understand their responsibility, what I expect from them, what the world expects from them, and what they must do to be successful, as they define success.

When my children were in nursery and elementary school, I drove them to school at three different locations before I drove to work which I had to arrive before 8:00 a.m. to open the building. We had to leave the house by 6:45 a.m., so when it was time to leave, it was time to go. The rule was, "You know you get up at a certain time and fix your breakfast and your lunch. If you don't, you'll be hungry. If you have not packed your lunch and your homework, when it's time to walk out the house, then you will not have it, I'm not going back." The children developed the sense that we've got to pull together to make this thing work, and that was what life was about.

I remember an early conversation with my ex-husband when the kids were quite young. I asked him, "How are we going to teach our kids about the birds and the bees?" And he said, "Well, that's a bit early for that." I said, "Well, still, we have to come up with some way now so we both know how to do it." He responded, "You teach the kids from the time that they're very young that they're responsible for the consequences of their behavior, if you don't clean your room, you can't watch television, the consequence of not cleaning your room. If you want to watch television, then clean your room." The lesson that was being taught and reinforced throughout our children's lives is that they are responsible for the consequences of their decisions. So as I raised our children, I reinforced that they are responsible not only for their behavior but also about the consequences of their mis-behavior. So the lesson that they were to learn is that if they chose to have unprotected sex, then they would become parents at a time when they might not be prepared to support their offspring.

I also used many of my parents quotes like, "The coward never starts, the weak die on the way, only the strong come through." If mother says do this or that, don't say "I can't" or "Why?" "Let her hear your gentle voice, Mother dear, I'll try." A lot of ideas of what it takes to be a responsible person were quotes that came from my mother, so I used literature to give the children a good sense of who they were.

I always had high expectations for myself and my children. It's so important to me that young people understand what's important and why. I did try to have some flexibility, but I was probably a more traditional mother. During most of the time, I was raising my children, we had limited resources, so it was imperative that we lived within our means. However, I did not want the children to feel that our limited resources meant that they could not achieve their goals. While three of the children were high school and one of them asked for an expensive stereo, which was not in my budget, I told them that the stereo was not in my budget. I repeated my mantra, "First degree, debt free." I also always told them, "You do your part, and I'll do mine." Most the time I was raising the children as a single parent, which meant that I could only depend on my income. I believed that I had to be both the stern authoritarian father who had to ensure that our children understood how to navigate being African Americans in racist America, while at the same time trying to be the compassionate understanding mother who encouraged them to set high morale and professional standards. I felt compelled to be both in the same persons which could have been confusing at times to them. At times, I am sure that they did not agree, but somehow we tried to disagree without being disagreeable?

My father became more active in my children's lives once they were as they matured as teenagers and for the rest of their adult lives. He instilled into them the importance of the values in the same poems he instilled in his own six children. His favorite poems were "Invictus" by William Ernest Henley and "If" by Rudyard Kipling. Once they were in the late twenties and early thirties, he developed his list of Diamond Makers, which enabled the young adults to rate themselves.

*Denise Thorne*

Parenting is a job that has many components, and you have to be able to recognize those various aspects and be able to either meet those requirements yourself or find resources to help you fill those requirements. I think parenting is something that prepares a child to go out into the world, to take on his or her place that that child has been put on this earth to do. And it's up to the parents to help that child meet and fulfill those requirements. That's the role of a parent.

# Ten Things about Parenting
## from the Elders

- Once you become a parent, your child becomes your number one priority. Parenting cannot be minimized.
- Parents should always have high expectations for themselves and their children and should communicate these expectations to their children. It is also important for parents to communicate their love to their children.
- Loving your children include setting boundaries. If you love your children, you monitor what they say and do, and you don't let them say and do whatever they want to.
- Parents' religious beliefs guide their parenting practices, and for these parents, it is important to raise children with a firm belief in God and his laws for our lives.
- Children are not born knowing what's good and what's bad. That's where parenting comes in. However, in today's world, children may know and experience things their parents were not exposed to.
- The generation gap is not a new phenomenon. Parents just have to embrace it and become knowledgeable of their children's out-of-home exposure and experiences.
- Parenting is a multifaceted responsibility, and parents should ask for help if and when needed to adequately respond to their parenting challenges.
- The challenging aspects of parenting include the lack of knowledge about how to parent, community and social influences on children and limited resources within the family to adequately provide for even the basic needs.

- One important responsibility of parenting is to help children fulfill their potential—to support and nurture them into becoming all that they can be.
- One ought not to become a parent if they are not prepared for such a responsibility. One should be intentional about taking on the important responsibilities of parenting.

# CHAPTER 2

# Elders Provide Advice on Raising Children Based on the Four Rs

Thinking of the values of respect, responsibility, restraint, and reciprocity, how can parents raise children to develop these values? Start with respect, including self-respect, and then we'll move to the others.

## Respect

*Herman Bostick*

Self-respect is very important, and it should begin with the child as an infant. Now let me give you some examples. I think that if there are a mother and father in the home, they have to demonstrate respect one toward the other, so that the child learns not only by precept, but also by example. Being respectful of each other will help the child to see the importance when they teach the child how to respect him or herself, how to respect mother and father, and how to respect their playmates and those persons that they come in contact with outside of the home. Respect given in the home will be lasting for the child throughout his or her life, so I give it very high importance. That is one thing that is going to be fundamental to the progress of the child and in his or her adult life.

How do you respect other people and respect me? How do you speak to other people? How do you answer them when they ask you questions? How do you show that you value yourself and you value them? You do so by being respectful, by treating them the way you want them to treat you, and that has to start in the home. The parent has to talk to the child about this importance, and not only as he's growing up and becomes a teenager, that would be the same thing, but respect has to be present in the beginning in the home, and it has to permeate the whole home setting not one day but every day.

*Derek Broomes*

The generation that I grew up in believed in certain biblical principles, and we had a foundation for everything. Parents taught us respectful behavior and trained us in how to respect others and how to speak to people because that's how they were trained. But now, in the younger generation, raising a younger child, it becomes difficult because the environment that you are competing with is greater than you are. You're competing with the Internet, you're competing with Facebook, you're competing with YouTube, so you could give your kids all the guidance and everything else and when you go, but you also want the hands of God to protect them.

What I'm saying is, those are the things you have to be very conscious about and something you have to work on every day. You have to cure some of your faults, you have to curb some of your anger, you become a partner of virtue or should be a partner of virtue in front of your kids. Certain language should not be tolerated, certain behavior should not be tolerated, and whether that brings you in conflict with your children, and also whether or not that conflict leads to some physical altercation and other things, those things you have to be very cognizant of because the state and the government are not going to be in line with what you as a parent believe is morally right. They will probably be in line with certain turpitude, certain behaviors the parents or the parents of yesteryear would never tolerate. I'm also thinking about the teachers, with whom kids spend most of their day and hours. Teachers hands are tied, and they cannot correct a child; they cannot remonstrate a child without getting themselves into trouble. So your child, boy or girl, can be out there unprotected but for the grace of God, and you pray dearly every day for guidance and their protection. So that's one of the things about being a parent now and before and will continue to be.

*Jean Bynoe-Singh*

Well, as a parent, you first have to set the right example; you have to show respect for each other you are the parents in the home and your children looking on will want to practice what they see you do. When you're disrespectful, the father and the mother disrespectful to each other, when parents treat the children disrespectfully, the children in turn will feel that that's the norm and so you will find them practicing that. But you, the parents, have to guide them; you are the first teachers, and you guide them more by what you do than by what you say. So when you are respectful to each other, then you explain to them why respect is important, why you do certain things, and eventually, they will want to practice it. But then again, you know, religion, the Bible for Christians, plays a big role.

Regarding the role of the Bible—or religion in general—because there may be some cultural groups that do not use the Bible, they may use the Quran, for instance. Well, I try to live according to the Bible. The Bible will teach you as parents how you must love and respect each other and how you must inculcate the same attitude in your children. So when you follow that principle, it will show dividends. Therefore, I try to mold my thinking in line with what Jehovah wants, what the Bible states, and I try to get my children and grandchildren to see the value and importance of being respectful. I show them the pros and the cons.

*Gloria Clanton*

Actually, I think that the values of respect, responsibility, restraint, and respect are all tied together. I feel that if your children see you respecting them, then they will respect you; and if they see you respecting others, your mate, your friends, people that you come in contact with in the public, and then they will hopefully mirror your actions. I guess you teach them by example.

How you act is how they act. If they see you being mean in your actions, in the way you talk about people, they'll all feel that that's okay and that they can do the same thing too. So you try not to do that in front of them. That's the answer I would give for all the values you are talking about.

*Rachel DeFour*

Respect to me comes in first place—I often reinforced to them how important they were. It's kind of hard for kids to show respect when they don't feel good about themselves and their environment. It's kind of hard for me to just pinpoint exactly how I did that, but one of the things that I did was to also respect them. If they didn't like mayonnaise, and they did consistently not like mayonnaise, I respected that, and I didn't push that on them. Even with their food, they had to taste it first—they just couldn't tell me they didn't like it—they had to taste it and then once I established that wasn't what they really liked, then I honored that. That was me respecting their choices. I often talked to them even in regards to when I was paying the bills. They would sit down with me and they would see just how much money I had left over and I would base their allowances on what I had available. In fact, I think I did that with them because I never had the sense of I never had that respect for money. I think you also have to respect property; you have to also respect people. You know how kids would just run into someone, if I were around, they had to say "I'm sorry" or "Excuse me." I just didn't let them do things without me observing what they were doing and anytime that I saw them being disrespectful to someone else, I would address the issue.

I'm learning as they're getting older that my daughter would do whatever I told her to do just because she didn't want the consequences. My son would give me a lot of opposition, and I would spend more than enough time repeating to him "This is not acceptable. You cannot hit a girl—I don't care if she hits you." I wanted to teach him respect for women. The way his daddy treated me showed him respect for women. When we would go out, even as a little boy, I'd have him opening the door for us to go in (I call it manners). All this comes in their formative years. You don't wait until they're teenagers to do this. When I learned that the formative stages of development is up to the age of nine and their personalities are formed, I really took that seriously and worked at instilling respect—first for themselves and for those around them. When they respect themselves, they tend to respect others. You can't treat somebody else the way you don't feel about yourself.

*Gretel James*

Parents must exhibit respect, including self-respect, not just speak these values, but also exhibit them in all they say and do. Being careful about their conversation of what they are saying, even if they're not speaking directly to the child, sometimes children overhear adult conversations and we are not being respectful. For example, when we start to gossip, we start the accusations and that kind of thing. So we must exhibit respect by what we say about people, what we do to people, and what we do to ourselves. We must have high standards and then demonstrate it in front of our children daily. And it has to be a constant thing. It may be difficult because of the influences of the outside world, but parents must be constant in exhibiting their values and making it known to their children that this is what I expect of you. I used a phrase with my children, I said, "You were not born to me crazy, and you're not gonna act crazy."

*Brenda Jones*

Respect is a feeling or understanding that someone or something has importance and should be treated in an appropriate manner. At an early age, children need to learn to respect themselves, as well as others. Parents should teach children they are unique and have individual traits which distinguish them from others. They need to impress upon the child that no one has the right to jeopardize his/her physical or emotional well-being. When parents model respect for others in words and actions, they have a powerful influence on the child's behavior. Having children emulate the Golden Rule is a perfect way to help them learn how to interact positively with others in respectful ways.

*Linda Hampton*

I think parents have to have a sense of what respect is to be able to teach children what respect means, what it looks like, by exhibiting the behavior that they would want their children to exhibit. So that means leading by example, respecting their opinions, advising, or thinking through, in allowing children to know what's going to happen next, so that they can be prepared to move forward. Respect to me is really a reciprocal thing; actually, it's just one of those factors that is almost hard to define, because it may mean one thing to one person and something else to someone else, but it certainly means that there has to be some basis to go forward in terms of treating others the way you want to be treated and operating from a spiritual place when it comes to your children and the concept of respect.

When I say a spiritual place, I mean having a consciousness that is beyond you, I mean looking to a higher source for guidance, having a God-centered life. If you are a believer, as I as am, I depend on this Judeo Christian teaching in everything that I do. So to operate from that perspective means to have a sense of what that means from a biblical perspective and how to apply it in my own life. Certainly, parenting is one of those things that you would want to incorporate your spiritual values. So what does it look like—what kind of behaviors, what does it mean? How do you lead by example, and how do you treat others, as the Bible says, the way you want to be treated, as in love your neighbor as yourself? I can equate it to etiquette, you know, how we interact with each other, not just when it comes to how we set the table, but behaviors that cause us to live in harmony with each other.

*Rev. Jeanie Martinez-Jantz*

I think the most important thing parents do is model behavior. If you treat your child with respect and you insist that they treat you with respect, you're teaching them not only to have self-respect but to give respect, and if you insist that other people treat them with respect, they will know how to claim respect for themselves. I think they will also, if they are given respect, they're going to be more willing to give it back. I've observed that children instinctively reflect what you do, so if you're treating them with respect and treating them as good human beings, unless they have been through more than they should have, then they're going to respond, because you're calling out their best behavior.

## Lyngrid Smith Rawlings

It's important first for parents to respect themselves to set their boundaries to know what's important, to take care of themselves in a way that they are honest and forthright and they do their best. The children often emulate their parents' behavior. You can talk about respect, but they look at how you treat your family, how you treat your parents, how you treat your siblings, how you talk to your friends. If you tell your kids not to gossip and they hear you gossiping on the phone, they will often model your behavior. Make sure you model the behavior that's important to you and make sure that when they hear you talk to other people, watch how you interact with other people, how you carry yourself with other people—that it represents what you want them to learn. That's how self-respect and respect for others are learned. I would tell my children, "When I was carrying you, I didn't take any medicine. I made sure that my body was a perfect place for you to develop. So you came into this world with a full deck, so don't ever say you didn't come with a full deck." When I carried the kids to school, we talked about things that were important to us. You can really have valuable conversations in the car with the kids going to school and coming back. Then at home I made sure there were set times for dinner, bedtime, homework, and other routine activities. A lot of it has to do with how you relate and respect yourself and how you relate and respect your kids, including how you talk to them to make them understand the rules.

## Denise Thorne

Respect is very, very important. First of all, the parents have to respect themselves, and if you respect yourself, then you should be able to respect other people. And when you maintain self-respect, you are demonstrating to your child what that should look like. Oftentimes, children imitate what they see their parents do, or the people do in their village. So if parents or the village is able to demonstrate self-respect, then automatically that child will learn self-respect as long as you keep them within the confines of the communities that demonstrate self-respect. So I think it's very important to maintain a village; and the village could be your parents, grandparents, the school or the afternoon activities that the child goes to. As parents, you have to be able to find those avenues that support and maintain your values. That is very important.

Parents need to model respectful behavior; we have to set the example. One day I was in the parking lot of a grocery store lot and a car was coming through. The driver almost ran over this woman in her car. She had her grandchild with her, and she just took off cursing. I understand that the driver was wrong and he was on his phone and wasn't paying attention, but she told the grandson, "I'm going to go over there and whip his ass." And the first thing that I thought to myself was, "What is the lesson that you just taught this child? Is this the only way to respond, instead of teaching that child that what the driver did was not right?" She could have gone over to the driver and said, "Do you realize that you almost ran over us?" But the ferocity and the force with which she went over to the driver, she taught that child, "Look, anytime you are faced with a challenge like this, or any situation where it looks like somebody is about to take advantage of you, this is how you respond—curse them out, start a fight."

In my opinion, it was a teachable moment for her to be able to say to the child, "It was not the right thing for him to do." And even if she wanted to confront the driver, all she had to do was go to him and say, "Did you realize that you almost ran over me and my grandson? Next time make sure you pay attention." The young man would have received the message a lot better and thought about what he did or realized he needed to pay attention in the future and that his phone is really a distraction. But instead, she was ready to beat him over the head—I mean, literally fight—and so he went into defense mode.

I have found that when my own children are respectful to people, they get that respect back, regardless of who those people are. It doesn't matter what color they are or how they look; they get the respect. We have to also think in terms of long-term everything; it can't be short-term. Whatever you do, it has to always be about down the road and how it is going to affect the child down the road.

# Responsibility

*Herman Bostick*

That's a big one. Parents are responsible for rearing their children. Parents are responsible for developing an atmosphere in the home that will nurture the child. That's an important responsibility. Parents must make sure that what is needed in the home is there. That you do not engage in unnecessary behaviors or purchases, for example, living beyond your means. You have to show the child what is important and what is valuable in life, what is needed and what is not needed, and you have to have to model that. You also have to model the importance of being honest, the importance of being truthful, the importance of being respectful, the importance of education—that's a big one, and the importance of appearance. I know there is peer pressure and children want to do what they see others do. But as a parent, I would have to explain to my child why this is important and to what extent can he do this. Because your dress says a lot about who you are, and it also says a lot about how people are going to treat you, how they're going to respond to you when they see you. Certainly, I understand that dressing and behaving like their peers is important to them, but I want them to understand—and I say this because I work with some young people in my church—that they're not going to change much when they get to be twenty-five years old from what they are when they are eighteen. They have to start now being that person they want to be as adults. That's my responsibility as a parent.

I have two adopted sons, and I would explain to them how to spend money, how to value money, and how to look at what to buy and what not to buy, what to say and what not to say, when to speak and when not to speak, and the importance of good manners. I notice that sometimes children don't say "thank you" very much or they don't say "please," and I try to instill that in them in front of their parents. Parents must teach these truly valuable words in our language—*thank you* and *please*; that will carry children a long way. So the responsibility of parenting is important, and it's also critical because you are molding that child to become an adult.

*Derek Broomes*

Parents, in order to pass along certain behaviors to your children, in raising your children, you yourself have to believe and practice those habits; that's a priority. You cannot pass on or you cannot develop something that you don't believe in. And so parents now have to take an introspected look at themselves and make a commitment. Today parents have extracurricular classes like good parenting and what to do with difficult kids. So parents have to educate themselves, and it's not going to come naturally; it is not going to come effortlessly. Parents, as they are raising their kids, have to participate in every educational or learning opportunity that will enable them to become conscientious parents, to become disciplined parents, and this is for both parents where the mother and the father are there. So as the children are growing and learning, parents have to learn to become parents too. And another way they can do that is by listening to other parents who have been successful.

There are examples all over the place of how parents can learn how to be successful. Some parents form clubs and join organizations on good parenting. You can find such groups in the church. And you learn from that, and you mold yourself from that so you don't have say, "Do what I say, not what I do." You learn to be an effective parent by looking at others who have raised kids, asking them the questions, comparing your answers, seeing what is your objective for your parenting—that's the only way I know how. And pray, of course, but I don't know any other way—maybe there are, but I'm saying what worked for me and what I have done as a parent and grandparent. That's my answer.

*Jean Bynoe-Singh*

Well, for me, from the time my children were able to help themselves, even as toddlers, I taught them to do things, little things around the home, and even little things for themselves, like putting on shoes, even if they put them on the wrong feet, I said, "Well, you tell me why it's not feeling right." And they should be able to see, "Maybe I didn't put them on right." And they learn by trial and error and correctly do things that they could do, like keeping their surroundings clean and helping me with little chores in the home. I know when they were all living in my home, when they became teenagers, I had a timetable on the wall with the various chores, and everybody, male or female, had to do work, and it wasn't specified that this is what boys must do and this is what girls must do. They all learned how to wash the clothes, they learned how to press the clothes, and they also had to learn to help cook our meals. And the times when I was not at home or I couldn't do certain tasks, they had to do it. And the beautiful thing was that, however the food turned out, everybody said, "Enjoy." So you teach them little things they have to do for themselves, then little things around the home, and then bigger responsibilities later on.

In terms of responsibilities pertaining to schoolwork, here children differ. There are those who you don't have to prod to do schoolwork—those who are just simply dedicated, and then there are those who you have to be behind. Sometimes as a parent, I would help. But then when I found that they became too dependent on me, I left them to suffer the consequences at school. For instance, I would tell them, "You didn't do the teachers homework, let the teacher see that you didn't do it, and you would suffer the consequence." I also told them, "If you don't understand a particular concept, I'll help you to understand it. But if you still don't understand from my explanation, you still do the homework. You do it as far as what you understand, and when you get it wrong, any teacher will realize that you really don't understand, and so you will benefit from doing the homework, and the whole class will benefit as well, because the teacher will to have to teach it again, so that everybody can understand it better."

*Gloria Clanton*

Personal responsibility, the way they take care of themselves and the way they interact with other people, is as important outside the home as it is within the home. If they see their friends going down the wrong path, I would hope that they would not follow them, that they would know what is the right thing, what is expected of them, and that they not follow others who might not be doing the right thing. I think my particular children might try to lead their friends onto the right path. I don't think they would hold back, you know, some people might be afraid that they would lose their friends if they told them that what they were doing was wrong. But I think that they would encourage them to do the right thing, because they carry themselves in such a way that they would do what was right, as I have seen them interact with people as they have grown up. Both of them are firmly rooted in Christian values. They are both very active in their churches, and they were raised from childhood to accept the principles of the Christian faith, and they seem to have stuck to it. For example, some of those principles are "Do unto others as you would have them do unto you," "Follow the teachings of Jesus," "Try to uphold as many of the Ten Commandments." I think that my husband and I were examples for them, as we were both very active in our churches and we didn't argue and fuss and fight in front of them. We showed respect for each other, which I think they try to carry into their lives.

*Rachel DeFour*

I believe that parents should give children responsibility. Whenever they do something, it has to have consequences; that adds to them being responsible. Responsibility is taught. The way in which its taught is that you give them responsibility and you also are responsible. That way, they are seeing it and they are also experiencing it. My children had responsibilities in the household, even at around the age of five, I'd have them stand on a stool and play and wash the dishes; when I was cooking things that would not hurt them, I'd let them become a part of that; when I was cleaning their room, even at the age of five, I'd have them pick things up and bring to me if it was something that they left on the floor. They had to be responsible to keep their room clean, they had to be responsible to have chores, and they had to be responsible for being a part of and respectful of the family.

Their father and I always had dinner together; we worshipped together; that was my way of instilling the Christ spirit into them. Once they got to a certain age, they had a choice, but at a young age, they didn't have any choices so that gave them an understanding that you have to have the Christ spirit in your life, and you also have to practice that; it just doesn't come from you seeing it on TV or reading it in books. When they became older, they had a time by which they had to come home; when they didn't come in at that time, then they were punished. I didn't believe in beating them, but I believed in taking things from them. And to me, I think it makes them responsible when they realize that there are consequences to their actions.

Personal responsibility is important outside of the home—even in the school environment. I was very blessed that my kids went to school where my friends were principals and people were looking out for them. I believe that responsibility comes when there is a village, and everybody within that village has some sense of responsibility for the raising of that child, so when people outside of the home would say things to my children, I would make them obey. I would tell them, they would say, "But, Mommy, but that isn't the way you do it." And I'd say, "Yes, but when an adult tells you to do something, if it's not detrimental to your health, and if it's not against your moral values, then you obey." And everyone who was around me, I allowed them to be able to give my children instructions and tell them what to do and what not to do. And when they didn't complete things, I made them go back and complete them. If they didn't do things well, I made them do it again. All that to me is helping them develop a sense of personal responsibility.

*Gretel James*

Parents can say and have children do simple things, such as, "Make your bed when you get out of it," "Keep your room clean," "Help the family by washing dishes," "Do other chores around the house in a timely manner, not waiting until the next day. I'm convinced that these kinds of things build responsibility in children.

Others have a routine for getting ready for the next day after dinner, have some kind of routine so that children are prepared and nobody's running around like wild folk in the morning—can't find this, can't find that. Allow them to help fix the lunches for school the next day and any kind of chore that they can do. I don't care how poorly they make the bed, because it's difficult for younger children sometimes. Let them do it and compliment them on it, and as they grow, the bed-making will smooth out. So let them do it early. Sometimes we think you're too young and we say, "No, you can't do that," and "No, that's the wrong thing," but if you don't let them start helping and doing things early, when they get old enough to really be able to do it, you can't get them to do it.

*Brenda Jones*
Responsibility includes being dependable, being accountable, keeping one's commitments, honoring one's word and agreements. Responsibility is not obedience. Following directions, complying with parents' requests, submitting to authority are obedience, not responsibility. Allowing children the opportunity for self-expression, to take ownership of their behavior, and requiring them to complete assigned tasks foster responsibility. Parents must learn to step back yet offer guidance which will increase the likelihood the child will make appropriate choices and decisions.

*Linda Hampton*
Responsibility is defining your role and having some boundaries to what that means and doing exactly what you said you were going to do. It's being truthful; it's being consistent in attacking expectations that are good not only for the parents, but also for the child. So to be responsible means you have expectations that you care for yourself and your child, but also some consistency in making sure that you do exactly what you said you were going to do. You are very truthful, you are consistent, and it does not change; although the roles may change, the expectations do not.

I think responsibility develops with practice, as do most areas of development; it doesn't just happen. Some behaviors in showing respect to children are listening, accepting guidance, doing some very simple things in terms of being involved with your children, helping them with their homework, showing kindness, giving support, playing sports, doing things that are in the moment with the children so that they come to understand that you're here as an individual because you have a responsibility to be there. Children understand that for them, responsibility means to respond positively to the parents' interactions, because it doesn't have to happen. Children are aware that all parents do not do the same things. They see that their parents do certain things and other parents do not; therefore, they have a sense of what that means in terms of what behaviors are expected of them if they are to grow up to be responsible individuals.

*Rev. Jeanie Martinez-Jantz*

I think one of the biggest things is parents not doing everything for their children. When I was a Girl Scout leader, there were some parents who would come with us on camping trips, and where the children are supposed to have jobs to do, the parents would do it, and I would see the kids running around. I would say, "Wait, you're supposed to be doing this, your parents are just supposed to be supervising here." And I think also that challenging children to do more than they think they can is making sure they succeed. One of the things that that I do in churches is as teenagers, and as children are able, I give them adult-type responsibilities. They don't have to be twenty years old in order to read the lessons in church. Once they are able to read and do it well, then they can do it, but they have to be responsible for showing up on time and so on. I think naming behaviors is really important and naming things, describing. Like if a person is a reader, we call that a lector, and then we say the lector has to speak clearly and has to know how to pronounce the biblical names. So you're a lector, which means that you will work at this. You have to earn the right to be a lector, and if you take it seriously, that way you're teaching them and requiring them, but setting the bar a little high enough so they can achieve, but then helping them do that. With children we need to set higher standards.

I think also the one thing that helps children gain responsibility, especially as teenagers, is giving them meaningful work. A lot of times in churches adults will say, "Oh, we need to move the tables, let's get the youth to do that. We need this done, let's get the youth to do that." That's not meaningful work, and that's treating them like objects. One thing I do is, according to Episcopal church law, a person is an adult when they are sixteen years old; they have voice and vote. So as children turn sixteen, I insist that they show up at annual meetings and pay attention, and I ask them, "What do you think you should vote for on this and that?" They are also able to serve the wine at the Eucharist to the chalice Eucharistic minister, so I work with them to move up to that. Right now two of our youth have turned sixteen, and we are training them in the roles of first server and Eucharistic minister. I've also invited one of our youth to serve on the safety committee because of his particular and specific personality traits that would be valuable in keeping people in the church safe. So these kids are working with adult mentors who will teach them. They are considered adults in the church, and so they need to take on adult roles, and they're excited about it.

*Lyngrid Smith Rawlings*

There are only so many hours in a day. When my children were young, I used to iron their clothes, and one day I was in the basement ironing their clothes. They were just cutting up and messing up, and I said, "Oh no, this is it." So I called them downstairs, and I taught them how to iron their clothes. I always washed them, and I always put them in the dryer, but the ironing got to be a bit much because they wore uniforms every day; that meant uniforms for five days, which meant there were shirts, jumpers, and sets of slacks, so I taught them how to iron. I also told them they were responsible for cleaning their rooms, for making sure they put their dirty clothes in the hamper so they can be washed; plus they had the other chores. I didn't make a distinction in work between the boys and the girls. But I could have done some things a little differently—for example, when the boys complained that it was unfair for me to have only them clean up outside and not the girls, at which time I told them those were my rules. It was a challenge, but I wanted them to know that in order for everything to work, it has to work in a certain way.

*Denise Thorne*

I watch the National Geographic channel on television a lot, and the one thing that has stuck with me over the years is a documentary that I watched with a lioness and her three cubs in which she was preparing the cubs to go off into the wild to hunt. For three years she's spent time teaching and training them. She was part of a pride. And then after a while she and the three cubs went off on their own and one of the cubs somehow got lost. Nobody knew what happened to that cub, but she had two cubs remaining. Then one day she took the two to the river, and in their own language, she perhaps said to them, "I have done everything that I could do for you, now you go out there and make it happen for yourself." She then turned away and ran back into the woods with the rest of the pride. I believe that is how we should do things as parents. We prepare the children to go out into the world; we give them all the tools they need; we take them to a point where we know they are ready; then we step back and let them go out into the world.

# Reciprocity

*Herman Bostick*

Reciprocity is important. As a parent, I must be ready to reciprocate. When my child does well, I need to say to him or her, "I'm very proud of you, keep doing what you are doing. I love you." That's the main thing. By doing that, I hope that the child will say to me, "Dad, I love you. I appreciate what you were telling me to do." I would have behaved in such a way that my child has confidence in me, and that's a very important thing for parenting—that a child has to develop confidence in you not being a buddy. He is not my buddy, he's my son, and he must know that. But he also must know that I love him and that my loving him will give way for him loving me or his parents. So reciprocation is very important; it goes along with, "What I do, I do it not out of selfishness, but I do it out of respect and out of love." I'll give you an example. My education experience has been teaching college, and you know, college students experience a lot of things. I've had many students say to me, "Dr. Bostick, I was at this party, and they were doing thus, and so I left, because my parents are not rich, but they have love in the home, and I will not do anything to bring embarrassment to my parents." When I hear that from an adult college student, I know that in that home there was reciprocity, there was responsibility, there was love, and there was respect. The parents had molded that young man or woman into the adult that we could cherish.

*Jean Bynoe-Singh*

That is something they may have to learn through trial and error. Because you never have to learn that, for instance, if you like someone, it doesn't necessarily mean that person will have to like you. There's no rule saying that because you like me, I must like you, or because I do this for you, you must do this for me. They will have to just learn that through their own mistakes, their own experiences. They would realize that when things are done to them, how they feel, and they would realize that similarly, harm is done to them, how they feel, from that experience, they will know that if you do this to someone, the person will most likely feel the same way you feel. So if you want to make people around you feel happy, well, do good things, then they would want to make you feel good as well. So there is a value in it that when you hurt people, they feel the same way you feel when you are hurt. And if you don't like to feel that way, then don't go about doing it to others, because they may do it back to you and you wouldn't like it.

*Rachel DeFour*

I have to attribute reciprocity to my faith, the doctrine that I was born into, the doctrine of the Universal Hagar's Spiritual Church. One of our beliefs is, "Do unto others as you would have them do unto you." What you think and say is the prophecy of its fulfillment. So I would help my children see when things didn't go their way that was a result of their actions that was a result of how they thought.

They would judge their friends, or something would happen to their friends, and they would talk about their friends, and I would say or my mother used to always say, "Judge ye not, that ye may not be judged." I didn't really understand that until I got older, but I understood it when I had my children and I would point out to them how what they did made this thing happen. When my son was writing graffiti on the school wall and his sister, because of what I had taught them, went and told the principal that it was her brother that had done it, when the principal called me, we went back to the school and we made him clean it up. We made him put on some gloves, and he was there for hours trying to get that graffiti off. We had to use a special kind of solution. He learned from that experience that whatever you do that is disrespectful to property and to people, you have to pay for; you can't blame that on someone outside of yourself.

I always explained to kids who would be making fun of a child, "How would you like to be in that child's position? What if you were Eddie and everybody was standing around and laughing at you because of the mucus coming out of your nose? You had a tissue on you and you didn't give it to Eddie but you just made fun of Eddie?" Those are small examples of how I tried to teach reciprocity. I tried not to talk too much; I tried to live it in front of them, and then when I didn't, they would bring it to my attention, "Mom, you said that we shouldn't do that, and I heard you talking about so and so and so and so." Then I'd own up to it, "You're right, I'm sorry, I really shouldn't have done that. That was not right for me to do that—I apologize to you, and I hope that you will not see me doing that again. I am so sorry I did that." Because they do as they see, I was very selective.

Nowadays, I would say to parents, "You know, it took a lot of time, because I didn't let them look at any show unless I looked at it first. Because all the electronic games—and even now with my grandson—I sit down to look at what he's playing with on his phone or I'm selective with what he does with the computer, and when the programs have a lot of violence and slamming things and killing people, I don't let him look at it again, and I told his father and his mother, "This is not a good game for him to watch because what children see goes into their subconscious." The present TV shows are a mess. They're about lust, drugs, sex, and people doing each other in. Children are seeing this, and this goes into their subconscious. So one of the things I think is very important is that we monitor what we let our children watch until they are able to be responsible and to determine right from wrong themselves.

### Gretel James

You define that as treating people the way you want to be treated. Right—always, always do that. That's a part of respect. Treat people the way you want to be treated. Treat people fairly, respect their rights and their dignities. I don't care who it is; all people deserve to be respected. As mad as people can make you at times, you speak to them with respect, and you treat them with respect, because that is the way you want to be treated. Do unto others.

### Brenda Jones

Typically developing children are attentive to others and develop social behaviors at an early age. Very early on they sense that they are not alone and their action, verbal and nonverbal, can trigger a response from individuals within their milieu. Parents encourage reciprocity by teaching children to take turns, engaging children in meaningful conversations, and teaching children to interact with their peers and others in acceptable ways.

### Linda Hampton

I interpret reciprocity as doing to others as you would have them do unto you. I think reciprocity definitely applies to our parenting style. Parental behaviors influence children's behaviors, whether they are positive or negative. These behaviors can be emotionally charged as well as filled with conflicts. If positive behavior is the goal of good parenting, then we must utilize reciprocity in more intentional ways.

Since reciprocity involves back-and-forth interactions and responses, as parents we must have certain beliefs our children. Our philosophy of children dictates how we treat them. If we think children are to be seen and not heard, our responses will often be negative and dictatorial. If we think children are to be guided and nurtured to reach their full potential, our parental practices will often be positive, encouraging, and more mentoring. I think the reactions we get in either of these thought patterns will coincide with the positive or negative approaches.

My goal as a parent was to raise children to be loving, happy, and well-adjusted, without the nagging, stress, and drama. Did I hit the 100 percent mark? No, but I do feel my adult children are well-adjusted, God-fearing, and focused. I never pursued parenting with the idea of reciprocity as an obvious method. I think we parent the way we were parented. So kudos to my parents and to others who influenced my life.

I think we use reciprocity all the time, but we seem less aware of how, when, and its effects. Thank God I learned along the way, through trial and error and more knowledge of human behavior, that positive reactions beget positive reactions. As my mother would say, you attract more bees with honey. During my parenting journey, I became more conscious of what motivated my children and how they were motivated. My reactions became more "nudges" to elicit good behavior which frequently preempted the bad behavior. Self-awareness begot self-awareness, and self-management begot self-management in me and my children.

Giving children your undivided attention, rewarding good behavior, and consistently practicing loving and disciplined parenting by correcting inappropriate behavior sends a message that they are always loved. The reciprocal effect for me has been children who love me, want to spend time with me, and appreciate how they were raised. I see that being past to my grandchildren. That makes me happy!

I thank God for blessing me to have children, and I never want to take that for granted. There are childless couples and women who would love to be able to bear children. My parenting experience improved me as a person as my children taught me to be more responsible. They helped shape my vision of who I was and my purpose in life. I know without a doubt that my relationship with my children has been truly reciprocal in a positive way. I am so grateful.

*Rev. Jeanie Martinez-Jantz*

I think this is with everybody, that we are interactive as human beings. God created us to be in relationship, and so when you're in a relationship that carries reciprocity, it's interactive. The way I treat you affects how you treat me. Bishop Desmond Tutu talked about the theology of *ubuntu* (humanity)—I am because you are. And that's reciprocity, very much so. I think that is what God was saying to Moses on the mountain when he said, "I am becoming who I am becoming." And God reaches out to interact with us the same way that we then should reach out to interact with others. The way we treat our children is going to be the way they treat us, and the way we want to be treated is the way we should treat them.

The same applies outside of the home. One of the things that I taught my children was that you always treat other people the way you want to be treated, and if someone is harmful to you, you don't accept that, but you also don't give it back. I think that's one of the most serious things I did as a parent was if my kids returned bad for bad, like if one of them hit the other and then the other hit back, they got worse time-outs, and they lost toys. If they just walked away, they said, "Well, I'm not going to be around you if you're going to behave like that." And I use that language too. When I was managing a church nursery, I used that language—"You choose to fight, you choose to hit."

*Lyngrid Smith Rawlings*

One of the quotes that my mother shared was, "There is a destiny that makes us brothers, none goes his way alone, all that we send into the lives of others come back into our own, double force." If you do something hurtful to somebody, that may not come back to hurt you, but it may hurt your children and by hurting your children, it's going to hurt you much more because women are taught to just bear up under whatever it is, just keep going.

That being said, if you know you don't want this to happen to you, then you don't do it to anyone else. You just do unto others as you would have others do unto you. This is not hard. Do you want someone talking to you like that? If not, then why are you talking to them like that? If you disrespect people, they are going to disrespect you. Sometimes what you can do the most to hurt people is just be silent. If they are trying to get you upset and you don't buy into it, after a while they see that you are not going to buy into it and so they leave it alone. I think that's part of what we have to do.

*Denise Thorne*

I think there is a much bigger picture here. The question that you have asked goes beyond the village. What we're talking about here is the influence of the media. When I say media, I don't mean only CNN, NBC, and those places. I mean anything that comes on television, whether it's in the form of a commercial, newscast, or podcasts on the Internet, a webinar, or any of those resources. Kids now have unlimited access to information, and that has taken away control from the parents, because now anything kids need, they can YouTube it or Google it. So parents no longer have control over a lot of things. What I find has happened is that parents have become too dependent on these various sources of media to raise their children, as opposed to understanding what it's doing to the minds of these kids. Now, the one thing that I have observed in my line of work as a caterer delivering food to corporate offices, especially in Washington, DC, is that no matter what happens, how many Internet comes and goes, how many Googles and Apples you have, the traditional approach to corporate management will always prevail. How it gets done is no different from in the past. The Internet will help you—the Internet of things—but every single day, people are being groomed to take over and maintain the traditional approach.

Parents have to understand these things in order to exercise proper restraint with their children; otherwise the kids are going to end up as being a part of the pack, so to speak, with the leaders all the way out there and they're just a part of the pack, marching with the rest of the group, being told what to do and never in a leadership position. That's one of the biggest problems I see with restraint.

# Restraint

## Herman Bostick

Let me first say that when I hear the word *restraint*, I don't know whether that is the word I would use. It might sound a little harsh, in a way. I would say that parents have to set borders. They would have to let the child know, "There are limits over which you, as a child, must not pass. We have rules in this house." Now, in my home, I have a little chart that says, "If you put it down, pick it up." Those were the border lines that we set, and youngsters may resist a bit at first, but as they grow older, they come to appreciate it; they want limits. They want parents to set limits; they don't want their parents to be their buddies. Now I would say to my son's teenagers, "On Saturday night you may be out until twelve midnight, but on a weekday you have to be in the house at eleven o'clock." I also had another limit that was, "If for any reason you get stranded, you call me. I don't care what time of night or morning, you call me." That was an understanding among us. So I think the restraint is that you have to set boundaries, and they have to be clear, and they have to be sensible, and I think you need to explain to the child or young person why these boundaries are important for them, for you and for the family.

## Derek Broomes

You will not find a lack of restraint in a denominational school as in a public school. Let me tell you the reason why it will always be a public school and the reason why parents are moving their children away from public schools and why the public school will always be a failure. The public school is no more than a reform school. For me, you need only focus on the parents involved. As a parent, you may foster good habits in your kids—they won't fight, they won't curse, they won't strike a teacher—but when they go out there to a public school, say, in Harlem or in the Bronx in the gang's presence, and the gang says, "I dare you," and there is bullying and other socially unacceptable behaviors, these behaviors distract from your kids receiving a good public education.

Whatever you may do with your kids at home, how you may counsel them, the home and school have to work in harmony. The parent and teacher have to be interdependent so that when the teacher sees something happening at school, the teacher can always pick up the phone and call the parent, likewise if the parent has concerns. The children know they cannot get away with anything concerning school. They're being watched in a positive way at school and at home, so if they violate a home rule, they also make it into a school rule, and they cannot get away with it. That used to be the old-time philosophy. If a teacher or any neighbor caught you fooling around during school hours or anytime, they would call your parent, and you were in for the consequences. If you were living at home, you got a whipping and you were always watched. One of the things that parents had for checks and balance was corporal punishment. You can't do that nowadays. If your kid goes to school and tell the teacher, you can expect a knock on your door from a police or a social worker and the next thing you know, your career is finished. And so, parents have become very conscious of these rules and have accepted certain societal requirements that somehow were prescribed by law. There should be punishment on the home. It is a difficult situation without those parameters and is one reason why parents have lost control of their kids in disciplining them. The only thing that they have now is to appeal to the kids with reasoning, and for some it works and for some it doesn't.

The results are there, we see it every day—young black men in jail, young Puerto Rican men in jail. Why? Some claim it's because they came from broken homes, but even if their homes are not broken, the street has more influence on them than their parents. How do you prevent that? Then you know there's no immediate answer. You got to get that child into an organization or into activities to divert that focus from doing bad things to doing good things. Mike Tyson, and other kids like him—famous people—what actually saved them was that they channeled that energy into sports. When you are a parent, you've got to reach out to the resources that are available and use them. Teaching the kids at the end respect—respect comes from respecting yourself, respect comes from knowing the consequences of your actions. If you're feeling that your actions have no consequences, then what is the motivation for respect?

*Jean Bynoe-Singh*

Yes. Self-control—that is something that's a little bit difficult. But we could only see the value of self-control when we experience bad consequences from a lack of it. Because if you find that you cannot control your temper, you will always be in trouble. And when you find on the opposite side that when you control your temper, things go well, you will realize that self-control is really good. If you cannot control yourself while eating, then when you're finished eating, you get sick or you hurt yourself in some way, you would learn that you must not be a glutton, that you must have self-control in how you do things.

As a teacher, I responded to children who did not practice restraint by letting them experience the consequences of their behavior. The consequences being certain privileges were taken away, such as favorite things that they liked. They didn't get recess. Sometimes you just let them be in a corner where no one spoke to them for a couple of minutes. Or you let them write why what is happening to them is happening to them, why they are going through the punishment, and how they can correct it.

*Rachel DeFour*

I have a temper. I can blow up in a minute. I tried not to holler at my children—although when they got on my last nerve I did holler at them, and I would say, if you're always hollering at them, then when you raise your voice, they have no respect for it, because you holler all the time. So I would lower my voice and get right up in their face and I'd say it in a quiet manner. They didn't often get spankings, but when they got spankings, I would talk to them before I would spank them and tell them, "You know, this is not acceptable." You cannot run out in the street when I tell you the first time, but when you go to do it the second time, you know, I would punish you or either I would spank you; it depends on just how drastic it was. When I say drastic, if it was real dangerous for them, then I would spank them, then they would pay attention to it because I didn't spank them often.

Another thing is when children see parents lose control. Kids are imitators, and if you don't exercise control over yourself, how are you going to expect them to have control?

*Gretel James*

*Restraint* means controlling your emotions, regarding the tone and regarding the behavior. That comes also from what we speak and what we hear. If the child is hearing the parent being critical of others and making statements like they ought to be whipped or that kind of thing; that's the attitude they're going to carry. So that is a part of respect—restraining yourself and making children aware that there are consequences for every action. If you don't restrain yourself and say the wrong thing, you could get hurt, or hurt somebody else, or cause all kinds of problems. Learn to respect self before you speak or count to ten before you say anything; these help build restraint, and that's so important because children can be impulsive. We can all be impulsive, and that is dangerous. We must exercise restraint by thinking before we act, but we have to teach children that, and they'll find out that it pays off. In the end they'll be glad they didn't say or do certain things.

*Brenda Jones*

Restraint and self-control can be used interchangeably. These terms relate to how well an individual can stop and think before reacting. It is the ability to remain goal-directed, despite the urge to deviate from a given course. Parents help children to develop restraint by setting limits and letting children experience what happens when they do not show restraint or self-control. Parents should also encourage children to delay gratification, to insist they pause before acting, and to think about the consequences of their actions.

*Linda Hampton*

Well, this brings me back to the old times when we knew when to behave in a certain way. We learned that there was a time and a place for everything and things that we might want to do, it was not necessarily a good time to do it. This was also about making good decisions about reacting and how to use those core capabilities of life that cause you to develop the capacity and the skills to master things over time as you interact with people within your environment. So you have to promote a sense of resiliency and consistency so that you're able to develop the more formal executive functions that help you self-regulate, to help you attack the impulses of your behavior so that you always respond appropriately and you know what brings about balance and what causes more stress. Then you can continue to practice behaviors that will have less stressful outcomes, thereby avoiding toxic stress, because you're able to balance out things and you can develop your own rules around new situations, teamwork, managing school, managing work, and managing relationships. Then there's always going to be a balance in terms of what's happening, even in the midst of a storm.

*Rev. Jeanie Martinez-Jantz*

That's a hard one, especially with teenagers. Sometimes I think it's easier to work with young children because they accept what you say. But the concern with young children is, if you tell them use your words, don't use your hands; you're trying to teach them not to act out but to speak out, and then they see an adult acting out and they're puzzled by what's true and what's real. So one of the things you have to do is protect them, especially when they're young from certain kinds of things, like you should not be watching the news with the children in the room right now because there's so much unrestrained, immature behavior of people in our political system and generally on the news. I don't think it's good for young kids; they learn hypocrisy too early that way. For four teenagers, it's hard because they see adults not taking control of situations, especially in our schools. They see adults giving up.

When my daughter started middle school, we were sitting at dinner one evening, and she just sort of sighed and said, "Well, I guess I'm going to have my first fight tomorrow." Her dad and I looked at each other, and we looked at her, and we both said at the same time, "No, you're not." And she said, "Well yeah, you can't stop it. These girls said they were going to jump me on the way to the bus." And I said, "No, they're not." And she said, "Well, it can't be stopped." and I said, "Yes, it can. Where are the administrators, where's the teacher?" She said, "They can't do anything." And I said, "Yes, they can." So the next day I went to school with her, and we sat in the office for two hours until an administrator would talk to us, and I demanded the assistant principal handle this and monitor it and make sure that those children got to the bus safely. Day in and day out, it takes showing children that adults are in control when adults don't want to be. Yes, it's a jungle out there, and we have to show children that they can act with restraint and not be hurt, and the only way to do that is to enforce civil rules of behavior. I think if the adults let things get out of control, you're teaching children not to be restrained.

I think parents and all adults have to be really aware of the messages that we're giving children. If they see us playing first-person shooter video games that are all about mayhem, then they internalize that, and they think that's okay. Some of that may be fun, but we've also got to step back sometimes and say, "Well yeah, that's gross." I think there are a lot of things we can do restraint wise. Last summer I went to the Renaissance festival with a friend of mine. And you know they have the jolts, and they have the show and it's all staged and it's supposed to be giving you a historical view of what competitions like that were like. But this year, it was different, and it was terrifying in a way because they had changed the script and they had the crowds rooting for different sides. Usually, somebody gets knocked off his horse, and if he loses everybody, he gets up says, "Good job," and that's it. But this time they did more of a realistic combat, and when one guy was down, they had the crowd going thumbs-up or thumbs-down to fake kill him or not. And there were these adults near us who were screaming, "Kill him, kill him!" Then this little girl, no more than five years old, started copying the adults, and some not very nice person turned to her and clapped and said, "Good job." We're horrified. Really? What are adults doing praising this type of behavior and teaching a child that this is good?

So I wrote a letter to the festival organizers, and I said, "Look at what you're doing. You're playing into this sort of behavior that we don't want in our society, and I don't think you wanted that. Think about this. If that's the kind of show you want to do, you're going to lose people, because that's creating a very bad world." We have to speak up. We have to model for our children. If I had a child with me, I would have said something, but I know I should have said something anyway. I should have turned and said, "Really, that's not what we want to do." But I didn't, so I didn't take responsibility.

*Lyngrid Smith Rawlings*

If there are considerable financial restraints when raising children that they understand the difference between wants and needs. Everyone needs water, air, food, good shoes, a good mattress, and a safe home. Just about everything else can be considered to be a want. Individuals have choices to make. So teaching your children this difference is very important.

Most of the women that I know practice restraint on a regular basis because most of the people that I associate with have goals in life, and they had goals before they got married. They had goals, and they had children, and they are trying to make sure that their relationship works in the marriage. Once you have children, often you put what you want on the back burner and try to look at what's the overall good of the family, what's going to help everybody else. Sometimes it probably works as a disadvantage to women. Every year I would put on my annual planner each child's name, grade, and age they were for that year and the next five years, because it reminded me of what they were experiencing. So decisions that I made would have to be in the context of the impact they would have on the children, and it got to a point that there was so much that I had invested in the children that when I said *I*, I meant myself and the five children; I was not able to separate myself from the children. Resources were limited, and I had to make sure that everybody's needs were met. I always bought my clothes the same place I bought my kids' clothes. I wasn't one of those parents who bought my clothes at a high-end store and bought the kids clothes at a cheaper store. It took a lot of self-control and restraint and trying to make sure that things worked as you managed the time, energy, effort, and money. When my youngest son was in the seventh grade, a former grade school classmate was the first person killed during that year. My last born had become unmanageable, and I was afraid that if he remained with me in Washington, DC, he would get himself killed, so I sent him to St. Thomas, Virgin Islands, to live with his father.

My oldest son went to West Point, so there was no tuition for me to pay for him. I had started saving for my children's education when they were very young. At that time interest rates were good, so I used their college savings accounts augmented by my salary to pay half of the girls' tuition. For several years, three of my children were matriculating at universities, which put quite a financial strain so a considerable amount of self-control was required. I reminded my children of my mantra, "First degree debt free. I'm not borrowing any money for your degree. I'll pay half of your tuition for four years." One of my children asked, "Suppose it takes us five years?" My response was, "I'm paying for four. That's what I'm willing to do; so you have to finish in four years or pay for whatever it takes for you to graduate. "I think that's how they get to know who they were. It took me a while to have children, and once I started, I continued until I was finished, and then I made sure I had no more. My first was born in 1971, followed by the next in 1972, the next in 1974 and the last in 1977, when I was two and a half months pregnant with my last child, my sister passed, and we adopted her son who is seventeen days younger than my second child. So once they started going off to college, I was in the tuition paying mode. Even to this day, I cannot comprehend how I managed, but I did not borrow any money.

*Denise Thorne*

You also have to teach your kids when to walk away from situations. We have to give them the tools so they understand how to use it, and by tools, I mean knowing when to look at the situation and say you know what this is not a good situation for me. And there is nothing wrong with walking away from a situation. You always have to assess what the effects are going to be if you respond in a certain way versus if you respond a different way. And if it is not to your advantage, if it's not in keeping with your goals and aspirations in life, there is nothing chicken about walking away from that situation. And those are some of the things we have to teach our children.

This business of "dissin" (disrespect), I think that's such a mis-used word. I don't think people really know what it means anymore. If someone says something to you that you don't like you have to be able to either talk about it sensibly or sometimes tell yourself that this is just not worth the way things are going to go. Above all, I think if you maintain a certain community, then things tend to be the same within that community. It's when you step out of the community—and sometimes you have to, but oftentimes you don't have to step out of the community. You could start off school in a certain place—I'll use that as an example—go all the way to a PhD and never enter an environment that's not conducive to your lifestyle, I've seen it happen time and time again.

As parents, you also have to exercise restraint when it comes to your own personal self. Your wants, not needs, but wants—if you are able to say to yourself, "You know what, I want those red bottom shoes, but it's going to cost me a thousand dollars, but I can take those thousand dollars, and buy a violin and give this child a year's violin lessons, which will put his mind set in a different place." That's what you have to do.

Parents have given up their control, but it doesn't have to be this way. I'm on the outside looking in at corporate America. With my job, we deliver food every day to corporate America, and you see the stress and the pressures that people are under to either perform or to not miss work. And so the marketing folks out there have created a very aggressive and vibrant platform to accommodate children whose parents don't have the time—and they don't have the time because they don't want to, the conditions of society are forcing them that way. It's easier for them to give the child a cell phone with the candy crush game on it, or something like that. The child engages in that even as they're eating dinner, later and later at night. Everybody's mom comes home and is on Facebook. Facebook has taken over the lives of human beings to the point you ask yourself, "Is this a college-educated person that's on Facebook and putting everything on there? Do you really understand how all this information is being used against you?" It's too late now, the horse is out the barn, but at the same time, if we understand how these things are affecting us, and then we would exercise better control. But the idea is for us to not understand how these things work so that we don't think about it.

We'll never find CBS or NBC or CNN putting out a documentary on how Facebook and Google affect you. Never. You'll have to watch PBS, but PBS is nerdy, nobody wants to be associated with that, so you don't watch it. But I'm talking about the public image of the masses. I live on PBS, and I had to make that choice. We just have to make that choice, but our thinking has become skewed; we're no longer thinking on our own. We have all these gadgets that are thinking for us, and we don't understand that we are slowly but surely giving up our responsibility for thinking for ourselves.

If you look at what has happened in society today, you'll realize that so many things have become acceptable. But it all comes down to education. If you are learned, if you know what is happening, if you educate yourself about the hostile environment that surrounds you and what has happened to you, you can take action. But if in the spare time you have, you spend two or three hours on Facebook, how are you going to educate yourself?

# Chapter 3

# Elders Express Concerns Regarding the Four Rs

Do you see in today's world, anything in the areas of respect, responsibility, restraint, and reciprocity that cause you any concern?

*Herman Bostick*

Oh yes, I do see things that cause me concern. In so many cases there is no borderline, there is no restraint; it's dangerous to me, and that gives me a lot of concern. And also there's another concern in modern families, and that is the way some parents speak to their children. I have heard parents in public use language that I would not use even to myself, much less to a child. When parents speak that way to a child, what can we expect from the child? So yes, that gives me great concern, and sometimes I have to restrain myself so as not to say something to the parent about this, because that may not be very helpful. There is one other thing. You can't let television raise your child, and I see that too much. You can't let the cell phone raise your child; that bothers me a lot. You know, children come home, and they are on their cell phones; they don't know how to converse or to talk intelligently in a conversation. Everything is technology. Everything is wired up that that bothers me. Because then you are building a society that is disconnected—I have no empathy for you, because I don't know you, I know Instagram, I know Facebook.

That's not good. I see that too much and that gives me a lot of concern about modern parents.

*Gloria Clanton*

I get concerned when I see the parents in the grocery store with their little children, sometimes even cursing at the little children, telling them in very vulgar terms, be quiet or, you know, stop running around or whatever. When I was in the school system, there were kids, who rather than the parents supporting them, they were the head of the family, especially the boys, telling the parent—the mother—what to do. So yes, you can find instances where you can be very concerned about what is happening, like the violence we are seeing. I think this comes from the way that the parents have not been there to teach their children Christian values, or just plain values of living good lives. Many times parents take up for the children who are doing the wrong things, rather than realizing that the child needs help of some kind. The bullying some children experience is a terrible thing that has very sad results for the children being bullied, and the child that's doing it has some type of a problem; otherwise they wouldn't be doing it in the first place.

Another example is a little girl I know who makes up tales, and we can tell that she's not telling the truth and is trying to live in a fantasy world. I think her older sisters realize it, but I wonder if their father does, and if he's doing anything about it. There are children in this world who you can say that their parents are not parenting them correctly, but you are leery about speaking to the parents about it.

*Gretel James*

I see things in today's world in the areas of respect, responsibility, restraint, and reciprocity that cause me concern. I am really disturbed and don't know what to do about it. I talk about it all the time. I see children not having respect for themselves, for anybody's property, or for other people; it's a widespread problem. They just don't know how to speak to each other, and there was a time when children did show respect when they spoke or interacted with adults. Nowadays, kids say anything to adults and do anything too. So yes, there is definitely a gross lack of respect among young people today and all that leads to greater problems. It's unfortunate. We have a high incarceration rate among young people because they commit crimes without impunity; they behave without impunity because they have not learned to respect anybody, and a lot of times that comes out of the home where parents say. If he hits you, hit him back; I'm going up there and tell that teacher off—that's what they're hearing a lot. Some words are too often spoken in homes, such as, "I'm gonna whip her—," "I'm gonna knock the—out of her." This is what they hear from parents a lot of times, as well as seeing adults attacking other adults if they try to chastise their children today.

When we were kids growing up, adults other than our parents could have talked to us. But we can't do that now, even with the children we are charged to teach. Some parents may get defensive and respond with statements like, "What you say? My child said that? I'm gonna do this or that to you," and saying that in front of the children.

As a teacher, I witnessed that in the classroom. As a matter of fact, on a Friday, I was leaving school and I stopped by my mailbox and I had a note, so I said, "Well, when I get home, I'll call this parent. I'm not going to make her wait all weekend. I called and got cursed out like I never heard before, about something that wasn't true that I had taken the child's jacket." So yes, I witnessed what parents saying that teachers lied about their children and what they would do to the teachers. When children know parents will stand up for them when they're wrong, they get even worse.

*Brenda Jones*

These four *R*s seemingly are less obvious in today's children than they were say fifty years ago. Many of today's parents have a more relaxed disciplinary style. Rather than assuming an authoritarian role, they prefer to have more of a partnership relationship with their children. Parents frequently establish rules and limits, but then make the mistake of not enforcing them. This leads children to believe it is not necessary to acknowledge authority, exercise restraint, take responsibility for their behavior, or show respect for their parents.

*Linda Hampton*

There are lots of messages that our children get nowadays within our society. They get messages that it's okay to do certain things such as being intolerant, not thinking, not being able to put yourself in someone else's shoes. It seems the emphasis now is me, myself, and I. I don't go outside of myself to try to assess how other people feel, in order to make society better, or for actually becoming better adults in a productive system. It bothers me that we tend to be so close-minded and intolerant of others, that we risk negating those good qualities we could develop as individuals. I see young people who, as they are growing up, don't have a sense of responsibility, or habits they need to be successful. They don't get the kind of academic guidance and support that they need and all those tend to be real risk factors when it comes to their development and to their parenting. Parenting is not just for parents. It includes those institutions and individuals that we have invited to have an influence in our children's lives, but there seems to be a disconnect, as this doesn't always give the children the kind of support that they need to ameliorate the risk factors that get in the way of their optimum development.

*Lyngrid Smith Rawlings*

I'm very concerned about the way our world is going and the way people are dealing with their own responsibilities. If you can't afford something you can't afford it, and the idea that we have can charge so much on credit cards keeps individuals in debt. It is not just individuals who are in debt, but also our nation is in very serious debt. We borrow money to spend it on what we want now, with little thought of how we are going to pay it off later. We don't plan for the future. I know my children won't have as good a retirement as I have; one of the reasons is because they are self-employed and are not saving enough for when they senior citizens. I'm not saying that's all debt is bad, but I am concerned about my country that's in debt and individuals that are in debt. I think a lot of young people are not having children and they're not planning to have children; it's just that they spend so much time getting higher degrees which means that they have so much college debt, which becomes a kind of indirect birth control. By the time they feel they're financially secure, their biological clocks have passed, and they are no longer able to have children. This decreasing birth rate could mean that our society is aging, and it causes me to ponder, there will be enough young people to ensure that there will be enough young people to sustain the economy of our country.

I am concerned about the level of violence that's going on all over the world, the whole issue of unregulated gun purchases, not providing mental health care for those who need counseling; these concerns coupled with the raising rate of unemployment, PTSD from so many former military personnel, toxic political climate, and white nationalism. These issues coupled with the broken criminal justice and biased immigration system is most concerning. I'm concerned about the impact that's going to have. Plus, the middle class is being eroded. Growing up we knew that if we did A, B, and C, we would live better lives than our parents, but now with the sum of their college debt, and the rapidly changing job market, young people don't have that type of assurance anymore.

Neither our nation nor the world is dealing with the negative impact that our habits are having on the environment. More people are becoming enlightened, but I'm not sure that it will be enough. But I am becoming more concerned about the impact on my grandchildren than my children because all my children are in their forties now. I am concerned about how the world is going to work then. I want us to start now to make it a better place, but now most people are only focusing on the short-term impact it has on them, not the future. Instead of people relating to one another in person, they are communicating on their cell phones and the Internet. They have many ways of communicating, but some of these ways do not enhance facilitate interpersonal relationships. A lot of the Facebook connections are not really relationships, those are just little snippets of things, and where are the people who will be with you when times get bad? A lot of people are not developing long-term relationships, and that's why we have so many problems with drugs, suicide, and depression. We have so many gadgets which could make things better, but those gadgets are not substitutes for close personal relationships.

So many young people who are successful work so many hours that they don't have time to develop their personal lives, and as they get older, it will not be about the number of hours they worked that will be important, it will be the quality of the relationships they have with those that they love. So I am concerned about trying to create situations where we can get together and have more fun with people of all ages, talking, sharing, laughing, and seeing how we can make our community, our country, and our world better places for everyone. This is the direction where we need to be headed.

*Denise Thorne*

Of course, I see many things that cause me concern. Stephen Hawkins was such a great predictor of things. I saw a documentary in which he said there are five things that need some restraint, and the Internet was one of them, and he went on to outline why it needs to be restrained, and I totally agree with him. He made a lot of sense, and some of the things I mentioned earlier are some of the things he talked about. I console myself sometimes by saying this is probably part of the evolutionary process.

I think understanding all the aspects of living and life should help a parent better position a child, because you can then explain to the child and help the child at a young age to understand the things that are happening and not wait until they turn eighteen, and they go to college, then all of a sudden the stuff hits them, or they're not in an environment where they're not exposed to all these changes and why and how or being a part of it because that's another thing.

We do deliveries to a lot of tech startup companies. Ninety percent of them have no blacks working there, none, not even the receptionist. The other 10 percent may have one, two, or three people of color. Interestingly, when you go in there and the black staff sees you, they gravitate to you and you discover nine out of ten times, the come from another country or their parents are from another country. We have to help our kids understand what's out there and how they can be a part of it, because one thing I know for sure, the days of keeping people out because of various reasons are slowly fading away. I say that because if you have a project that you're working on and here comes this black kid with the understanding and the brains and the knowledge, you're not going to turn that child away because he's black. You're going to bring him onboard. But that child coming onboard needs to understand how they can negotiate their way. If they don't understand those things, that's when they get used, but if they can understand how to negotiate their way into the process or through the process, they will get ahead. And parents can teach the young adults these things by themselves being aware of the process. I'm not saying you mustn't have fun, or you can't have any form of recreation, but at the same time you've got to keep up and understand what it is you're dealing with.

# Ten Things Elders Are Concerned about Regarding the Four *R*s in Today's World

- Parents who do not establish standards or limits for their children and let their children do whatever they want to do without any restraints
- The negative, derogatory manner in which some parents speak to their children, especially in public places
- The overdependence on the television, cell phone, and other devices to keep children entertained and occupied, thereby creating a breakdown in people-to-people communication and children not acquiring relationship-building and other social skills
- The violence in our communities that is likely linked to children not acquiring the knowledge and values necessary to deal with their anger and frustration in more socially acceptable ways
- Children not demonstrating respect for self, others, and property, and parents not doing anything to remedy these situations, rather, some parents say and do things that create or escalate these situations
- Parents making rules and setting limits and not following through with implementing them
- Children not receiving needed academic guidance and support in the home, thereby placing them at risk for academic failure

- Irresponsible money management and the creation of debt by families and our country and the impact of these situations on the future of our children and young adults
- The need for focused dialogue about what we can do to make our communities, country, and world better places for everyone, but most important, the children
- The negative messages children receive from society and the lack of consistent support to help them deal effectively with risk factors that are barriers to their optimal development

# CHAPTER 4

# Elders Provide Parenting Advice

What practical parenting advice do you have for twenty-first-century parents?

*Herman Bostick*

I'm talking about young couples. I advise them to communicate one with the other in an honest fashion. Communicate about every aspect of life and especially about finances. Communicate clearly so that each will understand the other's priorities, then they come to a consensus because that will be important in bringing up the child. If one parent is concerned about status, that's what he or she is going to make important, and the spouse may not see that as important. That's an important thing for me.

I know there are parents who do not do this, but I recommend that parents find a church and be a part of it. The church can do so much for you that even in the home where you do every positive thing we talked about, there is a missing link there that the church can fill. The church can fill this link—your life is not going to be a bed of roses. It's true that despite how much money you earn and how many degrees you have, life is not going to be a bed of roses. The church can give us that ethos, that strength to face the difficulties we are going to have in life somewhere along the way. That is what the church does. So bring the child up in the church. That's what I strongly advocate.

I'm being practical that this is what you need when things go sour. What you learn at home certainly will help, and what you learn in school certainly will help, but there is this thing that you get in the church that you hear, that "I am with you even to the end of the ages." You need that. I'm talking about once you're an adult. If you were brought up in the church, even though you might have strayed away—I've watched kids do this. They go to college, and they do not come back to church, but when they get to adulthood they come back, because they have something there that they know, that they got when they were growing up, that there is a group of people there who are going to embrace them with the word and who are going to help them through. So that's the gap that I think I would recommend. In this modern age, we think we can look at nature and all that, but I advise parents to bring the children to church and offer them to God.

*Derek Broomes*

Well, I think once you have children, because of the economic factor most parents have got to work. Single parents, parents that are together, mother and father, they have to work, sometimes two jobs. And both parents have to help with the housework. Now the babysitter takes over. Before it was the latchkey when the kids come home and they got the entire apartment to themselves until the mother and/or the father got home after six, so they got a lot of time, and this is where you find the emergence of some of the government programs, some of the social services programs. The hours between three and six are dangerous hours for school kids, especially those school-age kids who have nothing to do. So the advice that I have to offer, aside from the economics which is a reality, is that every spare time you get, spend it with your children. Some people want to be parents, but they also want to be free. They want to be doing the things they were doing as teenagers and leave the kids at some relatives or someplace, never finding time for the kids. When the kids' homework is too difficult, neither the mother nor the father checks it. And the cell phone makes it worse. Put down that cell phone, turn off the cell phone, and sit down with your kids, and ask them, "What did you do today?" Make them feel that they could come to you for the worst of things that happened in their life or happened in your life. When they meet their first love interest, let them know they could come to you. You as the parent, as the mother, talk to your daughter, tell her all the things she needs to know. Tell her what happened to you. They'll learn from that, let them know, be personal. As a father, talk to your son; mother, talk to your son; father, talk to your daughter. What are the challenges that face them out there? Don't shelter them from these challenges.

Don't be timid to go talk to your pastor, priest, or church leader. If you make confessions or you go to confession or you're telling the priest all these personal things about you—your marriage or who you may go with, then why is it so difficult to tell your priest about your child, your teenage daughter, your teenage son, the difficulty you're having? Why not bring your kids to church? Sit down one-on-one with the priest, the father, or whoever is the counselor. Let them feel that God is not the enemy, keeping them away from the church is not an achievement. You don't have to spend two to five hours every day or whatever. Try to have a conversation with God, a relationship in terms of asking will you guide me, you brought me success to this juncture—I need for you to do the same. And if you don't believe in anything, who do you believe in? What do you believe in? Who do you believe in that will not fail you? Man will fail you. Parents fail children. Children fail parents, so you have to have somebody there that is infinite that would not let you down. And that is something you have to be constantly seeking, because there are too many things out there that can lead you and your children astray.

You may not have all the answers. You may only be able to offer hypotheses for contemporary issues, but have the conversation. It's an evolving, symbiotic relationship between children and parent, and the only way you could help them is to listen to them, spend time getting their thought processes, and when it becomes too difficult, you need to figure out if there are other resources available to you. I always revert back to the church because that's why you're here. When you don't fulfill that role, you too shall be damned.

*Rachel DeFour*

Spend quality time with your children. I don't mean having your children around when you are spending time with others. I mean spend one-on-one time with your children and always listen to what they have to say. When they're talking, pay attention to them, and do that on a consistent basis.

You don't have to give your children everything they want. I traveled a lot for my job, and I brought things back for my kids, but I didn't give to my children because I went out on travel and was bringing something back. If I brought something back, it was because they needed it. I didn't buy all the up-to-date games and stuff; they had to play with pots and pans and make things to play with in the household. I didn't buy all the brand names, because then kids begin to have expectations and think that the world owes them something and that they don't have to earn anything. If you have two children, don't allow anyone to favor one child over the other child. I always made my children share. If somebody gave one something, if it was something that both of them could benefit from, I made them share. Another thing I always told them was to look out for each other, and I gave my older child the responsibility of looking out for his younger sister.

Don't let the TV raise your children. Read to your children, take them to museums, show them how to respect things in their homes, keep your homes clean. Sometimes you go into some homes and they're filled with garbage and dirt that you see all around the house—why do you think the children will be any different when they go out? Remember that things like cursing and littering the streets and neighborhoods start in the home. Children do what they see. Be the example for your children.

*Gretel James*

It's important how you talk to your child. Do you speak gently, or do you speak harshly? Do you speak with vulgar language, or do you speak with clean language? It goes back to being an example for your child. If your child gets a bad report whether at school, at church or wherever, don't be so quick to judge, for example, the teacher who has criticized your child or called them out on something, particularly in front of the child. The child has due process, but there are two sides to every story. Don't just take your child's story. I also think parents could talk about God in their homes. They don't even really have to know the Bible to talk about God. We all know God is a higher power and that he created us. They can talk about God and what God would expect of us. However, if parents are going to say that to the child, they also have to believe it and live it, they have to do what is right and good in the household.

Regarding parents as role models and the ones setting the example, nowadays I don't think a lot of parents know any better than what they are doing because that's what they lived for a few generations. They don't have the community that we knew in earlier times where everybody lived together whether you were professional or nonprofessional and it was like the rising tide lifted all the boats. But now we don't have this type of community; we have communities of people with lower resources who can't help each other, and that creates just generation after generation of problems. Many parents in these communities really don't know how to raise their children, but they love their children. Now one thing I've found, all parents love their children, but they don't always know the best way to love them. They love them by showering them with expensive clothes and shoes even when they can't afford it, and they value things more than spirituality and education, moral character, and that kind of thing.

Change is not going to happen for these parents unless there's a concerted effort with some legal backing to educate parents. They need to be educated and taught things like how to manage money and how to cook a healthy meal. I see a lot of fast food. I go to the store, and I see the basket piled up with frozen dinners, and I've had frozen food—it's gone in thirty minutes and I'm hungry again. Plus, it's all that unhealthy chemicals, and whatever they put in there to preserve it. So our lower-income parents need a lot of education as to how to parent, what's important versus what is not. It's a difficult job, because if you've lived in poverty and struggled, throughout life, things like Nikes or Jordan shoes make you feel like somebody. But we want parents and children to learn you'll feel like somebody when you behave properly, when you try to learn, when you help others rather than hurt others, when you speak well, guard what comes out of your mouth, strive to be a good student—it doesn't matter how poor you are, you can do those things. Because if it were not so, there wouldn't be a successful black person. We've come through the struggle of poverty, depravation, discrimination, but had a set of values—our first value was a belief in God, so we weren't allowed to do and say anything, and education was stressed as a way to a better life. And the parents are not offering that now because they didn't get it, and they really don't know. A lot of things we see children doing now could be because they really don't know any better.

*Brenda Jones*

Parents should limit and monitor the time children spend watching television, texting, talking on phones, and exploring the Internet. It is imperative parents bring back the human aspect of parenting. Technological devices are barriers to social engagement, as children and adults spend more time interfacing with their devices rather than with each other. Physical contact, i.e., hugs, kisses, pats on the back, and verbal communication help to strengthen the human bond between child and parent.

*Linda Hampton*

First of all, I think you have to want children. Please don't have children if you don't want them. But once you have children, your relationship with them is going to be a wonderful thing if you allow it to be. I think you have to be loving. You have to emulate certain behaviors because they are integrated into how your children will develop. As parents, being supportive, being present, being in the moment with your children—all are important. Young parents now have to be adaptable because things are changing so much. Sometimes you have to stop and think about the reasons behind certain behaviors.

Instead of always punishing, discipline with love. Create guidelines and stick to them, but also allow your children to have choices and hold them accountable. Consistency with rules is important, and some rules should be nonnegotiable.

Of course, respect is important. You have to teach your children what that means, and you have to have conversations about what your expectations are and why they are important, why you have these expectations, and how there are some things that you're never going to hear about because they don't change, but you should respect your children's opinions and listen to them but know that you the parent and you have the vision and there are some things they could never know; therefore, they have to trust you. In order to be trusted, you have to be trustworthy.

*Rev. Jeanie Martinez-Jantz*

Get outside, play, do real-world things with your families and eat dinner together. Studies show, and it's really true, regular family mealtime is crucial. Yes, it's hard, but even if that means putting off your kid's bedtime, and eating dinner at 7:00 p.m., because nobody gets home earlier, it's really important. Family time together is one of the most important things.

The second most important thing is to build into every day some real world experiences. Get outside, don't just do homework. Take a walk. Play a game and laugh together. Tell stories together, joke together, because if you take every day too seriously, the kids are going to be grown and gone before you had any fun.

*Lyngrid Smith Rawlings*

One thing about the computer is that knowledge is doubled, tripled, or quadrupled much quicker than when I was growing up. Now we must teach young people how to think, not what to think, how to make intelligent fact based choices, how to listen to what is said, and how to interpret the silences. We must teach them from a very young age how to read the situation they're in and how to become socially aware, how when you walk down the street and you feel that it's not a safe place, to choose another direction. We have to teach them to manage their time and money, how to work with people, how to develop relationships with people, and how to become active listeners questioning the validity of what is said, and not to think that because they have a lot of Internet friends, some of those people may not have their best interest at heart. We have to teach them how to make better decisions.

At a very young age, boys and girls are being introduced to sexually explicit information. Long before young children understand who they are as human beings, they are being introduced to sexual activities which can significantly impact their lives. This interest is often stimulated by information they receive on television, over the Internet, via Facebook, twits, or other media. I understand that young people are interested in learning about sex, but it is very important for people to discover who they are and what is important to them before they allow someone else to define themselves in terms that meet their needs and not what is beneficial to the individual. It is important that young people learn to set boundaries for their behavior and that they understand the impact that their decisions have on their future. There are a lot of negative influences in the world, and parents need to share their values with their children when they are young to talk about the implications and consequences of their behavior. Often parents would prefer to be friends instead of role models for their children. Helping children set their goals and develop pathways to achieving those goals are essential aspects of responsible parenting.

It is also important to ensure that our children engaged in meaningful activities which gives them purpose and a sense of direction in life. When I was growing up being a Girl Scout gave my life meaning, purpose, and a sense of responsibility for myself, my community, and the world. There are many different ways that people can pursue their dreams in ways that makes the world a better place. We can teach our children how to develop family budgets, and we can get them involved in cooking with us and teach them fractions as a part of it. We need to spend more time with family and friends instead of acquiring more things. Saying I have X number of games and X number of apps on my computer is not enough; it is our relationships with family and friends that keeps us going when things are really bad.

Parents can take their children to cultural events and spend time with them. It's the time you spend with them, not the money you spend on them that's more important. If all you do is spend money on your children, and fail to spend time with them, then someone with more money could lure them away from you. Think about it!

*Denise Thorne*

Parents, have discussions with your children, because oftentimes they're more in tune with the good and bad things than you are. The goals that you've set for them, especially if they are honorable goals, but sometimes kids will come up with stuff that you didn't even think about.

When our children were growing up, my husband and I used to have what we called "family night" every Sunday night. That was the children's opportunity to give their opinions and their thoughts, and if they thought that Mom and Dad were not doing something, or did something that was unreasonable, wasn't fair, wasn't right or was a good thing, that was their opportunity to tell us. But there were conditions. They couldn't be rude about it. They had to convey whatever it was that they wanted to convey in a civil manner and give everybody a chance to speak. Everyone had to listen to what everyone else had to say and to respect everyone's opinion even if they didn't agree with it. We taught them that everyone has an opinion, and that's their opinion. They may learn from it, so have an open mind. Not because they see the sky is blue and white, it means there's no yellow or green in it. You have to be open-minded.

# CHAPTER 5

# Elders Offer Advice on Supporting Parents

How can parents get the support they need in raising their children? Some parents may need support. As I look around, I see many parents needing support.

Does the federal government have a responsibility for supporting parents in raising their children?

Does the church have a responsibility to support parents in raising their children?

*Herman Bostick*

There are areas in which the government can help. I think the federal government needs to look at helping families in need and also there ought to be state and county support, not handouts. I'm not talking about welfare. I'm talking about sound, supportive programs with parents who are rearing children and whose income is not what it ought to be to make a comfortable home for these children. We pay taxes, and the government ought to be responsible for seeing that parents have what they need.

I went to Nova Scotia a few years ago and to Canada, and I was told that they don't have homeless people. The government sees that everybody has a home; the government sees that everybody has medical support. Parents shouldn't have to worry about what if their children get sick. In a country like this we ought to make those services available. We ought to also make it available for parents to ensure their children get a first-rate education without breaking the bank of the parent. That's a disgrace in this country. It's a disgrace, and this is a responsibility of the government, both federal and state, and also local.

*Rachel DeFour*

I think that we need to provide more parent training. A lot of the parents are having babies at thirteen. They're kids, they're not responsible, and they're not ready for that. A lot of what's happening with our kids have to do with the parents, society, the school systems, not treating them fairly and not giving them the things they need. They're not getting it at school, and they're not getting it at home. When we were segregated in school, the teacher was as important as the parent in giving instructions and correcting the children, and showing them responsible behavior. Even now, I'll say to young ladies when I hear them out in the street cussing, "Oh, baby, I know you got better vocabulary than that." My kids say to me, "Mom, they can hurt you—you should stop that."

And you know, she might cuss me too, but I'll go on if I think she's that violent. We as a nation feel it's not our responsibility, but I still think that we need to have more of the concept that it takes a village to raise a child, and when we see things in children in our neighborhoods, things that we can do to help them, I feel as though we need to be doing more of that.

I do believe that the government should be involved. I definitely feel as though, even in community centers, there needs to be more parenting classes. In the school system, there should be classes for the teenagers that are having babies and coming back to school and the grandparents are raising the babies. There need to be classes on child-rearing, the importance of bearing children and the importance of the formative stages of development. I do believe that this should be done in the home as well.

*Gretel James*

The government can do more as well to support families. But the government is headed by white people, and I still say welfare is designed to keep you back, so they're not holding anybody accountable. So black youth are often miseducated and incarcerated, and others make money off their incarceration. We have to demand more from the government too. We have to demand more.

One more thing I want to say about my own children is, they were easy to raise because they were gentle spirits. Even though I laid down the law, they just towed the line pretty much. Some parents may have children who are challenging and difficult to raise even for the best intentioned parents. It isn't that these parents don't do all that is good and right, but that there is something innately wrong with the child.

*Brenda Jones*

Parents need to access resources—other parents, school personnel, books, workshops, Internet, etc.—to help them put in place parenting strategies that are in the best interest of the child.

In addition, the government can promote child welfare and child protection by clarifying the legal obligations and rights of parents and children and providing assistance and safety nets which ensure the financial viability of parents, i.e., food stamps, childcare, housing, adult education.

*Linda Hampton*

I think parents don't get enough credit for the skills, knowledge, and abilities that they have, because we often treat them like property. In my own research, I saw that parents had just an enormous amount of knowledge about school readiness and what they wanted their children to know, to learn, and to do and what they needed to do on their own with their children, like spending time with their children, reading to their children, and being involved with their children. Even though that didn't apply to a majority of the parents, there was a significant number of parents who had a greater awareness of what they needed to do. But there were also a number of parents who came from environments where it was very difficult to overcome.

Poverty was the basis of almost everything that inhibited children and parents from being the best that they could be. There were food desserts in the midst of plenty. Even though we say parents are the foundation for what we do, we've gotten away from giving parents what's good for their children or listening to them. We tend to think we can fix them in some way regardless of their exposure to certain mental factors. My research showed there were parents who were exposed to risk factors, including being single-parent families, and their children were still able to have a good sense of who they were and were most likely to succeed. They were able to develop those resilient abilities to bounce back from negative experiences because they had competent functioning parents who were able to be examples of what it meant to be able to overcome adversity.

*Rev. Jeanie Martinez-Jantz*

Parents do not get the support they need. Where do I start? First of all, societies all know that families are crucial toward the building of society's well-being, and so the society has to take responsibility and support parents. If you have created a world where both parents have to work, then you as a society have to take responsibility for providing quality childcare experiences because children should not just be on their own. This society needs to make sure the schools are there to teach children. Parents are there to parent. Parents are not teachers. They are parents; let them be parents. I think parents need to quit pushing their children to be the brightest and the best. One of the things I've seen a lot is that parents are so desperate for scholarships that they have their kids in five different sports, six different college prep programs, and eight different STEM programs. And the kids are so busy; they don't have time to just be human beings. Make them pick one. If they don't like it, they have to stick with it a year, and then they can change. That teaches responsibility; it teaches how to make decisions and live with them even if you don't like them. When you do that, you're teaching the child to respect themselves enough to learn when to say no, how to budget their time and how to have downtime. And again, soccer is just a game. Football is just a game; treat it like a game, enjoy it. Most of the kids that I've seen who have played sports and have been in travel teams and so on in order to get a college scholarship. As soon as they get to college, they quit that sport because they're done with it. It wasn't fun.

In saying that society must support parents, I think that governments have this responsibility. First of all, I believe in universal health care because nobody can take care of children or raise decent, productive human beings if they're sick, if they can't get access to good medical care. And that's one of the things that really stratifies our society. Families should have liberal family leave programs because if a child is sick, they should not be in school. If they have a runny nose, they should not be in school. They need to be at home getting well, and doctors know that the pressures on parents, that parents have to work, and so they'll tell them to give the kids antibiotics for twenty-four hours, and then they can go back to school because they're not infectious. While they may not be infectious, they're not giving those children's bodies time to get well. So we need legislated family leave programs, and we need to support businesses so that they can afford to do it.

There are so many things that as a society, as governments, we can do to take responsibility for these children that we expect to grow up and pay into our Social Security system, and yet we're not treating them well. We're not giving them the opportunity to grow up and do that, and yet we want to take from them. I think finding ways to do on-site day care at work will be really helpful to parents. Studies show that parents perform better in the workplace, their relationship with their children is better, and the children are happier when they have on-site day care. That's one thing that will be amazing to support parents.

*Lyngrid Smith Rawlings*
Parents are responsible for raising their children. If grandparents live close to their grandchildren, and are willing to be spend time with their grandchildren, then both parents and children will be blessed with having older, loving adults offering a more seasoned

perspective on life. If there are no grandparents close by, you may be able to find older responsible adults who have similar values so you can share their ideas and provide you with good advice to pass their values to the younger generation.

There are a wide variety of programs that the federal government should provide to ensure that families have the needed resources to raise strong children. The federal government has a responsibility to develop, support, and enhance programs which positively impact the development of young people and strengthen families. Some of these programs should ensure that universal physical and mental health care is available and affordable for all people. Other programs should focus on providing quality universal free education from preschool to preschool to community college. Affordable housing programs can ensure that more families can afford to live in comfortable homes. The federal government can provide incentives for businesses to increase the number of entry level and upward mobility programs which will help more people to earn a living wage. The federal government can develop more family friendly immigration programs valuing more diverse programs. It's time to turn things around and become what we were mean to be. Young people are our future; we have to do better.

*Denise Thorne*

We really need to go back to the village because that's how you learn. You can't rely on what you read on Facebook; you can't rely on everything you read on the Internet because a lot of it is fake news. You can't rely on everything that is on the TV. Sometimes you just have to get back to the times when the parents will gather the children in the living room and talk about the issues and how to solve them in conjunction with the resources that are available out there. Don't get me wrong. The Internet is not a bad thing; Facebook is not a bad thing. How you use them is really what makes the difference. You just have to be vigilant.

The community and the church have a role in supporting families, and the government should be a part of it too because they're all interconnected. But more and more now we can't rely on the government to do everything. We have to be vigilant of the government too; you have to pay very close attention to what they're doing and saying.

The government has a major responsibility in terms of passing legislation and creating policies that will actually support children and families. I'm thinking particularly about law and order, because we need law and order; we just can't allow people to go crazy or run wild. The government needs also to better control the Internet. There are websites that push fake news and advertise products. Many of us, including our children, believe the false information on the Internet, and few of us check this information before we forward it to others. These websites make a lot of money from advertisers. We need to ferret out all the nonsense that's out there, and the government has a role to play in controlling the flow of false, unreliable, and damaging information into our homes.

# CHAPTER 6

# Elders Share Their Views on the Role of the Church in Supporting Parents

Does the church have a responsibility to support parents in raising their children?

*Herman Bostick*

Yes, but that's going to be a little tricky in a way. The church offers church school, and it offers young adults opportunities in leadership. There is church school, then as children grow up, they move into the youth group. The church also has the responsibility for integrating them into the total worship of the church. There ought to be a program for that. The church should also offer counseling. Some churches have a youth minister, and his or her responsibility is to fill that gap. All churches do not have the finances to do that, but any church can offer activities for the spiritual development through children and youth activities and also follow the students even when they go away to college. For instance, if a student is going away to college and he's a Methodist, the church should advise him of a Methodist church near the college. This is something that some churches do, and yes, the church should have that responsibility since its mission is to inculcate spiritual values throughout life for all its members from baptism, but also, the church has to foster respect for all age groups and also be responsible for training the young kids in the Bible and all aspects of worship and study and how it can enrich their lives.

Respect, responsibility, reciprocity, and restraint are social values, but they are also spiritual values. Social values have to do with how you behave in society. First of all, how you treat yourself and how you treat others. You want to do unto others as you would do unto yourself. You want to love your neighbor as you love yourself, even if he does not look like you, love like you, or vote like you. Love your neighbor. Those are spiritual values, and the church has to teach that.

*Gretel James*

Yes, the church should support parents in raising their children. Parents whose children are in the Sunday school don't know what's going on or what their children are being taught. The church should involve parents in everything it does with their children and not have activities just for the children, because I can teach a child a whole lot of stuff right here, but when they go back to their home environment, that environment is going to influence them greater than anything they did at church. The church should be doing more. It's a lot of work, but it can be done. Starting in small groups and gathering parents and children together and starting parent/child education. That's what's going to have to happen—parent/child education and a part of that education needs to be about sexual activity. That gets a lot of people in trouble too; they have so many children so early— you cannot go very far if you have a lot of children and are depending on public assistance. You can't make much of that, but everybody's scared to touch sexual behavior. Nobody wants to say anything about that, but we have to find a way to tell people this can be detrimental, and that's part of God's law too—that is, how we use our sexual drive and what it can result in.

Church/Sunday school teachers also have responsibility for helping children to acquire the best skills, knowledge, and attitude. Yesterday, at my church, I cringed when a child read the wrong scripture and no one corrected him. As a Church/Sunday school teacher, I taught children to perform and practiced with them before performance behaviors such as how to raise their heads and look out above the people, because they may get nervous if they're looking at somebody's face, but look above them in their direction and speak distinctly with their heads up, standing upright. Those are simple things we need to teach our children at church. Slouching and mispronouncing words that they haven't practiced can be improved. Yes, the church needs to be doing more.

There are reasons why some church members may not want to correct children. I once witnessed the biggest argument in my church's parish hall because a church member said something to a parent about their child's behavior. That's one reason we may just let it go, but it's not for the good of our children because I still say as we were always taught black children need to know to do better, to aim for the best because the world is stacked against them. Why would we let them do less than their best?

*Brenda Jones*

Whereas the church was a significant part of the community triad—school, home, church—in the past, it plays an increasingly diminishing role today. The church should advance biblical doctrine which guides the behavior of parents and children; pastors and church leaders should offer programs which help families function in a changing and chaotic world; the church should have a holistic perspective—i.e., concerned about the families' spiritual as well as its physical and socioeconomic well-being.

*Linda Hampton*

I think there needs to be a greater collaboration between and among the schools, the homes, the churches, and the communities. Everybody has a responsibility to do that. As for me and my kids, I am going to seek out what I believe is good for them. And that's how it was when I was raising them. So yes, I'm going to be involved in my children's schools. And sometimes I have to speak up for them or to at least provide a voice for them in terms of what's good for them when I see things happening. But I also have to be open to understanding that these institutions are not just there for my child only. I must be a part of collaboration with others to make sure that my child and other children are at the center of what's going on. So that not only are they a part of what their teachers need, but also what the leaders need. There's a real role for leaders in making sure that all these institutions provide what parents need and what children need.

We may not have control over all risk factors that a lot of kids grow up with, such as a lack of access to proper nutrition, or health care, or housing, or poverty, or crime, and other environmental factors that we see around us. I feel blessed to be able to recognize that my children were not completely inundated with that. They were exposed, but I worked very hard to make sure that that I limited the risk factors and concentrated more on home protective factors that supported their development.

*Rev. Jeanie Martinez-Jantz*

One of the things that I never get a chance to do, that I love to do with parents, is a course with parents on the spirituality of parenting, helping parents to see that every child, even an infant, has a spiritual life and how to see that and how to nurture that spiritual life inside that child. It is a sacred and beautiful thing when we can do that, when we learn to have those conversations with children about God, about who God is, about answering their questions and exploring the spiritual world with them.

One of the biggest things the church has failed at and needs to do is to put focus on children's ministries. One of the things that our church has done that's very dysfunctional, I think, is that they have, when a priest comes out of seminary—seminarians go to seminary to become priests—their first job is with a large church as an assistant rector. The assistant rector is only expected to be at a church a few years while they're getting on the job training, and then they move on to being in their own church. Who is it that's given the job as youth minister? The assistant rector. They're only going to be there a few years, and then they're going to leave. That sets up the children to have broken relationships with God, because that clergy person, just about the time that they start to bond with the children and the children can open up and start exploring deep questions of faith with them, that person has to say sayonara, goodbye, see you later. Children need more consistency than adults; they need a person that's been with them since they were little, that they look up to and they can trust, and that has been with them as they grow, to teach them, not this broken thing of youth ministers coming and going every few years. That's like raising children in foster homes, a different home every three years. Spiritually, that's what you're doing to them. But that's just my opinion.

Children don't ask to be born. We as parents are the ones who call them into being, and I think if we start, as parents, as faith communities to look at them and see that we called this new person into being, we are going to take more responsibility for the sacredness of the role that we're playing in their lives. And I think that's the best place to start. They didn't ask for it. We brought them here, and we owe them.

*Lyngrid Smith Rawlings*

Family-oriented, community-based churches can play an important role in raising children and instilling strong morals and positive values in young people. Some young parents can profit by becoming active in the church.

*Denise Thorne*

So are there any resources outside of the village that the village can bring in to support parents—and the church comes to mind. Churches need to do more, especially the mega churches that are a place where people gather every Sunday outside of working a nine-to-five job. Church is a place where people gather the longest outside of work or school, and I think more of them should be more available to the people. Churches need to move forward with some of the things that they could be doing to help people, because if you look back, that's what the church did. I know three mega churches right now that have these ministries, and they don't pay the people who manage them, so why the pastor should be owning a Lear jet—I have a huge problem with that.

I think the church should be a place where people can come and get help in preparedness and in solving their problems. Sometimes the church is not explicit enough in helping you understand the meaning of the parables as they relate to life today, and that's one of the reasons why young people are not going to church. I feel my grandson is going to need to go to church somewhere where the values of respect, responsibility, and other spiritual values are reinforced. Children need to be brought to church for the same purpose and to be with other kids to learn in a different setting about their spiritual connectedness.

# Ten Things Elders Recommend for Supporting Parents in Raising Their Children

- Federal, state, and local governments have a major responsibility for supporting children, parents, and families, not only through welfare handouts, but also by providing training and other programs that focus on building and strengthening families in ways that promote and foster positive child outcomes.
- The state of society is linked to the state of the family; therefore, the society in general has to take responsibility for supporting families in areas such as adequate health care and childcare—including on-site childcare; employment training, other upward mobility programs, and other programs that positively impact the lives of children and families.
- Parents will benefit from having parent training programs available to them through which they can learn how to successfully raise their children. These programs can be provided at neighborhood community centers.
- Concerned citizens need to demand that the federal government hold educational, child protection, and criminal justice programs accountable for assuring better outcomes for children and youth through well-thought-out, pro-family legislation and policies.

- Parents who experience high-risk factors, such as poverty and single parenting, need special attention and support in raising their children.
- It does take a village to fully support parents in raising their children. The village includes grandparents, other family members, governments, churches, schools, and the entire community. Each entity has a unique role to play.
- As in the past, the church can play an important and unique role in supporting parents through providing leadership, spiritual, moral, and social development opportunities for children and youth.
- The church can do more in areas of parent education and joint parent/child education, to include topics such as the spirituality of parenting, sexuality (often a taboo subject for churches), public speaking, child-rearing, and the role of the church as a member of the village that must support parents, children, and families.
- The church can also do more in areas of parent and family counseling and problem-solving.
- The church "must take responsibility for the sacredness of the role" it plays in the lives of children.

# Final Thoughts

It was a pleasure writing this book. It was also a thought-provoking and reinforcing learning experience. All contributors spoke openly, boldly, and honestly when responding to the many questions I asked. I was astounded by their passion for the topic of child-rearing and the commitment and conviction they expressed concerning future parents and the parenting of children. Parents and grandparents shared their personal stories about raising their children, their advice to current and future parents, and their advice to the younger generation about the importance of values-based parenting with a focus on the four *R*s. Young adults were by no means shy in sharing their concerns about the behaviors of some of their peers and children in today's world. Above all, all contributors wanted to make a contribution, however small, to improving the lives of children of the twenty-first century and interpersonal relationships between and among people of all generations.

Parents, you have in your hands power to effect change. So begin today, begin right now to work with your children, their teachers, your family members, your church, your communities to come together to develop and implement parenting plans that are values-based, including the core values discussed in this book. You decide as a family, as a community, as a church or school community. You've got to decide; you can't sit down and wait. The clock is ticking. It's time for change.

# Biographical Information about Contributors

Below is biographical information about a sample of the contributors to this book. These are the individuals who were interviewed and whose responses form the core of the book. Readers will be able to have an idea of the diversity of contributors in terms of age, gender, and race/ethnicity.

Marguerite Daniels Anderson is currently a stay-at-home mom. She is the mother of a young happy toddler who eats well and sleeps through the night. She was previously a web designer and a recipe developer with a background in lifestyle and health care writing and marketing. Marguerite earned a master's of fine arts in creative writing from the New School University and a bachelor of arts in creative writing/literature from Columbia University. Her parenting philosophy isn't well defined yet, but she believes in raising a child with gentle guidance, open discussions, and well-defined family rules.

Sean Anderson, PhD, is the father of a truly amazing toddler. He's also an optical engineer specializing in photonics. He has worked for start-ups, the military, and multinational companies. He holds eleven patents, with several pending and has authored over a dozen scientific papers. He earned his PhD in optics from the University of Rochester and received his bachelor of science in electrical engineering with high honors from Lehigh University. His parenting philosophy is to foster learning and growth by providing opportunities to be challenged.

Holly Blum, mother and grandmother, resides in Washington, DC. Her adult daughter lives with her adorable and confident toddler son in New Jersey. Holly is a retired early childhood professional who has supported classroom teachers in her many roles that included responsive classroom trainer, development and implementation of the success by eight multiage program, and working collaboratively with members of the English as a Second Language (ESL) office to provide professional development to pre-K and kindergarten teaching staff. Upon retirement, she became an adjunct professor at George Washington University Graduate School of Education and Human Development and an Early Childhood Leadership coach consultant. Her parenting philosophy was inspired by the wisdom of Khalil Gibran that states, "*Your children are not your children. They are the sons and daughters of Life's longing for itself.*

*They come through you but not from you, And though they are with you yet they belong not to you. You are the bows from which your children as living arrows are sent forth.*"

Marlon Bovell is the son of a lifelong educator and father of three children. Marlon has been married for fourteen years to Vickie Bovell, and they believe it is essential to ensure they are on the same page as it pertains to parenting. It's also imperative as parents to ensure the lines of communication are always open to their children. Marlon holds a bachelor of computer engineering degree and works in the software engineering field.

Alexis Braswell is currently a senior student attending Towson University located in Baltimore, Maryland. She will graduate December 2019 with a bachelor of science degree in health education and promotion with a concentration in community health. Upon graduation, Alexis plans to work as an emergency medical technician (EMT) with aspirations to become a physician assistant specializing in pediatrics.

Jean Bynoe-Singh is a retired schoolteacher. She taught in the primary school system in Guyana for thirty-eight years. She is the mother of five adult children and nine grandchildren.

She believes that education is most essential in all aspects of life and that those imparting it, whether teacher or parent, must believe that sincerely and do so with love, conviction, and compassion so as to have a positive impact on the minds of the children or learners.

Dorel Campbell-Adams is a married mother of three teenage children. She has a career in health care that has evolved over sixteen years into one that specializes in physician training and clinical sales for a medical device company. Her parenting philosophy is, "Parenting is not giving your child everything they want, nor is it being your child's friend. Parenting is about preparing your child to be a useful and respectful person in society."

Gloria Clanton is a retired music educator, having served as a junior high school music teacher for thirty-three years. During that time, she served in several administrative positions, including president of the District of Columbia Music Educators Association. After retirement she became active with her local AARP chapter, serving not only as president but in several other capacities. She has also chaired several ministries in her church as well as servicing as choir director and pianist. Gloria is the mother of two children and has three grandchildren. She raised her children using a philosophy based on an idiom she learned a long time ago—"As the twig is bent, so grows the tree." In other words, one's behaviors as a grown person are based on what he learned while he was a child. She is proud to say that with the help of God and her late husband, following this philosophy produced two great results, her son and daughter.

Dr. Desiree DeFlorimonte has a forty-five-year career in pedagogy which spans the spectrum from nursery through graduate schools. A reflective practitioner, she has been passionate about mentoring and inspiring students, both in the USA and Caribbean. Dr. DeFlorimonte was honored to obtain a Fulbright Scholar Award (2016–2017) and served as a literary studies facilitator at the University of Guyana. There she assisted in the literacy development of children and aided teachers in implementing best practices in their classrooms. Dr. DeFlorimonte resides in Maryland, and she enjoys traveling, reading, deepwater aerobics, singing, and dancing. She is the loving mother of Angel and proud grandmother of Jayson.

Ryan E. H. Dickson, Esq., is the father of three young children and the child of immigrants in the United States. He is an attorney and an entrepreneur, counseling businesses in creative growth strategies and scaling. Strongly believing in business, personal development, and forward-thinking ideologies, his parenting philosophy is similar to training young entrepreneurs of life—allow them the space to take risks and to fail.

Richlyn Ophelia Emanuel is the mother of a teenage son. She is a mother first and a career accountant. Her parenting philosophy is, "Expose your child to everything possible, making sure they are rounded and understand that the world is their competition." She is a firm believer that it takes a village to raise a child.

Anastasia Foster is a graduate student at Central Connecticut State University (CCSU) working on her master of arts in mathematics. She graduated from the University of Saint Joseph in December 2017 and works as graduate assistant in assessment and technology in the Career Department at CCSU and as an after-school teacher at Trinity Christian School in Windsor, Connecticut. In her spare time, she plays the harp, the piano/keyboard, and draws Batman symbols.

Martine Sadarangani Gordon is the mother of two young children. She has worked in the education space for over a decade, with a particular focus on early childhood education. Martine is currently a program officer with Washington Area Women's Foundation where she works to advance racial and gender equity in early education systems and to advance the early care and education workforce. She believes that parents and caregivers should respect children as individuals and encourage their self-confidence.

Dr. Linda Hampton is president of LC & Associates Inc., a consulting firm specializing in early childhood education, organizational and leadership training, and technical assistance to the Head Start and childcare communities nationwide. Linda was the first Head Start state collaboration director for more than fifteen years, a position requiring developing statewide partnerships among state and local entities and influencing policies relative to children and families in Alabama. Linda has been married for more than forty years, has two adult children, and three awesome grandchildren. Her parenting philosophy is "Saying what you mean and meaning what you say." It is important to provide guidance, consistency, and transparency while encouraging independence. She and her husband live in Montgomery, Alabama.

"As the twig is bent, so grows the tree," is a proverb Brenda Williams Jones has applied during her forty years of work with parents, teachers, and children. Dr. Jones, mother of two and grandmother of four, is keenly aware that how parents and teachers engage with children during their preschool years will ultimately make a significant impact on their early growth and development and beyond. In formal and informal settings, Dr. Jones seizes the opportunity to help parents recognize and develop parenting goals, strategies, and practices that will equip and shape their children to live productive and meaningful lives in a rapidly changing global society.

Joseph Kijewski is a husband, the father of three adult children, and a practicing attorney specializing in corporate ethics and regulatory compliance. His career has included service as an assistant director of the Civil Division of the US Department of Justice under Attorney General Janet Reno. He and his wife, Cheryl, have lived in the Northern Virginia area since graduating college together in 1982, and both are graduates of Georgetown University Law School. They are active members of their church and a number of public service and educational organizations. Joseph's parenting philosophy is, "Model for your children the person you would like them to be."

Lyngrid Smith Rawlings, Ed.D, is the mother of five adult children and grandmother of two, one who is a young adult. She is a retired Foreign Service officer, who served in Chad, Ivory Coast, India, Algeria, Pakistan, and Benin. Since retiring, she has served overseas on short-term assignments in Afghanistan, Algeria, Bahrain, Libya, Dubai Jordan, and Kyrgyzstan. Prior to becoming a diplomat, she served as an administrator of various adult education and manpower development programs in DC public schools, where she also developed, piloted, and received approval from the board of education to award a high school diploma to adults who successfully documented their life skills and had their career experiences assessed. Once her children completed high school, she joined the Foreign Service. In raising her children, she taught them that they were responsible for consequences of their decisions and tried to instill in them the confidence that hard work and integrity will eventually enable them to achieve their goals.

Jacqueline Rose, M.Ed., is parent to four adult children and grandmother to eight ranging in ages of two to twenty-five years. She has shared her parenting knowledge coupled with expertise in early education and childcare systems development and policy with other parents and professionals in classrooms and training programs. She also has provided policy support to members of state-governing bodies and leadership to national, state, and local organizations that are mission-driven to support parents, teachers, and policymakers. Currently she provides consultation services through her business, Rose Resources. Her parenting philosophy is *"Guide through the action of deep listening."*

Nyeim Risien is an IT Professional. He grew up in Largo, MD, and graduated from Largo High School. He was selected to participate in the Year Up Program during which he studied informational technology (IT). Upon graduation he completed his internship with the Carlyle Group in Washington, DC. He has completed several IT certification courses and works as a systems administrator. Nyeim was raised by his mother, grandmother, and older brother. Growing up he was taught to treat people how he wants to be treated and to have respect for himself and others. He plans to pass on these values to his future children.

Denise Thorne is the mother of two adult daughters and grandmother of one. After migrating to the United States, Denise began her career in banking. However, after having her daughters, she and her husband realized that it was of great importance to raise their children to understand the importance of being upstanding contributing citizens and the value of taking advantage of all opportunities. Denise walked away from her career in banking and stayed home with her children. Though balancing an asthmatic child, a child with severe digestive issues, the traditional demands of having children in multiple extracurricular activities, and the birth of her boutique catering business, Denise followed a mantra that allowed for clear boundaries and consistency with her children. P—persistence, R—resistance, I—insistence, and C—consistency allowed her to always remain steps ahead of her children. "The beauty of the hard work in parenting is the reward in the end."

# THE AUTHOR

Dr. Carmen Bovell is an early childhood professional, having spent her entire fifty-year career in this field. Her professional experiences include teaching at the preschool, elementary, and university levels and leading and managing early childhood programs at the local and federal levels. Dr. Bovell has also served as a visiting Fulbright Scholar and Fulbright Specialist at the University of the West Indies (UWI), Mona campus, Jamaica, and as Fulbright Specialist at the University of Guyana. Dr. Bovell was born in Guyana, where she attended primary school and high school and graduated with a teacher's diploma from the Guyana Teachers' Training College. She immigrated to the USA in 1969 and continued her professional education, earning a doctorate degree in early childhood special education, with a concentration in social and emotional disorders of preschool-aged children, from the University of Maryland, College Park. Since her retirement from federal service, Dr. Bovell has continued working in her field as an independent consultant, mentor, and coach. Dr. Bovell resides in Maryland and is the proud mother of three and grandmother of seven.

Pledge to Children by the Members of the Midcentury
Conference on Children and Youth

## Pledge to Children

To YOU, our children, who hold within you our most cherished hopes, we the members of the Midcentury White House Conference on Children and Youth, relying on your full response, make this pledge:

From your earliest infancy we give you our love, so that you may grow with trust in yourself and in others.

We will recognize your worth as a person and we will help you to strengthen your sense of belonging.

We will respect your right to be yourself and at the same time help you to understand the rights of others, so that you may experience cooperative living.

We will help you to develop initiative and imagination, so that you may have the opportunity freely to create.

We will encourage your curiosity and your pride in workmanship, so that you may have the satisfaction that comes from achievement.

We will provide the conditions for wholesome play that will add to your learning, to your social experience, and to your happiness.

. . . .

We will provide you with rewarding educational opportunities, so that you develop your talents and contribute to a better world.

We will protect you against exploitation and undue hazards and help you grow in health and strength.

. . . .

# About the Author

The author of this book, Dr. Carmen Bovell, is an expert in the field of early childhood education and has spent more than fifty years in the field engaging with, advocating for, and fostering relationships with young children and their families. Most of her years engaging in this work were with the federally funded but locally operated Head Start Program for children birth to five years old and their families. Dr. Bovell is steeped in parenting information, parenting advice, and parenting advocacy and is by far the best person to write such a compelling account of what "real parents" both current, past (grandparents), and future parents have to say about the subject of parenting in today's world.

—Dr. Marsha Carter McLean